MEDIEVAL POETICS AND SOCIAL PRACTICE

FORDHAM SERIES

IN MEDIEVAL STUDIES

Mary C. Erler and Richard F. Gyug,

series editors

Ronald B. Begley and Joseph W. Koterski, S.J. (eds.), *Medieval Education*

Teodolinda Barolini and H. Wayne Storey (eds.), *Dante for the New Millennium*

Richard F. Gyug (ed.), *Medieval Cultures in Contact*

Seeta Chaganti (ed.), *Medieval Poetics and Social Practice: Responding to the Work of Penn R. Szittya*

Devorah Schoenfeld, *Isaac on Jewish and Christian Altars: Polemic and Exegesis in Rashi and the Glossa Ordinaria*

MEDIEVAL POETICS AND SOCIAL PRACTICE

Responding to the Work of Penn R. Szittya

EDITED BY SEETA CHAGANTI

FORDHAM UNIVERSITY PRESS

New York   2012

Fordham University Press has no responsibility for the persistence or accuracy of URLs for external or third-party Internet websites referred to in this publication and does not guarantee that any content on such websites is, or will remain, accurate or appropriate.

Fordham University Press also publishes its books in a variety of electronic formats. Some content that appears in print may not be available in electronic books.

Library of Congress Cataloging-in-Publication Data

Medieval poetics and social practice : responding to the work of Penn R. Szittya / edited by Seeta Chaganti. — 1st ed.
     p. cm. — (Fordham series in medieval studies)
  Includes bibliographical references and index.
  ISBN 978-0-8232-4324-2 (cloth : alk. paper)
  1. English poetry—Middle English, 1100–1500— History and criticism. 2. Great Britain—Social life and customs—1066–1485. I. Chaganti, Seeta. II. Szittya, Penn R., 1945–
  PR317.S6M43 2012
  821'.109353—dc23

2012002986

Printed in the United States of America

14 13 12   5 4 3 2 1

First edition

CONTENTS

INTRODUCTION

Seeta Chaganti

This book pays tribute to the career of Penn R. Szittya, who retired from the English department at Georgetown University in 2009. The collection's title derives from Georgetown's Lannan Center for Poetics and Social Practice, an institution to which Penn lent considerable support while chairing the English department. Named and founded in 2006 by Mark McMorris, the Lannan Center currently bases its mission description on Adrienne Rich's belief in "art's social presence."[1] The Center's statement that poetry "traverses the fields of aesthetic, social, political, and religious thought" and "reconfigures these fields according to the designs of imagination" is, I think, what inspired Penn to support an institution concerned with contemporary poetics and social practice.[2] This faith in poetic culture's potential power in the world, its participation in social definition and even critique, has always characterized his work. In placing this volume's essays under the rubric of poetics and social practice, I hope to foreground their perspective on medieval poetic language as not only reflecting but also shaping social, political, and religious worlds.

Because both *poetics* and *social practice* can seem dauntingly capacious terms, I will attempt to set some parameters around them in their own right and in particular within the context of the medieval. The words *poetry*, *poetic*, and *poetics* are perhaps nowhere else so suggestively indeterminate as they are in the late Middle Ages. In the scholarship of the last several years, medieval poetics have been described as contrarian, visual, oral, sacrificial, Lancastrian, documentary, and memorial, to provide only a very partial list of approaches to the topic.[3] Medieval poetics are also implicated in the turn to historically and materially inflected new formalist studies, which might consider the politics of metrics and manuscript *ordinatio* as part of a medieval poetics.[4] For the purposes of the present volume, however, I propose first that we orient ourselves by considering, relative to our own sense of this term, the poetic as a medieval quality of expression. Second, I shall briefly outline the critical traditions that understand medieval poetics as ethical and rhetorical. These designations, and the relationship between them, are the most relevant to the following essays' engagement with poetics.

In one sense, the late-medieval idea of the *poetical* seems to correlate with a category of expression that in our modern context we might label as poetry or the poetic. Some criticism has seen the fourteenth-century poet Eustache Deschamps as deliberately making choices to invest his work with a poetic quality.[5] His *Art de dictier* (1392), for instance, has been read as a vernacular *ars poetica* describing the need to be "expressive," to showcase the poet's natural talent and the pleasure it brings an audience.[6] The word *poetical* as a qualifier appears mainly in the fifteenth century, referring to muses, meter, books, and art.[7] When, in an envoy to *The Fall of Princes* (ca. 1431–39), John Lydgate says, "The profunde processe was so poetical," he is describing the nature of a narrative account in a manner that might somewhat approximate our sense of how *poetic* is used or the qualities it might designate.[8] He calls his source "profunde" to designate its subtlety and even its resistance to being understood easily.[9] It is also "entirmedlyd with chaunges of fortune / And straunge materys that were hystoryal" (9.3326–27). Furthermore, Lydgate takes pains to note in this envoy the difficulty of writing his own version because "Ynglyssh in ryme hath skarsete" (9.3312). In communicating the source's challenging unfamiliarity and complicated interminglings, as well as mentioning the associated labor of containing this ineffability in verse, Lydgate uses his qualifier "poetical" in a way that potentially resonates with our sense of the poetic.[10]

At the same time, concepts like *poetic* and *poetics* did other work as well for a medieval audience, and these functions have sometimes been categorized as ethical or rhetorical. Medieval poetry was not simply synonymous with verse form but rather could encompass the learned, the moral, and the philosophical, existing in complicated relation to the more contained and occasional beauty of courtly "making."[11] Judson Boyce Allen has proposed an "ethical poetic" for the late Middle Ages in order to address the possible differences between medieval and modern senses of the poetic. Allen reformulates his own earlier understanding of the poetic in the Middle Ages by replacing the very category of "literature" with that of the "ethical." In doing so, he proposes a medieval understanding of text whereby "the verbal act which makes a poem and the moral act which leads a life are the same." A dynamic of "assimilation" and "constant reciprocity" exists between the text and the lived ethical experience of the audience.[12] This model of absorption between text and world offers a possible structure through which to understand poetics and social practice; a version of it also obtains in Paul Zumthor's medieval poetics. For him, "history embraces the text; the text absorbs history," and poetry is functional, like an event.[13] To some extent, Zumthor is providing an alternative to the idea of "rhetorical" poetics, in which poetic form and rhetoric intersect. As Rita Copeland and Ineke Sluiter suggest, poetic figure and ornament can exist not merely as "artificial surface" to rhetorical thought but rather as "the completion of a process of artifice that . . . culminates in the technical control of effective language." Building on Quintilian, medieval theory about poetic composition sees "the articulation of form as a dimension of representation, not as a separate process."[14] The spectrum implied between ethical and rhetorical poetics usefully corresponds to the approaches of this volume's essays. As a group, they ask us to think about not only the intersection of poetic form and rhetorical technique but also the intersection between poetics and action or prescription in the world.

The point above turns us toward the idea of "social practice"; we might approach the task of understanding this term's meaning and significance by returning to the Lannan Center's use of it in relation to poetry and poetics. In addition to Rich, the Lannan Center also invokes Roman Jakobson, who argues in his essay "What Is Poetry?" that "art is an integral part of the social structure, a component that interacts with all the others and is itself mutable since both the domain of art and its relationship to the other constituents of the social structure are in constant dialectical flux."[15] Thus, poetry exists in dialectical relation to every component of social interaction and behavior; it "transforms the other elements and determines with them the nature of the whole."[16] This statement might appear so broad as to lack meaning, and yet I would caution us against perceiving it in this way. Social practice itself does encompass a dizzying range of possibilities—from specific material acts to what Michel de Certeau, in his meditation on worldly practices, characterizes as " 'ways of operating' or doing things."[17] But what is crucial here is to consider this broad term's juxtaposition with *poetics*: such a juxtaposition makes a claim for the indispensible role of poetic language in the formation of social structures, actions, utterances, and behaviors. This claim is subtly and implicitly reflected in the volume's examination of medieval verbal and visual poetics.

The juxtaposition of *medieval poetics* and *social practice* gains further conceptual specificity when we consider the content of the present volume and what it contributes to the field. First, the collection offers some new perspectives on the power of specific features of poetic culture to shape social behaviors and attitudes. As Kara Doyle demonstrates, poetically expressed protocols of patronage could reflect and influence the positioning and perception of women in late-medieval society. A poetic figure might, as in Nick Havely's essay, define the structure of a power dynamic between two agents. Poetic figure can also, Anne Middleton shows, interact with the proverbial in order to elucidate didactic practices. For Moira Fitzgibbons, poetic language and form also enable the reader to think through the ethics of pedagogy. In examples such as these, considering poetics also means considering practices of teaching, learning, and social negotiation.

In addition to viewing the volume's arguments as examining social modes and practices through poetics, we should also note that many of its essays bring somewhat underexamined texts to readers' attention; these two different categories of contribution are, I will suggest, related to each other. Along with Fitzgibbons writing on *The Prick of Conscience* (1340–50) and Doyle on *Amoryus and Cleopes* (1449), we also find John C. Hirsh examining the carols of James Ryman (1492), as well as John T. Sebastian treating John Lydgate's lesser-known lyrics. And as Richard K. Emmerson points out in introducing his study of a *Pilgrimage of the Soul* manuscript (ca. 1413), such fifteenth-century English manuscripts have not enjoyed the kind of comprehensive investigation as textual and visual objects that Continental manuscripts have. The volume's inclination toward less heavily studied artifacts is deeply related to the integration of poetics and social practice, particularly as Jakobson articulates this dynamic. For Jakobson also points out in his essay that in order for poetic language to perform its work in the world, we must be able to experience it not as "mere representation of the object being named" but rather as words that "acquire a weight and value of their own instead of referring indifferently to reality."[18] It is precisely when we turn to unfamiliar texts, I suggest, that we heighten for ourselves the possibility of this experience of poetry. In reading medieval poetry that is new to us, we might combat the indifference or inattention that the canonical or overly familiar might induce. If we can see clearly the weight and value of words because they are novel to us, then we can also see anew, as Jakobson suggests, their dialectical engagement with the world's social structures. Thus, the two main contributions that this volume makes—an examination of poetics and social practice, on the one hand, and an exposition of noncanonical texts, on the other—function interdependently. Ultimately, it is our honoree who has inspired this dynamic. This collection aims to reflect Penn's commitment to thinking about the place of poetry in society along with the catholicity of expertise that characterizes his scholarship.

The volume's critical readings begin with Richard K. Emmerson, whose essay "Visual Translation in Fifteenth-Century English Manuscripts" evokes Penn's interest in the relationship between medieval literary and visual cultures. Emmerson's piece suggests that a painting or illustration is an absolutely appropriate and important place from which to begin speaking about poetics and narrative; that, indeed, so many visual or otherwise nonverbal elements of a culture can be the right place from which to start speaking of textuality. As Emmerson puts it, the manuscript image "visually translates" its accompanying text, and this creative and interpretive activity must form part of our understanding of the creation and reception of late-medieval texts. Reading an illustrated fifteenth-century *Pilgrimage of the Soul* manuscript (an English translation of Guillaume de Deguileville's French original), Emmerson shows how illustration can foreground a text's most important themes by anticipating, delaying, manipulating, and otherwise energetically interacting with the textual narrative.

J. Patrick Hornbeck's contribution, entitled "Barn of Unity or the Devil's Church? Salvation and Ecclesiology in Langland and the Wycliffites," considers the relationship between the twentieth-century Jesuit priest and cardinal Avery Robert Dulles, on the one hand, and the fourteenth-century writers William Langland and John Wyclif, on the other. He illuminates their shared investment—despite their many differences—in ecclesiological accounts that give "preference to a communion model of the church over an institutional one." By including in his essay a theologian whose father was a U.S. secretary of state, Hornbeck reminds us of another interesting element of Penn's career. With its combination of Jesuit affiliation and inside-the-Beltway location, Georgetown University—Penn's longtime professional home—has always been deeply concerned with questions about the relationship between statehood and religion. Within this frame, Hornbeck considers the implications of a communal model of the church. Specifically, Langland and Wyclif felt a responsibility to recognize a "rustic rather than corporate" social reality in their ecclesiologies, and they expressed this view in opposition to a political climate that increasingly attempted to assert the church's institutional power.

Another important aspect of Penn's scholarly legacy is its encouragement to us to recognize the cultural influence of friars in the Middle Ages. In "Christian Poetics and Orthodox Practice: Meaning and Implication in Six Carols by James Ryman, O.F.M.," John C. Hirsh, a member of Georgetown's English department, responds to this legacy. Hirsh suggests that the intervention of friars into different arenas of culture could give rise to unique and subtle poetics. Hirsh turns our attention to James Ryman, a fifteenth-century Franciscan who was also a poet and musician. Hirsh argues that while the simplicity of Ryman's songs and carols generally relegates him to a place below the critical radar, this very simplicity in fact "enabled both composer and audience to become engaged in a powerful and considered spirituality." By avoiding overt response to Lollard and other reformist dissent, Ryman's carols can "construc[t] a nuanced representation of certain central Christian teachings in a way that responds to Franciscan thought and spirituality." In the six carols that Hirsh examines, syntax, form, and imagery "gently reflect" rather than aggressively argue. This tonal strategy allows Ryman's carols to articulate a critical understanding of hypostatic union while at the same time sustaining "a degree of poetic wonder."

For Moira Fitzgibbons, the modern term "mindfulness" becomes a lens through which to consider medieval poetry and social practice. In "Enabled and Disabled 'Myndes' in *The Prick of Conscience*," she argues that the fourteenth-century *Conscience*-poet emphasizes "mynde," "resoun," "skil," and "wit" in order to foreground the role of self-aware cognition in the human encounter with death and judgment. Within this context, Fitzgibbons also explores the inevitable problem of disabling madness, as the *Conscience*-poet describes it, showing us through this text "the complications involved in yoking the soul's salvation to the mind's activity." Fitzgibbons's essay deeply engages the poetics of this work by tracking subtle shifts in the meanings and resonances of specific words—such as "mynde"—repeated throughout the text. *The Prick of Conscience*, Fitzgibbons demonstrates, depends on its formal features and diction to make its point: that pedagogical intervention into any community requires a mindfulness "both rigorous and humane."

John T. Sebastian conceives of social and religious communities through the articulation of "common voice." Building on Anne Middleton's formulation that public poetry speaks in a common voice on behalf of a common good, Sebastian asks: "What happens if we read Middle English devotional literature as public poetry?" In "The Idea of Public Poetry in Lydgatean Religious Verse: Authority and the Common Voice in Devotional Literature," Sebastian proposes to extend the category of public poetry by including within it John Lydgate's devotional verse. He begins by suggesting that in the poems he examines, speaking voices sustain complex relationships to their audience. Sebastian then goes on to argue that the multivocal networks produced in those interactions can express a devotional community's thoughts about religious imagery and other contested issues related to theology and vernacular piety.

The next two contributions investigate the social placement of women as understood through poetry. In Nick Havely's essay, entitled "Nature's *Yerde* and Ward: Authority and Choice in Chaucer's *Parliament of Fowls*," the poetic deployment of a specific phrase comments on marital practices enacted by and imposed on women. Havely focuses on Chaucer's use of the phrase *under youre yerde*, which has gone somewhat unremarked in Chaucer criticism. *Under youre yerde*, he argues, should open our eyes to the institution of medieval wardship and its legal and social features as articulated in English, French, and Latin. Having established the connotations of wardship in a Chaucerian context, Havely shows how acknowledging this concept can enrich the existing critical discourse concerning the formel's position and choice in the *Parliament*. Nature's wardship of the formel, Havely contends, implies a subtle matchmaking dynamic that oscillates between the ostensible interests of the formel and the deeper and more powerful interests of a "mildly coercive" Nature as noble guardian. This situation allows us to understand the formel's response as "a combination of caution and resolution," strategically phrased to defuse its relationship to any action.

Kara Doyle develops this investigation of women's roles by focusing on medieval women as literary patrons. Doyle's essay, "Fabulous Women, Fables of Patronage: Metham's *Amoryus and Cleopes* and BL MS Additional 10304," argues that the increased presence of female patrons in the century after Chaucer's death not only changed depictions of classical women in poetry but also opened up a space for reexamining some fourteenth-century literary models. Traditionally, poets like Chaucer and Boccaccio dictated prescriptions for female behavior. In the fifteenth century, by contrast, women's participation in patronage networks compelled authors to respond to their demands. Their patronage thereby changed poetic traditions surrounding the perception of women. The works of John Metham and the anonymous Middle English translator of part of Boccaccio's *De mulieribus claris*, Doyle demonstrates, reflect the power of their female patrons and audiences to revise the meaning of classical feminine ideals as well as of the fourteenth-century canon.

The collection's final critical essay begins with *Piers Plowman*'s use of the adage "Do well and have well," a phrase that elegantly interweaves poetics and social practice. It prescribes practice within a form that reveals the relationship of Langland's poetics to other figural and didactic realms. In "Dowel, the Proverbial, and the Vernacular: Some Versions of Pastoralia," Anne Middleton argues that by looking at other occurrences of the phrase "do well and have well," we discern how the register of the proverbial and popular provides Langland with a way to think about pastoral didacticism in relation to his own work. Middleton surveys different occurrences of this phrase, focusing, for instance, on its appearance in the *Similitudinarium* of William de Montibus (d. 1213). This work provided an important source for the *summae confessorum* that influenced *Piers Plowman*. Rather than simply pinpointing in William's text another possible origin for a Langlandian formulation, however, Middleton suggests instead that we read such texts as "illuminating commentary *avant la lettre* on the poet's pivotal deployment" of the "Dowel" dictum. Investigating the implications of the proverbial, Middleton shows how "ordinary and extraordinary language declare their interdependence in the 'arts' of both pastors and poets."

Following a bibliography of Penn's works, Jo Ann Hoeppner Moran Cruz, who worked with Penn for many years while she taught in Georgetown's Department of History, surveys the diverse content of this scholarship. She illuminates the subtle threads in his early work that start to weave the tapestry of his major study on antifraternal tradition, but she also demonstrates the breadth of his scholarly interests and the range of topics and texts on which he has written. Penn's work spans the early and late medieval periods, exploring, for example, the Old English *Andreas*; millennial apocalyptic texts; the *Song of Roland*; Peter Abelard; Chaucer, Langland, Gower, and other late-medieval authors; and less well-known but highly intriguing works such as James le Palmer's fourteenth-century *Omne bonum*. In addition, Penn published an influential article in modernist studies on Joseph Conrad's 1911 novel *Under Western Eyes*. As this piece, as well as his interest in Wallace Stevens, both suggest, Penn's work has long engaged in an important conversation about the relationship between the medieval and the modern. Cruz also details the contribution that Penn's most recognized work, *The Antifraternal Tradition in Medieval Literature* (Princeton, 1986), has made to the field. Her essay ends by acknowledging Penn's equally important contributions as a teacher.

Finally, as an acknowledgment of Penn's affection and support for the Lannan Center, its founder and former director (2006–9) Mark McMorris has written what he evocatively describes as a poetic palimpsest on a lecture Penn once gave. The inclusion of a contribution by a distinguished poet and scholar of contemporary poetry and poetics honors Penn's belief in exploring the social meaning of all poetic culture, whether medieval or modern. Building on Penn's examination of the *Omne bonum* manuscript, as described in Cruz's essay, McMorris draws inspiration from Penn's thesis about the text as "conceptual palimpsest" to find a structure for describing the relationship between poetics and social practice. McMorris constructs a palimpsest of his own, layering manuscript pages and modern life. Building an analogy between medieval civil servant and modern poet, he considers how medieval and contemporary poetics might speak to each other in their shared engagement with worldly practices and objects.

In closing, I offer an anecdote that demonstrates the productive power of the relation between poetics and social practice in Penn's professional life. As a Georgetown master's-degree student in the fall of 1993, I enrolled in Penn's graduate seminar on the *Canterbury Tales*. At the time, I, along with several of my classmates, was a teacher at a D.C.-area secondary school. Every week, Penn taught us more than a thing or two about how to teach, conducting one of the most rigorous, exciting, collegial, and also equitable and respectful seminars I have had the honor to take. One day, Penn asked the class to meet at the National Gallery, where we gathered in front of Jan van Eyck's Annunciation panel (ca. 1434), the image decorating the cover of this volume.

Penn began by calling attention to the material history of the painting, using its provenance to illustrate the workings of the past's relationship to the present. As McMorris suggests, and as Penn's commitment to a center for contemporary poetry indicates, the humanist discourses of the past and the present might have important things to say to each other, and Penn used the Annunciation to illustrate the complexity of such a dialogue. The painting vividly demonstrates how our present perspective and condition always necessarily inform the project of encountering the past. Penn told us that, while held in St. Petersburg during the nineteenth century, the painting was transferred onto canvas from its original wood-panel support.[19] I remember his dramatic presentation of this fact, his desire to convey how easily the painting could have been harmed in the noble attempt to preserve it.[20] For me, and probably for others as well, the story of the Washington Annunciation's precarious transfer would come to exist as a compelling allegory for the risky but crucial inextricability of the past and the present.

Within this context, the features of the painting constituted a poetics. Through its details and dense allusion, Penn painstakingly constructed a world made of symbol and textuality, what McMorris here calls "the leaves of the universe." This perspective was profoundly important for Penn's teaching of Chaucerian poetics, which also revolved around this idea of multiple textual worlds. Reading the painting alongside the *Tales* allowed us to see medieval poetics as Penn saw them—structural, architectural, kinetic, built of symbols as strata. At the same time, the discourse networks generated between the different media of painting and poetry revealed to us how the world of medieval literary production was part of a larger world of aesthetic, philosophical, ethical, and social endeavor.

Finally, we noted that this lesson about medieval poetics took place in the Washington National Gallery of Art, a museum that belongs genuinely to the citizenry. By taking us there, Penn encouraged us to think about what it meant to have access to this piece in the nation's capital and about the importance of ensuring that humanist scholarship and discourse—present and past—are recognized in the public sector, not as a luxury but as a necessity and a public good. Institutions like the National Gallery offer aesthetically saturated spaces where provocative inquiries into poetic culture can take place in the midst of civic life. Penn showed us how to stand in the museum and work against the perception of art as mere leisure commodity, asking us to use the features of that public space as a shaping vessel for rigorous thought. Many former students of Penn's who accompanied him on this outing have gone on to become scholars of poetry, trying to contribute positively to the lives of students and to conversations in our fields and in the culture more broadly. Penn used this painting to teach all of us how medieval poetics reach into many worlds.

VISUAL TRANSLATION IN FIFTEENTH-CENTURY ENGLISH MANUSCRIPTS

Richard K. Emmerson

Although the role of linguistic translation in the expansion of medieval literature and the establishment of English as a literary vernacular is well known, the role played by visual translation, the creation of manuscript images to picture and interpret verbal texts, has yet to be fully appreciated.[1] This essay investigates visual translation in illustrated fifteenth-century literary manuscripts not only to expand our understanding of translation as a creative activity but also to encourage scholarship to consider certain manuscript illustrations as visual translations: related, but independent, responses to literary texts, worthy of analysis in their own right. I will argue that an image accompanying a text should be approached not as a visual copy of the text—what David Freedberg calls "the accuracy that mirrors"—but as "a resemblance that re-produces,"[2] that is, as a translation from one imaginative medium to another capable of producing new meaning just as new meaning may be produced by translations from one language to another. As we shall see, literary scholarship has generally misunderstood this creative process and, as a result, has failed to appreciate the kind of "transformative adaptation" of a text produced by visual translation, an adaptation analogous, for example, to what Chaucer often achieves in his translations.[3] This misunderstanding is unfortunate, because recognizing the conventions, codes, and methods of visual translation—what Alex Potts calls "the how of meaning"[4]—can provide fresh insights into the reception of late medieval texts extant in often visually elaborate manuscripts. If Roger Chartier is right that reading practices depend on the forms in which texts are transmitted to the reader, that indeed "forms produce meaning,"[5] then the packaging of Middle English literature in illustrated manuscripts is a significant development of the later Middle Ages, and visual translation deserves study that is more extensive and methodologically astute.

I focus on visual translation for both positive and negative reasons. The positive is the increasing scholarly recognition that illuminated English manuscripts proliferated in the fifteenth century, which has directed attention to "the material features of translation in a manuscript culture."[6] These are often *visual* elements of the manuscript's *mise-en-page*: glosses, colophons, rubrics, pen-flourished paraphs, colorful interlinear fillers, ornate borders, historiated initials, and, of course, images, including framed miniatures, *bas-de-page* scenes, and marginal drawings.[7] More than twenty years ago, introducing the "New Philology" issue of *Speculum*, Stephen Nichols stressed that "the dynamic of the medieval manuscript matrix . . . involves cognitive perception as two kinds of literacy: reading text and interpreting visual signs."[8] This perception, furthermore, results in complex reading practices, because, as Ardis Butterfield argues, the manuscript page "is not a mere transparency through which the author's 'original' is to be viewed but rather an artifact of independent visual interest."[9] Attention to "the visual as well as the verbal status of medieval textuality" is therefore most welcome and, as I have noted in a survey of interdisciplinary medieval scholarship, "represents our own 'pictorial turn,' the next phase of humanistic scholarship that is beginning to reassert itself after 'the linguistic turn' that—according to Richard Rorty—so dominated twentieth-century thought."[10]

Despite this "pictorial turn," literary scholars have failed to respond adequately to images or acknowledge the interpretive significance of visual translations. For example, although recognizing that "the translation of text into visual image helps to focus the economic, political, and possibly gender, relations underpinning translations produced by and for the nobility," Roger Ellis suggests that such visual translation may involve "the possible simplification of complex sources so translated, a sort of glorious 'dumbing-down' of the word"![11] This statement is particularly dismaying because Ellis is discussing the illustrated *Estoire de Seint Aedward le Rei* (Cambridge, University Library, MS Ee.3.59, ca. 1255), whose sixty-four miniatures are integral to the hagiographic narrative, and whose manuscript, as Thelma Fenster and Jocelyn Wogan-Browne point out, "offers multiple ways of reading Edward's life."[12] Ellis's comment regrettably typifies a failure to understand the role played by images in medieval manuscripts, which, as Mary Carruthers has shown in her work on mnemonic images, are tools for invention and contemplation as well as recollection and illustration.[13] Perhaps the Gregorian dictum that pictures are the books of the illiterate has helped devalue images among textual scholars, but whatever the dictum meant in the early Middle Ages,[14] it had little practical bearing on the often sumptuous manuscript culture of the later Middle Ages. As Jeffrey Hamburger notes, when vernacular texts were first widely illustrated, the purpose of images "was less that of providing an aid to the illiterate, . . . than of lending to the vernacular an authority associated with Latin illuminated manuscripts."[15] Yet the notion that images dumb-down the word—even if rarely stated so bluntly—characterizes much literary historical scholarship, which is why this paper will not only stress the widespread significance of late-medieval English illustrated manuscripts but also critique some mistaken assumptions about manuscript images. Following an approach to visual translation that seeks to respect both its visual and verbal texts, it will conclude by briefly examining an illustrated Middle English manuscript.

FIFTEENTH-CENTURY ENGLISH ILLUSTRATED MANUSCRIPTS

The production of illustrated English manuscripts increased tremendously during the fifteenth century, as did the copying of vernacular literary texts. Tony Edwards and Derek Pearsall have stressed the "decisively significant" early years of the century for the history of the English book, noting that only about thirty literary manuscripts are extant from the seventy-five years before 1400, whereas about six hundred are extant from the seventy-five years after.[16] This comparison of the rate of literary production before and after 1400 is even more lopsided when we examine *illustrated* English-language texts by comparing two standard surveys of fourteenth- and fifteenth-century manuscripts illuminated in Britain.[17] Of the 158 fourteenth-century illustrated manuscripts in the survey edited by Lucy Freeman Sandler, only one is "literary," a French *Lancelot* copied around 1300, with two miniatures added in England around 1370.[18] In contrast, of the 140 entries in Kathleen Scott's catalog of manuscripts produced in fifteenth-century England, 55 have Middle English texts and another three mix English with other languages. Thus 42 percent illustrate Middle English texts, even though this survey likely underrepresents such manuscripts, since it selects those primarily of art-historical interest.[19] Since art historians have generally been as unsympathetic to fifteenth-century English manuscripts as literary critics have been to fifteenth-century English poetry, manuscripts that usually attract art-historical attention are in French and Latin and often produced by Continental artists.[20] Further research will likely reveal that the proliferation of illustrated English manuscripts in the fifteenth century is even greater than Scott's survey suggests, a visual analogue to the reestablishment of English as a literary vernacular.

Before the fifteenth century no English literary manuscript compares to the deluxe books associated with French collectors such as Charles V, Jean of Berry, and Philip the Bold.[21] The one earlier illustrated anthology of English romances, the Auchinleck manuscript, only reinforces the contrast between the manuscript presentations of French and English literature.[22] Two transitional manuscripts, though, hint at the emergent status of English around the turn of the fifteenth century. The immense Vernon Manuscript (1390–1400), which collects hagiographic, devotional, and didactic texts, includes two narratives illustrated by miniatures: *La Estorie del Evangelie en engleis*, a poetic account of the Gospels translated from French, and *The Miracles of Our Lady*, also translated from French or perhaps Latin.[23] This linking of image and translated word—highlighted by the title of *La Estorie*—is significant because it both reminds us that images usually draw on available iconographic models and points to images as aids to translation. The second transitional manuscript—Bodleian Library, Bodley 264—embeds a brief Middle English poem between two lengthy French texts: a verse Alexander romance and a prose account of Marco Polo's journey to the court of Kublai Khan.[24] The poem, which relates a series of letters between Alexander and Dindimus, king of India, is accompanied by nine miniatures (fols. 209r–215v) framed within the verse columns, a layout common in fourteenth-century French literary manuscripts but new to an English literary text. One of the earliest illustrated Middle English secular works, its miniatures repeatedly depict the acts of sending and receiving letters, while distinguishing Alexander from Dindimus and his orientalized court. As typical for early vernacular illustrations, the images authorize the inserted English text by stressing its epistolary "authors" and means of transmission.

A more famous, if also more problematic, early illustrated literary manuscript is British Library, Cotton Nero A.x, the sole copy of the works of the *Pearl*-poet. Although copied in the last two decades of the fourteenth century, its twelve illustrations were probably added in the early fifteenth century.[25] As Paul Reichardt notes, until recently they have received scant scholarly attention, because critics thought they failed to depict "significant features" of the poems and art historians found them "crude."[26] For example, John Bowers's The Politics of "Pearl," which takes seriously the magnificent visual culture of Ricardian England, does not examine these images, mentioning them only as evidence of Cheshire's "backwoods manorial culture" after the fall of Richard II and deeming them the product of the artist's "utterly provincial imagination."[27] This assertion epitomizes an aesthetic rather than critical response to images, a major impediment to appreciating medieval visuality. This is unfortunate, for, as Edwards notes, the pictures "are conscientious attempts to reflect the texts and significant moments within them,"[28] such as the Dreamer asleep in the garden (fol. 41r), the handwriting on the wall during Belshazzar's feast (fol. 60v), Jonah's preaching in Nineveh (fol. 86v), and Gawain's feigning sleep when visited by Bercilak's lady (fol. 129r). Unifying this authorial anthology, the images are noteworthy for their full-page format, providing evidence of reception through some of the earliest narrative illustrations of secular English poetry.[29]

Literary historical approaches to the manuscripts of Geoffrey Chaucer are both better known and more representative of scholarship on medieval illustrated texts. The Canterbury Tales is the first extensive Middle English poem to be illustrated in a deluxe manuscript, the Ellesmere Chaucer.[30] Unfortunately, art-historical attention has been minimal, whereas literary scholars have scrutinized its depictions of the taletellers to determine the extent to which they capture the verbal portraits of the pilgrims described in the General Prologue.[31] Such an approach typifies literary historical treatments of manuscript images, in that they relegate the visual to illustrations of the verbal, according praise to pictorial features that capture verbal details, while ignoring the figural aspects of the image that are crucial to visual form and meaning but are apparently unrelated to the accompanying literary text. It is worth stressing that the twenty-three portraits are painted in the margins next to the tales told by the pilgrims, not next to their descriptions, as in Caxton's edition.[32] As I show elsewhere, the primary purpose of the portraits—probably based on instructions to the artists—was not thematic but functional, to serve as visual guideposts to contents and identify speakers.[33] Ideology and iconographic conventions, rather than textual representation, motivate the pictures. The Physician (fol. 133r), for example, holds a vial of urine, not because he would carry it on horse-back as he rides toward Canterbury, but as a marker identifying his pro-fession. Similarly, the Cook wields a meat hook as an occupational sign (fol. 47r), the artist's goal being the identification of the speaker through a recognizable visual shorthand. Nevertheless, critics typically discuss the Ellesmere portraits as "realistic," so that Ellesmere becomes to Middle English manuscripts what Chaucer is to literary history—a herald of Renaissance realism.

Perhaps the most celebrated attempt to understand Chaucer's poetic in terms of medieval iconography is V. A. Kolve's *Chaucer and the Imagery of Narrative*.[34] It argues that each of the first five tales can be understood in terms of specific images "created by the narrative action itself, which it in-vites us to imagine and hold in mind as we experience the poem, and which later serve as memorial centers around which we are able to reconstruct the story and think appropriately about its meanings that are symbolic and around which the narratives are formed."[35] In two methodological chapters, Kolve explains how he uses iconographic traditions, noting that he does not argue that "Chaucer looked upon any of these pictures, only that he would have understood them, and that he could have counted on some substantial part of his audience to share with him that skill."[36] This methodology, how-ever, tends to treat images as mere illustrations, as "the vast store of conven-tional imagery."[37] It mines medieval visual culture for illustrative images with little regard to cultural, geographic, or historical factors or to particu-lar media, audiences, or forms of reception. It is as if medieval iconography was frozen in time, carrying uncontested meanings for a monolithic medi-eval culture passed on by a thousand-year tradition. Yet, as Jonathan Alex-ander notes, "meanings in images could vary for different spectators, . . . are not static over time, and . . . may often be sites of contested and conflicting meanings. As such these meanings are only intelligible in the social con-texts in which they were created."[38] It is therefore troubling that Kolve's earlier problematic methodology continues to inform his recent *Telling Images: Chaucer and the Imagery of Narrative*.[39] Curiously, although con-cerned with the "imagery of narrative," Kolve never addresses "a crucial question concerning Chaucer and medieval visual culture: why were the *narratives* of the *Canterbury Tales* not illustrated in the fifteenth century (as were the poems of Gower and Lydgate)?"[40]

More scholarly attention that is contextualized and detailed has been paid to manuscripts of Gower's *Confessio Amantis*, which are often deluxe, large-format books inscribing texts in double columns on brilliantly decorated folios.[41] At the higher levels of English society Gower is the vernacular author of choice in the first two decades of the fifteenth century, and the *Confessio* is the most widely illustrated Middle English text. Its several illuminated manuscripts typically depict two scenes that encapsulate the poem's themes: Nebuchadnezzar's dream of the statue symbolizing world empires, and the confession of Amant.[42] Two later manuscripts also include narrative images (Oxford, New College, MS 266; and New York, Morgan Library, M. 126), which show how miniatures are crucial to the fifteenth-century packaging and reception of Gower.[43] The *mise-en-page* of these and other *Confessio* manuscripts varies in placing the illustrations in relation to Gower's Latin texts and English verse, implying, as I have argued elsewhere, three distinct ways in which Gower was received during the fifteenth century: as a public poet speaking forthrightly to the court of Richard II and then of Henry IV, as primarily an English storyteller, and as a humanist whose vernacular mythmaking is buttressed by Latin verse and explicated by Latin commentaries.[44] Scholarship on Gower manuscripts demonstrates the value of affording meticulous analysis to manuscript images as visual translations.

The enhanced status of the vernacular in the mid-fifteenth century is exemplified by the manuscripts of the most prolific and popular English poet-translator, John Lydgate. If the *Confessio Amantis* is the most widely illustrated poem, Lydgate is the most widely illustrated poet.[45] His many lavishly illuminated texts serve as a signature establishing authorship, a principal function of manuscript illustration.[46] Many of his manuscripts were produced by metropolitan workshops and show a consistent design resulting from commercial publication.[47] Of the twenty-three manuscripts of *Troy Book*, based on Guido della Colonne's Latin *Historia destructionis Troiae*, eight were originally illustrated, some with lavish narrative scenes.[48] Their images visually translate the poem's new organization, marking Lydgate's prologue and five books by a standard set of prefatory images. By mid-century, images had become interpretive guides to Lydgate's poetry, responding to patronage, directing reading practices, and highlighting key narrative moments. The illustration of the *Fall of Princes* in

British Library, Harley 1766, for example, includes 157 narrative images in its margins.[49] It deserves the attentive scholarly analysis Anne D. Hedeman has given to the manuscripts of Lydgate's French source, Laurent de Premierfait's *Des cas des nobles hommes et femmes*.[50] A popular work extant or extracted in some sixty-five manuscripts, the *Fall of Princes* exemplifies how the moralizing of the public servant that some critics consider dull was in step with Continental innovations that other critics hail as humanistic evidence of Renaissance New Learning. Manuscript images, in fact, link Lydgate directly to the Italian humanists. The Philadelphia *Fall of Princes* (Rosenbach Museum, MS 439/16, 1465–75), for example, repeatedly depicts Boccaccio writing at his desk next to the manuscript's narrative scenes, visually eliding the French intermediary and stressing the ultimate Italian authorial source for the reader of Lydgate's English.[51]

William Langland's *Piers Plowman*, although clearly popular, was not widely illustrated, an indicator of its social status and reception in the fifteenth century when it aroused political and religious suspicion. Its single extensively illustrated manuscript (Bodleian Library, Douce 104) is unusual in its seventy-three marginal drawings and Irish provenance (1427).[52] The drawings represent the visionary's experience, even if personified characters and narrative actions hover in the margins seemingly detached from the poem's text. Antichrist, for example, is depicted as a disembodied head, a visual translation of the phrase "in mans form" (C.23.52; fol. 107r).[53] These intriguing pictures have been studied by Denise L. Despres and Kathryn Kerby-Fulton, whose *Iconography and the Professional Reader* suggests how valuable insights can result from analyzing manuscript images in detail.[54] The debate between these authors and Ralph Hanna also shows how difficult it is for literary scholars to credit visual evidence. Although Hanna astutely details the book's historical missteps, his conclusion is not fair: "On virtually every level—as a model for others to use in their investigations, as a definition of a literary community, as practical criticism of either *Piers Plowman* or its tradition—it just won't do."[55] Focusing on images to understand a text's early reception and interpretation is a useful approach that has been highly successful in recent studies, though.[56] The authors, furthermore, rightly note that Hanna's opposition to their methodology reveals serious critical blinders: "Hanna seems to feel we have slighted the post-Romantic notion of the author by deigning to appreciate the interpretive creativity of nameless scribes and artists on something more like a level playing field than is traditional in literary studies."[57] If we are to make progress in the study of late-medieval literary cultures, we must accept fascinating manuscripts such as Douce 104 as evidence of the reception of fourteenth-century poems within specific fifteenth-century interpretive communities.

IMAGE AND WORD: THREE MISTAKEN ASSUMPTIONS

To do so we need a methodology that takes visual translation seriously and counters three mistaken assumptions that often influence image and word studies. The first, the "aesthetic," assumes that images must be as aesthetically pleasing or as sophisticated as the texts they illustrate. This often unstated but widely held misconception explains why the stunning frontispiece of *Troilus and Criseyde* in Corpus Christi College, MS 61 (ca. 1420), receives so much attention, whereas the pictures of pilgrims and vices in the Cambridge Chaucer are mainly ignored.[58] The aesthetic judgment, for example, motivates Pearsall's gibe that the Cambridge manuscript was made for a patron "with plenty of money but little taste."[59] It also affects responses to the *Pearl* manuscript, as in Barbara Nolan's account, in *Gothic Visionary Perspective*, of her introduction to manuscript imagery: "A chance encounter with a thirteenth-century English illustrated Apocalypse on exhibit in the British Museum first suggested the directions of this book. I had been studying a group of thirteenth- and fourteenth-century French, Italian, and English poems concerning eschatological visions when I came upon an illuminated manuscript in its glass case opened to a vision of the New Jerusalem. Closer examination revealed striking similarities between the elegant miniatures in this book and the poems I had been reading."[60] Those "elegant miniatures" are a far cry from the images of the *Pearl* manuscript, which may explain why Nolan's chapter on *Pearl* does not acknowledge, much less discuss, them. Yet as Freedberg shows in his study of responses to images over millennia and by cultures worldwide, the power of images does not primarily reside in their widely varying aesthetic achievements.[61] Even humble manuscript images can serve as valuable aids to reading, as Hilary Maddocks demonstrates for an illustrated translation of Deguileville's pilgrimage poems, in which pictures give unimaginable personifications "concrete shape and credibility as well as real presence."[62] Images not in deluxe manuscripts may also provide local knowledge necessary to understand an interpretive community, as demonstrated by studies of the Middle English Carthusian Miscellany (British Library, Add. 37049).[63]

A second methodological dead end is to focus on the "accuracy" of an image, judging its efficacy by the extent to which it precisely depicts the text. The assumption that the visual must correspond closely to the verbal, as noted earlier, informs studies of the Ellesmere Chaucer, but it is commonplace in literary critical discussions, "as if the significance of the image began and ended in its fidelity to the text."[64] Although it is the nature of an illustration to be referential, it is nevertheless necessary to analyze an image as a semiotically distinct if related work of art in its own right, not just by how closely it parallels a text. We would not judge a Middle English translation of a French poem simply by its linguistic fidelity to the French (e.g., as a "word-for-word" translation) but would analyze it as a literary work reshaping the meaning of the original (as a "sense-for-sense" translation) for a new audience.[65] Discussing Stephen Scrope's translation (ca. 1440) of Christine de Pizan's *Épître d'Othéa*, for example, Helen Phillips notes that the translator "distinctly obscures Christine's status as the author in his prologue and later blurs the sharpness of Christine's representation of women as sources of advice and wisdom."[66] This is an important insight, but it says more about mid-fifteenth-century English anxieties than about Christine's status in France under Charles VI. Similarly, attention to images may highlight the anxieties of later patrons and readers, as Michael Camille shows by tracing the visual transformation of the personified Idolatry from the fourteenth-century French *Pèlerinage de vie humaine* to Lydgate's fifteenth-century translation.[67] The Middle English manuscript in one image conflates two scenes of Idolatry while adding a new miniature depicting proper devotion to sacred images. These changes, which likely respond to contemporary Lollard polemics that equated images and idols, exemplify how a visual translation can transform a text for a new audience. Scholars can be alert to such interpretive insights by respecting the meaningful choices evident in an image rather than lamenting its lack of textual precision. As David Summers notes, "The *what* of representation—subject matter—is most significant for what it reveals in having been chosen."[68]

Manuscript images sometimes disappoint because of what they "fail" to represent, so that critics consider the elision of textual details as not only a form of inaccuracy but also a "simplification" or "dumbing down." Just as words cannot fully capture a work of art, since "intellectual thinking dismantles the simultaneity of spatial structure,"[69] so an image cannot fully express the superfluity of detail conveyed by a literary text unfolding serially as it is read.[70] As in the medieval art of memory—which recognizes that remembering some things necessitates forgetting others[71]—visual translation requires that some textual details be elided to highlight others in a new visual composition. What is accentuated informs the fresh artistic interpretation, which may represent an essential meaning rather than picture a naturalistic surface. The nonrepresentation of verbal details is not a failure, therefore, but a fundamental technique of visual translation, which results in a new creation: an image with its own emphases, perspectives, and communicative power. By expecting a close correspondence between word and image, furthermore, critics have often ignored visual features that are not discursive, not based on the text, but are nevertheless crucial to the image's figurality, what Norman Bryson tags as features "which belong to the image as a visual experience independent of language—its 'being-as-image.'"[72] These include details of background, color, texture, composition, size, symmetry, and form as well as figural features—such as expressions, gestures, clothing, architectural interiors, natural locales, and so forth—that, although not explicit in the text, are necessary to depict characters and settings. Here it is useful to distinguish between the subject and the content of an image.[73] Owing to its referential nature, a manuscript illustration will likely share a subject with its accompanying text, yet it can never fully share a content, since the verbal text is incommensurate with the image's dense visual field. To appreciate the complexity of a manuscript image, therefore, we need to avoid privileging the unachievable, and undesirable, model of accurate content and instead focus as much on *how* the image represents as on *what* textual features it represents.[74] This crucial desideratum in approaching a visual translation recognizes the heuristic principle that an interpretation of an image should not separate form from content.

The third and most common misunderstanding of medieval images assumes that a picture simply illustrates an idea, theme, belief, social structure, worldview, or even "real life." The image is conceived as a mirror that "reflects" the past, a notion Michael Camille critiques in his *Mirror in Parchment*. Describing the ways the Luttrell Psalter's images have been misused as pictures of "real" fourteenth-century English life, he notes that historians on both the left and the right "have fallen into the same trap of confusing what is representational with what is real" and concludes that scholars must move "beyond this real/unreal dichotomy and see the manuscript as producing, not reflecting, reality."[75] The corollary of the mirror analogy is the treatment of a manuscript image as if it were a transparent window to look through to an unmediated "reality" requiring no analysis since the window/image is transparent, "rudimentary and intuitive," and therefore easy to understand.[76] Deeply ingrained in literary scholarship, this assumption is based on a parochialism, stated more than sixty years ago by Ernst Robert Curtius, that "knowing pictures is easy compared with knowing books."[77] An image, however, is as opaque, complex, and coded as is a literary text; such is clearly evident when "realistic" visual features, such as clothing, are examined by specialists.[78] To interpret an image therefore requires a trained eye, for, as Tom Mitchell notes, "the innocent eye is blind."[79] Paradoxically, treating images as merely illustrative both empowers and debilitates them. On the one hand, they are given compelling authority as "windows" into the past and are treated as indisputable evidence to support an argument. On the other hand, they are reduced to passive "reflection," cited out of context and without regard to their patronage, audience, medium, or function. The critical assumption is that there is no need to analyze the visual text, since it simply illustrates another, more important, verbal text.[80] As Hamburger notes, "Even the most brilliant iconographic interpretations can reduce images to cyphers linked more by what they signify than the means by which that significance was created and conveyed."[81] This problem is exemplified by Sister Mary Clemente Davlin's *Place of God in "Piers Plowman" and Medieval Art,* which cites art ranging from the early-Christian mosaics of San Clemente to fifteenth-century manuscripts without providing visual analysis or considering the relevance of juxtaposing such a wide range of art with the Middle English poem.[82] As Elizabeth Sears has emphasized, however, to interpret a medieval image, it is essential to "pay particular attention to the specific physical context in which a work functioned—who had access to it and what social and religious practices governed its use."[83]

These three mistaken assumptions are challenged by theoretically informed studies interrogating what is at stake in the intricate relationship of visual and verbal texts.[84] For example, visual analysis drawing on semiotic approaches establishes neutral terminology based on sign systems to counter the primacy of verbal texts, a problem that bedevils image and word scholarship.[85] Mieke Bal's *Reading Rembrandt: Beyond the Word–Image Opposition* argues that images and words are co-texts that need not correspond to one another, at least directly, but may share a third—possibly absent—"pre-text," literary, visual, cultural, or historical.[86] It may inform a visual translation based on an established iconography as well as a translated text, as in the Vernon Manuscript miniatures noted above. Manuscript images may also create their own "systems of significations" to translate meaning, as Brigitte Buettner has shown in an illuminated French translation of Boccaccio's *De mulieribus claris.*[87] Hedeman has further stressed the role played by visual rhetoric "to make the past come alive and be relevant to readers and viewers of manuscripts in the medieval present."[88] To avoid privileging word over image, Mary Olson has even argued that there is no essential difference between texts and images, since both are forms of "graphic signification."[89] Although sympathetic to her argument, I think Olson overstates the similarities of iconic and symbolic signs, fails to recognize how images develop distinct sign systems, and risks devaluing the figurality of the image. As Nelson Goodman shows, there is a "boundary between description and representation."[90] To understand visual translation, we need to respect both the figural and discursive—both visual and verbal sign systems—without equating them or eliding their distinct functions.

GRACE DIEU AS VISUAL TRANSLATION

I conclude by briefly examining visual translation in an illustrated manuscript of *The Pilgrimage of the Soul,* the anonymous Middle English version of Guillaume de Deguileville's *Pèlerinage de l'âme* made in 1413, probably for a noblewoman.[91] Seven of its manuscripts are illustrated, and its other extant manuscripts were designed to include pictures, "which indicates the integral role played by illustration in the Soul's manuscript tradition and suggests that illustration must have been present in the earliest copies of the text."[92] Although unusual for a Middle English text, this visual emphasis is not surprising, since the French original was widely known and illustrated and was even recast as a deluxe Latin manuscript for the duke of Bedford.[93] The English translation is also of great interest, reinforcing the orthodox nature of Guillaume's otherworldly allegory by converting it, as its editor shows, "into a polemical text offering material in the vernacular that . . . would answer Lollard attacks on Roman Catholic doctrine."[94] As we will see, this concern with orthodoxy is further underscored by the manuscript's images.

This generic shift from verse dream vision to prose treatise is exemplified by *Grace Dieu,* the work's title in New York Public Library, Spencer 19, produced around 1430.[95] After an added table of contents comprising its first six pages, it opens with a beautifully decorated page (fol. 7r; Figure 1) that encloses the prose text within a richly floriated vinet border.[96] The top third of the folio is dominated by a miniature that establishes the setting of the entire work. A Latin rubric ("Incipit liber qui nuncupatur Grace dieu. Cap[itulum] primum") is inscribed immediately below, further authorizing the repackaging of Guillaume's poem as an orthodox treatise. It separates the miniature from the Middle English text, which is introduced by a six-line sprynget initial *A,* for "As I lay in a Seint Laurence nyght slepynge in bed, me bifel a ful mervaylous dreme which I shal reherse." The narrative, marked by a blue paraph, then begins: "Than cam cruel deth and smot me wyth his venomous dart." Toward the bottom of the text box, the names of "Misericordie" and "Prayer" are highlighted in red. With its table of contents, division into five books and 142 chapters, Latin apparatus, rubricated character designations, and alternating blue and red paraphs, the manuscript epitomizes "the articulation of the text" characterizing late-medieval reading practices, which, as Armando Petrucci notes, were directed "by a rich series of graphic interventions and tools . . . , all of which enclosed, delimited, and cut up the text, rendering it thus accessible in small portions that could easily be found again."[97]

Grace Dieu's twenty-six miniatures similarly direct reading, fashioning a visual translation that supports and interprets the text.[98] A large opening miniature (Figure 2) is set off by a three-paneled frame painted orange, blue, and rose and highlighted by a gold band that is slightly notched in the lower right to draw attention to and accommodate a burial scene. The tooled gold ground distinguishes the picture's eschatological upper half from the interior setting of the bed—which dominates the left side of the scene and rests on a black-and-white checkerboard floor—as well as from the exterior setting of the grave, placed on grass in the foreground of a spired church on the right. Although five characters are depicted within this miniature,

Figure 1: Dreamer/Narrator in bed. *Grace Dieu* (ca. 1430), New York Public Library, Spencer 19, fol. 7r. (Spencer Collection, The New York Public Library, Astor, Lenox and Tilden Foundations.)

it significantly omits "cruel Deth," who begins the text's action by smiting the narrator. The artist has instead highlighted the elderly, curly-haired, and bearded Dreamer/Narrator in bed, who has completed his "fleshly pilgrimage" (fol. 7r). His relatively large size gives him prominence as he experiences his "ful mervaylous dreme" in which his body is buried while he morphs into the Pilgrim/Soul. The scene visually emphasizes three stages of this visionary transition. First, the living Pilgrim of the past is shown as a small man dressed in blue and wearing red hose who emerges from the church, having arrived at "þe holy cite of Ierusalem" and no longer able to "ferther trauayle vpon my foot" (fol. 7r).[99] Second, his shrouded body is buried in a tomb by the blonde Dame Misericordie, also dressed in blue, who stands in the grave. Next to her is a ladder that leads the eye from the grave up to the bed and on to the New Jerusalem, symbolized by the church. Its cruciform nave and transept cradle Misericordie's nimbus, accentuating this visual and orthodox *ars moriendi*. Third, the narrator's Soul, now young and not bearded but still curly-haired, stands by the bed gazing into the distance, ready for his journey. He holds a pilgrim's staff, a visual prop linking him to the Dreamer, whose status as a pilgrim is suggested by the gold scallop shell lying on the bed next to his right shoulder, a figural rather than a discursive detail.

Standing next to the Soul, who is dressed in blue here and in all other miniatures, is a red-winged figure repeatedly misidentified by scholars as Dame Prayer, probably because she is the next character introduced by the text.[100] She, however, is not depicted in the image. Instead, the figure in white, who is linked by his youth and curly hair to the Soul, is his guardian Angel, "a ful fair ʒongelynge of ful huge beaute" (fol. 7v). He is not introduced by the text until the next chapter, however, not until after the Soul is harassed by Satan. The miniature's figural elements, therefore, both elide and anticipate discursive details to place the Soul from the outset of the pilgrimage next to his guardian Angel, whose crucial role is emphasized visually by his large golden nimbus shown breaking the frame's boundary. This visual translation thus only partly corresponds to the text, but not because it "dumbs down" the narrative, "fails" to depict Death and Dame Prayer, or "inaccurately" adds a character not yet present in the literary text. It instead represents the central doctrinal theme of *Grace Dieu* by stressing the promise of salvation. The image significantly replaces Death and its "ven-

Figure 2: NYPL, Spencer 19, fol. 7r, detail. (Spencer Collection, The New York Public Library, Astor, Lenox and Tilden Foundations.)

omous dart"[101] with the Angel holding the chalice and host—figural details not mentioned in the text. They emphasize the church's salvific role from the very beginning and thereby strengthen the manuscript's orthodoxy.

The representation of Satan, who is active in the narrative from near its beginning, is delayed until the second miniature (Figure 3). It shows three characters walking on a grassy visionary landscape against a gold ground. The scene is placed below an English caption ("How þe soule is led to þe iuggement be twene þe aungel and þe fule satanas," fol. 9r) and a Latin rubric identifying the fourth chapter. Its text, introduced by a champ initial S attached to the demi-vinet border, states that the Angel is on "my right side." The image's composition, however, visually translates this verbal detail by placing the red-winged Angel—depicted as in the first miniature—on the Soul's left and thus on the *viewer's* right. This allows the Angel to lead the pilgrim by his left arm, while gesturing with his right hand toward the place of judgment. The Soul's status as pilgrim is highlighted by his script as well as his staff, visual details not in the accompanying text, but significant because in an earlier chapter Satan had ordered the pilgrim to "Cast doun þi scrippe and þi burdon, for al þi pilgrimage is come to a iape" (fol. 7v). Their inclusion exemplifies how the figural elements of an image—here motivated by the need to depict the Soul as a pilgrim—can have thematic potency and recall an earlier discursive scene. The composition of the narrative scene also contests Scott's description of this miniature: "Soul as pilgrim led to judgement by Satan and Guardian Angel."[102] The image, however, visually emphasizes that the pilgrim is *not* led by Satan. Instead, the fiery red, club-wielding devil, who in the second and third chapters aggressively menaced the Soul and fiercely debated the Angel, is first depicted here meekly trailing behind on the left, rather than leading on the right, where he would have been placed had the artist followed the text. The compositional transposition is striking and gives prominence to the protective Angel, who shelters the Soul within his right wing. Satan's threatening gaze, furthermore, is directed at the reader/viewer, who is to learn from this allegorical treatise, not at the Soul. He has made a good death, has sustained a preliminary victory over Satan, and has earned his guardian Angel's guidance and protection during the forthcoming judgment.

These first two miniatures demonstrate how a visual translation can depict crucial discursive details while emphasizing by means of figural elements the larger thematic concerns of a verbal text. Their interpretive value

Figure 3: Guardian Angel leads Soul to Judgment. NYPL, Spencer 19, fol. 9r. (Spencer Collection, The New York Public Library, Astor, Lenox and Tilden Foundations.)

counters Pearsall's verdict that "what modern literary interpreters are always looking for in illustrated medieval literary manuscripts, and what they are never or rarely going to find, is 'expressiveness,' in which the meaning of a story, moral or emotional or psychological, will be communicated in visual form."[103] The miniatures of this and of many other late-medieval illustrated literary manuscripts, however, *do* translate meaning into visual form. Although space constraints prevent analysis of *Grace Dieu*'s other twenty-four miniatures, they similarly accentuate the protective role of the Angel leading the Soul from personal judgment through the otherworld, eliding some characters while depicting the allegory's main players, such as Justice, Reason, Truth, Synderesis (the worm of conscience), Lady Doctrine, Mary, and Satan. Many details of the text and the *sentence* of its dialogues are not represented; the images do not replace the Middle English version of the French poem but re-produce it. As a visual translation, it both directs reading by contributing to the rich matrix of the manuscript page and interprets the literary text by emphasizing its major themes. In representing souls in Purgatory, for example, the miniatures picture discursive details to accentuate suffering, whereas through their figural composition, placement of characters, and use of color and size, they stress the Angel's defense of the pilgrim Soul.

This thematic emphasis on angelic protection is rendered near the manuscript's conclusion by the miniature (Figure 4) introducing book 5 (fol. 109v). Placed below a caption ("How the soule was taken out of purgatorie and led up thurgh the hevenly spere toward the blisse"), it concentrates on the large Angel dominating the scene's center. Swooping down from blue clouds, its open wings are now a shaded white that contrasts dramatically with the bright crimson flames threatening the Soul. He reaches up to his guardian, who places a protective right hand on the pilgrim's head. To recognize how this image visually translates the Middle English, it is essential to note that the text does not here mention the Angel. Instead the Soul recounts: "Thanne semed I to my self so light that I bygan to fle with oute eny lettynge an[d] saugh into heuen," including "seint michael sittynge as a ȝuge" (fol. 109v). The miniature, however, focuses not on the pilgrim's glimpse of Michael, who earlier judged him, but on a later scene where— seeing and hearing a multitude of singing birds—the Soul asks about their significance (fol. 110r). They are larks, the guardian Angel explains, embodying praise and prayers rising to heaven. Placed in the dark fissure

Figure 4: Angel lifts Soul up to Heaven from Purgatory. NYPL, Spencer 19, fol. 109v.
(Spencer Collection, The New York Public Library, Astor, Lenox and Tilden
Foundations.)

separating the hot red of purgatory from the cool blue of heaven, they are intermediaries surrounding the Soul and the Angel. The Angel is shown here near the manuscript's end for the same reason the opening miniature depicts him well before he is mentioned in the text (Figure 2)—to stress how the Soul is *always* guided by his Angel. Balancing the structure of the picture cycle, the image underscores the orthodox doctrinal allegory of *Grace Dieu*. Through both form and content, this image and the others in the picture cycle create new meanings that as visual translations supplement and reinterpret rather than accurately copy or merely illustrate the accompanying text, just as the Middle English prose translation reinterprets the original French poem for its fifteenth-century audience.

BARN OF UNITY OR THE DEVIL'S CHURCH?
SALVATION AND ECCLESIOLOGY IN
LANGLAND AND THE WYCLIFFITES

J. Patrick Hornbeck II

very Dulles, the late Roman Catholic theologian, may seem an odd starting point for a discussion of religious reformers in late-medieval England. The son of an American secretary of state, a Jesuit priest, a cardinal, and a frequent defender of the conservative orthodoxy of Pope John Paul II, Dulles would appear to have had little in common with William Langland, the author of the poem *Piers Plowman*; or with John Wyclif, the Oxford philosopher and theologian exiled from his university and condemned posthumously as a heresiarch; or with the several hundred women and men tried for heresy in the fourteenth, fifteenth, and sixteenth centuries. Dulles was born into prestige; they, with a few notable exceptions, were of no great social or economic standing. He was a convert to Catholicism and grew to maturity in a church rocked by divisions about biblical interpretation, sexual ethics, and the theological standing of non-Christians; they were born into, lived, and died in a world more culturally and religiously homogeneous.

Yet Dulles' work on ecclesiology—the subdiscipline of theology that seeks to understand the mission and organization of the Christian church—can offer a helpful framework within which to situate late-medieval dissenters. The ecclesiological categories and tropes that Dulles systematized have their roots in twentieth-century Roman Catholic theology, even as they claim to capture perennial themes in the history of Christianity's self-understanding. They are, as a result, not the only categories one might use to assess competing theologies of the church, but neither are they totally irrelevant outside their own historical moment. In fact, if we are careful to avoid anachronism, the lenses that Dulles's ecclesiological writings offer us can enable us to perceive much about the intellectual and religious worlds of people who lived centuries earlier. At the same time, to borrow from Dulles is all the more appropriate in a volume dedicated to the contributions that Penn R. Szittya has made to the study of the Middle Ages: In Dulles's life story, the intersection between the concerns of the American state and the Roman Catholic Church parallels quite neatly the intersection of faith and reason in the mission of the university where Penn spent the bulk of his career, Georgetown.

In 1976, Dulles published *Models of the Church*, an economically written treatise that, over the course of multiple editions and reprintings, became his most influential intervention in Roman Catholic ecclesiology.[1] In that work, Dulles provided a topography of the many vocabularies that Catholics have used, and continue to use, to describe the church. He distilled these multiple and sometimes conflicting discourses into five broad models: an institutional model, which emphasizes the hierarchical organization of the church with the pope, bishops, clergy, and laity and focuses on the visible structures that connect members of the church to one another; a communion model, which (borrowing heavily from the language of the Second Vatican Council) highlights the mystical bonds linking members of the church, both living and dead; a sacrament model, which emphasizes the role of the church in symbolizing and bringing about salvation for its members; a herald model, which puts greatest emphasis on the church's task of preaching the gospel; and a servant model, which highlights the church's concern for promoting social and economic justice. Each of these five models, Dulles explained, is necessarily incomplete: The church is not only a hierarchy, a mystical communion, a sacrament, a herald, or a servant but rather an amalgam of all these roles. To unduly accentuate any one model at the expense of the others is to commit an act of theological violence: Thus, for instance, Dulles argued that ecclesiologies that overly stress the church's temporal role as an agent of justice in human societies neglect its spiritual role as an agent of salvation.[2]

Dulles's models thus purport to describe—albeit, as Dulles himself admitted, not without some rough edges—a set of intersecting ways of thinking about the church that have been contested throughout the history of Christianity. For this reason, they usefully foreground for the present study a series of crucial tensions in Christian theology and ecclesiology. Dulles's first two models, in particular, characterize well the age-old distinction between the visible community of worshipers gathered around the Sunday altar and the invisible community of believers and saints destined to enjoy the fullness of heaven. This binary was a way of thinking promoted strongly, though hardly exclusively, by Augustine of Hippo and enlarged on by a host of his successors. It also figured prominently in the writings of the individuals I will be considering in this essay: In late medieval England, William Langland, John Wyclif, and many of the dissenters who operated with a Wycliffite theological paradigm drew on the distinction between visible and invisible churches. Their ecclesiologies differed (in some ways conspicuously) from one another, but if analyzed in Dulles's terms they all gave preference to what Dulles called a communion model of the church over what he termed an institutional one.

———————

The striking similarities in their theological and ecclesiological methods may well have influenced the growth of a cottage scholarly industry in comparisons between Langland, Wyclif, and the Wycliffites. It is against the background of more than four centuries of such scholarship that this essay ventures to suggest not that Langland was a Wycliffite, nor that Wycliffites were "Langlandian," but that both groups privileged a particular set of ways of thinking about the church.[3] The tradition of making such comparisons may have begun in 1548, when the ex-Carmelite reformer John Bale included a poem entitled *Petrum Agricolam* in the list of works that he attributed to Wyclif. He withdrew the attribution a decade later, but the damage had already been done.[4] In 1550, the printer Robert Crowley wrote in the preface to his first edition of *Piers Plowman* that its author was one of Wyclif's followers, and other Edwardian propagandists lauded the poem as a harbinger of the reformation that they sought to impose on the English church.[5] To be sure, to draw analogies between Langland's poem and Wycliffite writings is tempting; they are all vernacular writings interested in making the text of scripture accessible to a lay audience, and, as Penn Szittya has done so much to establish, they all participate in a long tradition of antifraternal criticism and satire. In recent years, though, scholars have shown that, while the author of *Piers Plowman* was a religious reformer, he did not share many of the characteristic theological positions of Wyclif and his followers.[6] Thus, it is worth reiterating that to set Langland and Wyclif side by side, and to establish that their theologies of the church were methodologically similar, is by no means to attempt the resurrection of a Wycliffite Langland. Far from it, in fact: If this essay succeeds in bringing Langland and the Wycliffites closer together, I hope that its net effect will be not so much in painting a picture of Langland as a heretic than in contributing to the gradual dismantling of the claim that Wyclif and Wycliffites were interested in nothing short of the utter overthrow of late-medieval Christianity.[7]

For both Langland and Wyclif, the reform of the church is inseparably bound up with claims about the church's mission, about how the Christian community on earth helps to bring about the salvation promised in the suffering, death, and resurrection of Jesus. The connection between ecclesiology and soteriology is of course not unique to these two writers; it appears across the whole spectrum of Christian thought. Indeed, all five of Dulles's models describe not just what the church *is* but also what it *does*, so that it is possible to speak of an institution that mediates salvation through the lines of apostolic succession, or a mystical communion of individuals who will be saved, a sacrament of salvation, a herald of Jesus' saving message, or a servant that aims to make the present world more like the one to come. Particularly in the Middle Ages, when the end times and the church's place in the eschaton figured far more prominently than they do for most Christians today, the doctrine of salvation and the doctrine of the church cannot but be intertwined. In approaching Langland's and Wyclif's ecclesiologies, then, we may find it helpful to begin with their theologies of salvation.

The desire to be saved and to know with certainty of one's eventual salvation has long been a central feature of Christian thought and practice.[8] As successive generations of theologians have formulated their ideas about salvation, they have left behind them a bewildering array of terms in which to describe the process by which human souls are liberated from the effects of sin. In the West, discourse about salvation has revolved primarily around the Pauline metaphors of justification and redemption, but the interpretation of these terms has been hotly contested. Labels such as *Pelagian, semi-Pelagian, predestinarian, fatalist, universalist, Calvinist,* and *Arminian* may appear to delineate particularly influential or controversial positions in the history of discussions about salvation, but few such words are free from ambiguity.

There is not space here for a detailed discussion of these and other terms, but briefly it is worth observing that the position I will be referring to as *predestinarianism* holds that human beings can in no way merit grace and that salvation is solely dependent on God's gratuitous election. On the strictest version of this doctrine, the logic by which God makes salvific choices is inscrutable; God's election, moreover, is irresistible, and therefore the elect cannot forsake their status, nor can those not elect earn salvation. At the other end of the soteriological spectrum is the position I will be calling *Pelagianism*, which holds that human persons can earn salvation as a result of their freely chosen good deeds. This position has most infamously been associated with the fifth-century British monk Pelagius; whether or not it was in fact held by him, it nevertheless provides a helpful shorthand for the often reviled, but actually rarely articulated, view that human beings can, in effect, compel God to save them on account of their good deeds. Other soteriologies appropriate elements of both predestinarianism and Pelagianism. Insofar as a particular theology of salvation borrows from predestinarianism an emphasis on the sovereignty of God's grace, I will call it *grace-oriented*; likewise, insofar as a particular theory focuses on human freedom and agency, I will call it *works-oriented*. One epithet that I will generally avoid is *semi-Pelagian*, which in scholarly analyses of late-medieval literature and religion has appeared too often as a catch-all for ideas about salvation that are neither predestinarian nor Pelagian.[9] That is not to deny, however, that in the history of Christianity the vast majority of theologies of salvation have fallen into the gray area between predestinarianism and Pelagianism. Langland's and Wyclif's do as well, and this fact carries with it substantial implications for the ways in which both authors think about the church.

Salvation is among the most visible of Langland's preoccupations. The prologue to *Piers Plowman*, with its vision of the field of folk situated between "a tour on a toft trieliche ymaked" and a dungeon "with depe diches and derke and dredfulle of sighte," positions humankind between heaven and hell, and as the poem develops Langland frequently returns to the question of salvation.[10] In passus 1, for instance, the narrator's conversation with Lady Holy Church turns quickly to soteriological themes. Holy Church admonishes him not to seek his treasure in "the wrecched world" but instead to "go to the Gospel . . . that God seide hymselven," and she repeats Jesus' words in the Gospel of Matthew: "*Reddite Cesari . . .* that *Cesari* bifalleth" (1.39, 46, 52–53). The narrator's response merits reproduction in full:

I courbed on my knees and cried hire of grace,
And preide hire piteously to preye for my synnes,
And also kenne me kyndely on Crist to bileve,

That I myghte werchen His wille that wroghte me to manne:
"Teche me to no tresor, but tel me this ilke—
How I may save my soule, that seint art yholden."

(1.79–84)

Holy Church does not again appear in the poem in the form in which she
is personified here; after she introduces the vision of Lady Meed in passus
2, she departs the scene altogether. The reappearance of the church in the
form of the barn of Unity in passus 19 and 20, though, provides a bookend
to Langland's extended attempt to answer the narrator's question.

But how, exactly, does Langland believe that human beings are saved?
Scholarly opinion has fluctuated over the years, with some students of *Piers
Plowman* arguing that Langland takes a predestinarian stance, and others,
a works-oriented one; more recently, David Aers has rightly critiqued the
widespread tendency of scholars to reduce the complexities of Langland's
soteriology and its christological resonances to a dialectic between these
two competing positions.[11] It is worth noting, though, that many analyses
of Langland's soteriology have focused on a single disputed episode in the
poem, the famous pardon scene of passus 7 in the B-text. For scholars like
Denise Baker, the pardon scene represents Langland's repudiation of "semi-
Pelagianism"; according to her account, Piers's decision to tear up the par-
don sent by Truth and to abandon the plowing of the half acre testify that
only grace can enable human beings to do good and, therefore, to attain
salvation.[12] For others, such as Robert Adams, the tearing of the pardon
does not imply a rejection of its terms: "There are simply too many passages
scattered throughout the poem that emphasize the primacy of good works
and human effort for all of them to be explained away."[13]

Taken on its own, the pardon episode in the B-text may be ambiguous,
but the evolution of the pardon scene in the successive versions of *Piers
Plowman*, the resonances of that scene in medieval documentary culture,
and other episodes in the poem all suggest that Langland's soteriology is
not predestinarian. We should remember, first, that Piers's pardon comes
from Truth, one of Langland's personifications of the divine. Its terms are
worth repeating:

In two lynes it lay, and noght a letter more,
And was ywriten right thus in witnesse of Truthe:

Et qui bona egerunt ibunt in vitam eternam;
Qui vero mala, in ignem eternum.

(7.109–10)

In short, if human beings must "do well" in order to earn eternal life, then there must be some connection between human actions and salvation. The pardon is therefore not unlike the equivalent, in scholastic terms, of God's *potentia ordinata*, the set of rules God has put in place to govern the universe, even though God could have created the universe in some other way. The pardon imparts salvific significance to certain human actions, even though its existence is entirely contingent on the will of God. That salvation is available only through the terms of the pardon rules out Pelagianism; human beings cannot earn salvation without God having acted first. Recently, Emily Steiner has compellingly interpreted the pardon as an enactment of Augustine's commentary on the *chirographum Dei* of Psalm 145 (Psalm 144 in the Vulgate); in her view, Truth's pardon represents a "textual encounter with salvation history" whose terms enable Langland, as they do Augustine, to distinguish between God's absolute and God's conditional power.[14] For Steiner, the tearing of the pardon is not an act of rejection but rather of faith and affirmation. She points out that Langland's evocation of Augustine's *chirographum Dei* would have conjured up a specific image for late-medieval audiences:

> In a ceremony analogous to the Mass, the scribe would draw up in duplicate or triplicate a deed called a chirograph or indenture. As in the case of the consecrated wafer, the notary or scribe would ceremoniously rip or, more commonly, cut the indenture in half and distribute the parts to the legal actors. . . . The ritualistic "tearing" of the document, in sum, had at least three important effects: it enacted the conditions of the deed, it attested to the security and validity of the transaction, and it implicated the actors in the preservation of the contract.[15]

At the same time as they neglect these historical resonances, some arguments in favor of his predestinarianism also overlook the revision of the pardon scene in the C-text of the poem. For Baker, the most important element of the scene is Piers's tearing of the pardon; she interprets his action as evidence of his realization that "natural man is unable to do well . . . he cannot earn grace and salvation through his own works," and she ascribes Piers's angry ripping of the pardon to his frustration with the works-oriented soteriology that had motivated the plowing of the half acre in the first place.[16] However, while Piers does tear the pardon in both the A-text and B-text of the poem, in the C-text the document survives intact the confrontation between Piers and the priest. There, the narrator remarks that "the prest . . . and Perkyn of þe pardon iangelede," but the vision ends before Piers can take any action more drastic than that.[17] After waking, the narrator comments that he has often thought "of that y seyh slepynge, if hit be so myhte, / And of Peres the plouhman fol pencyf in herte / And which a pardoun Peres hadde the peple to glade / And how þe prest impugnede hit thorw two propre wordes."[18] The C-text appears to confirm that the terms of the pardon are to be taken literally. Piers is presented as having thought that the pardon *a poena et a culpa* promised the salvation of all; as a result, it is unsurprising that he argues vehemently with the priest.[19] Throughout the rest of the poem, it is the priest's doctrine that prevails: The pardon is effective only for those who act rightly. Piers's tearing of the pardon in the A- and the B-texts reflects a similar frustration with its terms, but Langland's decision to remove the tearing from his final revision allows the theological message of the pardon scene to emerge all the more clearly.[20]

Yet, as I suggested above, much scholarship on Langland's soteriology has handicapped itself by focusing too narrowly on the pardon scene, and episodes elsewhere in the poem call into question the idea that Langland endorses a predestinarian theology of salvation. Prior to the pardon episode, for instance, the seven deadly sins present themselves to Repentance and are shriven. The narrator notes that "Roberd the robbere on *Reddite* loked, / And for ther was nought wherewith, he wepte swithe soore" (5.462–63). Robert (or Hobbe) the robber, who figures not only in *Piers Plowman* but also in several of the epistolary fragments written by the protagonists of the 1381 "Peasants' Revolt," stands in this scene for the possibility of the conversion and repentance of sinful humanity.[21] Not only is it the case that Robert must choose to confess his sins in order to be granted grace, but the language the narrator uses here also foreshadows the poem's closing passus. That Hobbe looks on *Reddite* is all the more significant in light of the phrase that Langland employs in passus 19 to describe the condition for entry into the barn of Unity: *redde quod debes*. This phrase has its source in Matthew's parable of the talents, in which Jesus tells the story of a king who offers to settle the debts that his servants owe to him. When he forgives one servant his debt and yet that servant nevertheless imprisons one of his own debtors, the king exacts revenge and turns the hypocritical servant over to his torturers.[22] Its themes of forgiveness, salvation, and community make it unsurprising that this parable is the source of the phrase Langland uses to describe the characteristics of church members.

Given this background, let us examine more closely Langland's ecclesiology. In passus 19 and 20 of the B-text, Langland deploys his most extensive metaphor for the church. He envisions the founding of the church by Grace and Piers Plowman, who drives a team of four oxen (the evangelists) and four horses (the doctors of the church) to sow a field with the four cardinal virtues. When it comes time to harvest the crop, Grace instructs Piers to build a barn in which to store his produce. This building, constructed from Christ's crown of thorns, his blood, and the scriptures, becomes "Unite—Holy Chirche on Englissh" (19.330). Immediately after Piers finishes his work, however, Pride begins to plan an assault against the barn of Unity. Piers disappears, and passus 20 describes the cataclysmic conflict between his "conestable," Conscience, and the forces of Pride (20.214).

Embedded among the apocalyptic images of this final scene—for the understanding of which scholars owe Penn Szittya a great debt—are Langland's most direct comments on the doctrine of salvation.[23] Conscience, who all along has been narrating the story of the church's establishment, tells the narrator that Christ

> yaf Piers power, and pardon he grauntede:
> To alle maner men, mercy and foryifenesse;
> To hym, myghte men to assoille of alle manere synnes,
> In covenaunt that thei come to kneweliche to paye
> To Piers pardon the Plowman—*Redde quod debes.*
>
> (19.184–88)

For Langland, then, *redde quod debes* is the criterion that distinguishes those who deserve salvation from those who do not. Those who are able to pay what they owe merit the forgiveness of Piers and, through his agency, the forgiveness of Christ. As David Aers has argued, only those who *reddunt quod debent* to God and their fellow believers are members of the church and can receive the sacraments: the Eucharist, for instance, is available for "men to ete it . . . / In helpe of hir heele ones in a monthe, / Or as ofte as thei hadde need, tho that hadde ypaied / To Piers pardon the Plowman, *Redde quod debes*" (19.388–90).[24]

Just what do we owe? Langland furnishes one possible answer earlier in the poem, in the narrator's conversations with Abraham (Faith), Spes (Hope), and the Samaritan. In passus 17, Abraham tells the narrator that God saves those who believe in the Trinity and are "sory for hir synnes," while Spes explains that the love of God and neighbor together suffice for salvation (17.29, 22). Revealing a tablet on which are written the words *Dilige Deum et proximum tuum*, Spes notes that "whoso wercheth after this writ, I wol undertaken, / Shal never devel hym dere, ne deeth in soule greve" (17.16–17). Finally, the Samaritan synthesizes the advice of Abraham and Spes, adding an explicitly Christian gloss: Not only are faith and love required for salvation, but so also is the death of Jesus. Langland's *redde quod debes* thus seems to refer to each individual's debt of faith and love, and the term functions in *Piers Plowman* in a way quite reminiscent of the scholastic dictum *facere quod in se est*.[25] Earlier thinkers, from Irenaeus of Lyons to Langland's near-contemporary Robert Holcot, had argued that if human beings do what is in them, God will not deny them salvation. According to Holcot, God established the rule *facere quod in se est* at the time of creation; it is an act of God's *potentia ordinata*, but it assures human beings that by doing all that they can, they can ensure their salvation.[26] Likewise, Langland connects the maxim *redde quod debes* with the actions of Christ. It was Christ who entirely freely chose to appoint Piers "my procuratour and my reve, / And registrer to receive *Redde quod debes*," but once Christ had done so, that decision and its consequences became part of the fabric of the universe (19.260–61).

For Langland, then, those who fulfill the requirements of *redde quod debes* can enter the barn of Unity and become members of the church. The poet seems hopeful that a great number of people will do so, and indeed, the barn of Unity in passus 19 and 20 holds nearly everyone. When Pride begins to threaten the church, Conscience invites all Christians to seek sanctuary within it, and this invitation meets with an overwhelmingly positive response: "Thanne alle kynne Cristene, save comune wommen, / Repenteden and refusede synne . . . [C]lennesse of the comune and clerkes clene lyvynge / Made Unitee Holy Chirche in holynesse stonde" (19.371–72, 383–84). Those outside the barn of Unity are few in number, and they are the very characters one might expect to find outside the church—namely, unrepentant prostitutes and the servants of Pride. This group constitutes a minority that is outnumbered by those inside the barn—those who, in Langland's vocabulary, have paid what they owe.

It should be clear from this discussion that Langland's ecclesiology is a communitarian one, offering a way of thinking about the church that stresses the invisible bonds that bring together those human beings who have fulfilled the terms of the maxim *redde quod debes*. As James Simpson has argued, Langland's ecclesiology describes the church as neither a purely material nor a purely intellectual assembly; it is rather "psychological, volitional."[27] Indeed, Langland's theology of the church is closest to Avery Dulles's model of the church as a mystical communion. Both the image of the church as the barn of *Unity* (rather than of sacramental grace, or of hierarchy) and Langland's description of the Christian community gathered together in the barn downplay some of the distinctions that are characteristic of Dulles's institutional model. That we read of both the "clennesse of the comune" *and* "clerkes clene lyvynge," for instance, suggests that the laity as well as the clergy are essential to the spiritual health of the church. In contrast to the institutional model, which dominated the Middle Ages in the forms of an increasingly centralized papacy, the regulation of new models of religious life, and the development of inquisitorial procedures to deal with suspected heretics, Langland describes the church in terms far less authoritarian.

Indeed, the images Langland draws on as he depicts the foundation of the church are rustic ones. Conscience first describes Unity as a house, but he quickly adopts language that is more agrarian: "My counseil is to wende / Hastiliche into Unitee and holde we us there, / And praye we that a pees weere in Piers berne the Plowman" (19.359–61). To bolster his master metaphor of the church as a barn, Langland introduces a number of figures borrowed from the same field of human activity: "Grace devysede / A cart highte Cristendom, to carie home Piers sheves, / And gaf hym caples to his carte . . . / And made Preesthod Hayward" (19.332–35). Taken together, these and other images point to Langland's interest in the practice of the *ecclesia primitiva*, the supposedly pristine original church to which many medieval reformers looked as an example. These images reflect agricultural sensibilities reminiscent of the manger in the Christmas stories and of the humble occupations of Jesus' early disciples, and they also leave the reader with a sense of the ideal church's rustic simplicity. At the same time, Langland's definition of church membership in terms of those who have paid what they owe emphasizes the role of human agency in the dynamic of salvation. Just as human beings must cooperate with grace in order to pay what they owe and, thus, earn salvation, so also must Piers cooperate with a personified Grace in order to construct the church. Grace provides Piers with the raw materials with which to build the barn of Unity; Piers molds them into a kind of mortar; and Grace then takes that mortar and begins to lay "a good foundement" (19.328). This dynamic brings the key themes of Langland's ecclesiology together with those of his theology of salvation: Grace enables human beings to pay what they owe, human beings may choose willingly to do so, and grace then rewards them with salvation. The relative size of the armies of Conscience and Pride depicted in the final passus of Langland's poem seems to imply that an overwhelming majority of Christians, rather than a small remnant or a clerical elite, will ultimately pay their debt. His communitarian ecclesiology is thus also an optimistic one.

<hr>

Optimistic is a word not often used to describe the thought of John Wyclif, the fiery Oxford philosopher and theologian who was condemned by the Council of Constance (1415) as the first English heresiarch. Wyclif's reputation is that of an intellectual and polemical grouch; even his most sympathetic biographers have not failed to comment on the bile he directed at those whom he held responsible for the corruption of the fourteenth-century church. Nevertheless, Wyclif's doctrine of salvation—and the theology of the church that it undergirds—is not as divergent from Langland's as one might think. Both emphasize the role of human agency in cooperating with grace; both distinguish between the visible, institutional church and the invisible community of those who will be saved; and both ultimately give priority to a vision of the church that shares many similarities with Dulles's mystical communion model.

When it pronounced its posthumous sentence against Wyclif, the Council of Constance condemned him for teaching, among other things, that "all things that happen, happen from absolute necessity."[28] Until recently, much scholarship on Wyclif has followed suit, describing him as both a predestinarian and a philosophical determinist and tracing these positions back to his ultrarealist metaphysics. According to this approach,

Wyclif's soteriology is but one among many of the theological doctrines shaped by his metaphysical realism: God's foreknowledge necessitates the operation of double predestination, since the saved and the damned "represented two distinct modes of being . . . two universals which were eternally distinct from one another."[29] In turn, the story goes, Wyclif's predestinarianism affects other elements of his theological vision. For instance, in his treatise *De ecclesia*, Wyclif distinguishes between two "churches" whose members together constitute the institutional church on earth: on the one hand, an invisible congregation of those who will be saved, and on the other, an equally invisible gathering of those foreknown to damnation.[30] Predestinarian language also shapes Wyclif's doctrine of civil and ecclesiastical dominion, where he argues that only the predestined can justly exercise temporal and spiritual authority.[31] Finally, Wyclif's distinction between *predestinati* and *praesciti* calls ecclesiastical authority itself into question: His conviction that the true church exists independently of the institutional church results in substantially attenuated claims about the powers of the pope, bishops, and priests. After all, if the pope were "on his way to Hell . . . it was obvious that the pope did not have to be obeyed."[32]

While this account of Wyclif's soteriology reigned unchallenged for most of the nineteenth and twentieth centuries, a different consensus has recently begun to emerge among scholars.[33] In a wide-ranging study (2005) of Wyclif's doctrine of grace, Ian Christopher Levy convincingly demonstrated that Wyclif believes free will, God's foreknowledge, and predestination to be compatible. This is no mere philosophical sleight of hand on Wyclif's part: For Levy, as for many contemporary historians of philosophy and theology, it is unimaginable that Wyclif could have articulated a doctrine of salvation that did not involve the active cooperation of the human will.[34] But how, exactly, did this work for Wyclif? His soteriology relies on the distinction between absolute necessity and hypothetical necessity. Absolutely necessary propositions cannot not be true. Hypothetically necessary propositions, on the other hand, are constructed in such a way that while the truth about the connection between the two terms is absolutely necessary, it is contingent only that the first of the two terms itself is true. For instance, it is hypothetically necessary that if God knows that my dog is named Indie, then it is true that my dog is named Indie. But God's knowledge about my dog's name is only contingent, and were I to have a dog by another name, or to have no dog at all, then God's knowledge would reflect that state of affairs instead. What is crucial is that God's knowledge is at no time the *cause* of that state of affairs.

Wyclif leverages the concept of hypothetical necessity to explain that God's omniscience and foreknowledge do not entail that all events are predetermined. "Hypothetical necessity," he writes, "is consistent with supreme contingence."[35] This claim provides Wyclif with the space to assert that even though human actions are foreknown, God nonetheless does not cause them. Two things follow: On the one hand, God is not responsible for sinful human actions, and on the other, freely performed actions can be said to play a role in the process of salvation. According to Wyclif, God's will is to save all people, and therefore God makes prevenient grace available to all. Those who accept God's offer receive merit as well as additional forms of grace, including the grace of predestination, while those who either reject prevenient grace, or accept it at one point but reject it later, are for that reason excluded from the congregation of the elect. Levy explains:

> Wyclif paints a picture of God knocking on the door of people's hearts, even as some resist and refuse to let him in. . . . Thus, on the one hand, no one can be excused, since all people do have the capacity to receive God's grace. On the other hand, one can be sure that Christ does assist those wayfarers who efficaciously will to be saved.[36]

Since, for Wyclif, God is outside time, God's offers of grace happen simultaneously in one sense. In another sense, the offer of prevenient grace is causally prior to all the others. Wyclif thus argues that the *praesciti*, far from being damned by a capricious decree, are "those whom God foreknew he would punish on account of the sins they freely committed. While all were lost in sin, the predestined are those who have accepted God's grace, and the damned are those who have rejected it."[37] Thus, Wyclif's soteriology is neither as innovative nor as controversial as many earlier scholars have suggested. Nevertheless, the predestinarian metaphors that can be found throughout his writings have prompted many, not least his antagonists at the Council of Constance, to impute to Wyclif a soteriological fatalism that he never embraced.

It is this fact that has most obscured the similarities between Wyclif's and Langland's theological methods. For both men, soteriology provides the basis for ecclesiology. In Langland's case, as we have already seen, the

soteriological maxim *redde quod debes* serves to define the community of
church members; in Wyclif's, the distinction between the predestined and
the reprobate does the same. Earlier commentators on Wyclif have been
right to point out that many aspects of his thought revolve around this
binary, but the argument has sometimes been carried a step too far. It is
true that Wyclif speaks often of the predestined and the reprobate, but to
impute to him a radically predestinarian soteriology reminiscent of later
Calvinism is anachronistic. Instead, according to the account of Wyclif's
theology that I have been sketching above, the predestined and reprobate
occupy their respective places only as a result of their own choice either to
accept or to reject God's grace.

In light of this account of Wyclif's soteriology, his ecclesiological claims
take on radically different meanings from what they have traditionally
been thought to hold. It is true, as I mentioned above, that Wyclif defines
the true church as the congregation of the predestined, standing in opposi-
tion to the congregation of the reprobate. But this means less that Wyclif
denies church membership to morally upright individuals because they
are unlucky enough not to be elected by God and, more, that the members
of the church are those people who have responded positively to God's
offer of grace. Likewise, Wyclif's infamous claims about *dominium* do not
so much grant lordship only to those who have been chosen by God as
members of the elect, but rather acknowledge that a proper disposition
toward God's grace, and therefore a proper disposition toward keeping
God's commandments, is necessary for the exercise of authority. It is not,
then, that Wyclif's theology points toward the total abolition of ecclesiasti-
cal authority. Instead, his ideas point toward the restriction of positions of
authority to those morally worthy to hold them.

The net effect of these claims, for Wyclif, is to draw a distinction be-
tween the visible church, with its institutionally sanctioned theology, law,
and organizational structure, and the invisible community of those predes-
tined to salvation on account of their response to God's grace. In Dulles's
terms, Wyclif's ecclesiology stresses the church's existence as a commu-
nion of souls and downplays its existence as an institution. Wyclif does
endorse some ecclesiastical institutions, but he takes the invisible spiritual
realities they mediate to be far more important. In *Trialogus* and *De officio
regis*, for instance, he acknowledges that ordination sets a cleric apart from
a layperson, although he cautions both that the ordination rite does not

automatically make a man a member of God's clergy and that episcopal ordination is not necessary for a priest to exercise his ministry.[38] Apart from a few extreme statements in the polemical works he wrote in his last years, Wyclif also makes similar claims about the papacy, commenting in *De civili dominio* that while the pope enjoys the primacy of the apostle Peter, he can exercise that primacy only insofar as he governs the church in accordance with scripture and the example of the apostles.[39]

The distinction between the visible institution and the invisible community of the church was a focal point for Wyclif and later Wycliffite authors, just as it was for Langland.[40] *The Lanterne of Liȝt*, a vernacular Wycliffite text written between 1409 and 1415, distinguishes between three "churches": God's church of "þe chosun noumbre of hem þat schullen be saued," the devil's church of those who will be condemned in hell, and the material church here on earth.[41] The last of these churches, which corresponds to the visible institution, includes members of the first two. Only at the end of time will the separation between God's church and the devil's church become visible for all to see, but for the time being it is incumbent on believers to learn the attributes that distinguish God's faithful from the devil's minions. As in the case of Wyclif's own theology, some scholars have read the *Lanterne's* distinctions between the three churches as signs of its author's predestinarianism, but the text itself belies such an interpretation. In the last chapter of the *Lanterne*, the author exhorts his audience:

> Neþeles assay in þis lijf, if ȝe may leeue þe fendis chirche and brynge ȝoure silf boþe bodi and soule in to þe chirch of Iesu Crist while grace and mercy may be grauntid, axe of him þat offrid him silf . . . to saue vs alle whanne we were loost.[42]

This is not the utterance of a writer who believes that a person's status in the afterlife is independent of her actions in this world, to be sure: People irreversibly condemned to hell by divine decree would have no chance to succeed in leaving the devil's church. Instead, even though he employs predestinarian metaphors, the author of the *Lanterne* seems to have taken the position that human cooperation with God's offer of grace can bring about salvation; this is the most likely explanation for the author's call for people to actively *leeue* the devil's church and *brynge* themselves into the church of Christ.[43] Just as for Wyclif, then, for this writer the true church is an invisible gathering—in Dulles's words, a mystical communion—of those who will be saved on account of their choice to cooperate with God's grace.

This position was not universally adopted by all Wycliffite writers, nor was it taken up by all of the men and women who were charged with heresy in late medieval England. There is not room here to survey the whole map of doctrines of salvation and of the church that English dissenting authors and heresy suspects professed, but it is helpful to note some of its main contours. In the long Wycliffite sermon cycle, for instance, some sermons stress the operation of God's grace and downplay the cooperation of the will, while others do the opposite. Three excerpts from the sermons illustrate various points on the spectrum between these two positions:

> For þese þat God wot schulle be sauede, al ȝif þei synne for a tyme, neþeles here synful liȝf schal turne to hem to fruyt of heuene. And so þese men þat schal be dampnyde, al ȝif þei don good for a tyme, ȝit þei han an yuel maner þat qwencheþ þe good þat þei don.
>
> Do we now þat in us is, and God wole haue us excusid. And to þis secounde euydense a man shulde neuere ceesse to aȝenstonde þes synnes, wher he be alyue or deed; for, lyue a man riȝtfuly, and for hym God helpiþ his chirche. And þus eche holy deed man helpiþ aȝenus eche synne heere in þe chirche.
>
> [F]or eche man þat schal be dampned, is dampned for his owne gylt, and eche man þat schal be saued, is saued by his owne meryȝt.[44]

It is possible that these views, each of which are echoed in other Wycliffite texts, represent something of a difference in theological emphasis among the individuals who composed the cycle. They may also reflect what the writers perceived to be pastoral necessity: In some liturgical contexts, they may have thought, it is more appropriate to emphasize the grace that saves those who will be saved despite their evil deeds, whereas in other contexts it is better to remind the congregation that salvation and damnation depend on an individual's meritorious choice to cooperate with the grace of God.

I have elsewhere sought to position other Wycliffite texts on the continuum between predestinarian and Pelagian soteriologies, but it is more important here to note that, despite their divergent viewpoints on the doctrine of salvation, the majority of Wycliffite authors agreed with the writer of the *Lanterne* in defining the church as the congregation of those who will be saved.[45] Their emphasis on the invisible church bound together by grace, over against the visible church bound together by institutional structures, is of a piece with Wyclif's own thought; it also recurs in the trials of many of the men and women brought before English bishops and inquisitors on the charge of heresy. The relationship between soteriology and ecclesiology appears most visibly in the trials of some eighty defendants before William Alnwick, the bishop of Norwich, in the years 1428–31. Three of Alnwick's defendants alluded to the themes I have been pursuing in this essay: John Godesell confessed that he had believed that "the catholic church is the congregation of only those who are to be saved," Thomas Mone was accused of teaching that the church is "the soul of any good Christian," and Margery Baxter was charged with saying that "the holy church exists only in those places where her sect exists."[46] Admittedly, it may have been that the formulaic nature of medieval heresy trials and inquisitorial record-keeping caused these defendants' views to be presented as more similar to one another than they actually were.[47] Nevertheless, it is striking that the views attributed to these and other dissenters—views expressed in quite different terms, which would undermine the argument that they owe more to ecclesiastical stereotypes than to the defendants themselves—both cohere with one another and echo the main themes of Wyclif's ecclesiology.[48]

Similar resonances between Wyclif and those who followed in his footsteps can be found in their use of metaphors for the church. It is not surprising that biblical imagery dominates the ecclesiological rhetoric of Wyclif and later Wycliffite writers, given their well-known devotion to scripture and opposition to their contemporaries' use of extra-biblical stories. There is space here to mention only one of the parables that appear repeatedly in Wycliffite writings, as it highlights important elements of Wycliffite ecclesiology. The *Lanterne of Liȝt* uses the parable of the fish in the sea, drawn from the Gospel of Matthew, to describe the mingling of the saved and the damned in the visible church:

þe rewme of heuenes is lijk to a nett þat is sent into þe see and gadriþ to-gidre in to his cloos of alle þe kynde of diuerse fisches, and whanne þis nett was ful of fisches, þe fischers drowen it to þe lond, and þei . . . chosen þe good in to her vessellis; þe yuel forsoþe þei sentten oute and kesten hem aȝen in to þe see. . . . Þe secounde chirche here in erþe is lijke to a nett sent into þe see for as þe see ebbiþ and flowiþ, so þis chirche now riseþ and falliþ.[49]

Here the author of the *Lanterne* uses Matthew's parable to distinguish between the church as it currently is and the church as it will be at the end of time. The church as presently constituted moves with the fluctuations of temporal affairs: It rises and falls with the sea of time and contains both those who will be chosen and those who will be cast back into the sea. In this sense, the material or visible church is not to be equated with the church that will be revealed at the time of the final judgment, when God will separate the saved from the damned. It is this pure church, which the *Lanterne*-author elsewhere calls "God's church," that is the true church. Since this church possesses many of the same properties as Wyclif's congregation of the predestined, it is fair to say that the two are conceptual analogues.

———

Thus John Wyclif—and many later Wycliffite authors and heresy defendants—described the church as an invisible community of those who will be saved. Giving priority to ideas about the church that emphasize invisible, spiritual criteria of church membership, rather than visible criteria such as whether a person has been validly baptized, these Wycliffites adopted an ecclesiology similar to Dulles's model of a mystical communion. In doing so, they constructed a model of the church that shares many important features with the one to be found in Langland's poem *Piers Plowman*. Both models emphasize invisible grounds for membership of the church—in Langland's case, whether a person has satisfied the maxim *redde quod debes*; in Wyclif's, whether a person has chosen to cooperate with God's grace. Both models appeal to biblical images, and both consciously set themselves apart from mentalities that define the church primarily in terms of officially sanctioned institutions.

None of this is to revive the old argument that Langland was a secret Wycliffite, or to minimize the distinctive features of Langland's and Wyclif's ecclesiologies. That these two individuals, as well as those who came after Wyclif, borrowed features from the same archetype in setting forth ideas about the church is hardly to say that they set forth the same ideas. Nevertheless, it is striking that Langland and Wyclif made some of the same theological moves—separating the visible institution of the church from its theological reality, employing rustic rather than corporate images—especially in a historical and political climate not well disposed toward models and images of the church that deemphasized the institutional. Seen in this context, Bale's mistaken ascription of Langland's poem to Wyclif's pen becomes even more understandable. The connection between the two is not merely that both harbored aspirations for the reform of the church in England, and not merely that both extolled the theological potential of the English vernacular. It is, instead, that both men articulated soteriologies and ecclesiologies that privileged the model of the church as a mystical communion over the model of the church as an institution. Whatever the limits of Avery Dulles's typology, it provides a useful lens through which to view the shared assumptions and values that underpinned the theological views of two of the most significant writers of late medieval England.

CHRISTIAN POETICS AND ORTHODOX PRACTICE: MEANING AND IMPLICATION IN SIX CAROLS BY JAMES RYMAN, O.F.M.

John C. Hirsh

Though rarely announced publicly, Penn Szittya's thoughtful and progressive social attitudes have for many years found powerful if indirect expression in his teaching and his scholarship, in his chairmanship of Georgetown's English Department, and in his founding, together with his friend and colleague Jo Ann Hoeppner Moran Cruz, of Georgetown's Medieval Studies program. In these multiple roles, both his actions and his interactions have been invariably inclusive and democratic, responsive both to the representations of his colleagues and to the requirements of the profession and the university. During his time at Georgetown, his practices as a teacher and as an administrator seemed to his friends and colleagues rooted in ethical judgments of the highest order, while he also remained both attentive to what was best in and for his students and proactive in whatever could be done to engage and support them, both in and out of the classroom.

It may have been these traits, among others, that drew him not only to the study of as demanding a topic as the tradition of English dissent but also to an interest in such adversarial practices as were recorded in English literature in the fourteenth and fifteenth centuries and were disclosed and championed in the scholarship of the twentieth and twenty-first.[1] One of the more powerful effects of Penn Szittya's scholarship has been to make all of us think more critically about the circumstances and the content of fraternal dialogue and to reconsider the impact of the fraternal orders generally. It thus seems altogether appropriate, in honoring him, to turn to James Ryman, O.F.M., a fifteenth-century Franciscan poet and musician, once of Canterbury, whose critical reputation is still not entirely secure, and to consider, however briefly, the nature and effect of his practice and his art.[2]

In the study that follows I will present and examine six of Ryman's lyrics so as to argue for their evident connectedness and their interest not only as religious song but also for the degree of the theological teaching that they encode. Throughout, I shall be concerned less with his attitudes toward devout practices than with his considered understanding of certain central Christian teachings that effectively underpin his lyrics, particularly when they engage Christ's divinity and humanity. These teachings were informed by his distinctly Franciscan theology and yet are infused with a simplicity that was intended both to instruct and to delight his audience, but that has largely escaped contemporary criticism. This teaching aspect of his work is linked inescapably with the circumstance of its musical performance, so that it avoids the markedly inflected diction present in many Middle English lyrics, while preserving a role for theological instruction, albeit on a fundamental level. He was at pains, in his lyrical texts, to avoid theological controversy as such. He followed traditional teaching, even in as controversial a sacrament as the Eucharist,[3] with a theological sophistication that, though presented simply, is considered and orthodox.

Yet for such an obviously considered and productive musician, James Ryman has not been well served by critical commentary, and one recent editor in particular has proved remarkably deaf to his accomplishments. Writing in the introduction to his *Early English Carols*, a work that contains texts of most of James Ryman's lyrics, Richard L. Greene represents that "there is perhaps little to attract the casual modern reader in the 166 pieces contained in the manuscript [sc. Cambridge University Library MS Ee.1.12] to which his name and the date 1492 have been set. But we should not be too hasty in assuming that these pedestrian poems were equally uninteresting to the author's contemporaries."[4] Faint praise indeed. And, as so often in criticism of Ryman, sent fourth from a very great height!

But it must be allowed that one of the difficulties involved in examining Ryman's lyrics lies in the evident but also studied simplicity of his language, his syntax, and (to all appearances) his religiousness, all of which seem, when first encountered, innocent of any larger social meaning; indeed, for some of his critics, innocent of any larger meaning at all. But it is exactly this apparent simplicity that has enabled both composer and audience to become engaged in a powerful and felt spirituality, and to do so in the context of a sung performance. The religious attitudes these songs encourage, at once theological and devout, are present in representations of

Christ's humanity and his divinity, his nativity and his passion, all of which interact theologically and sympathetically throughout the lyrics. Part of Ryman's art lies in his ability to avoid entanglement in the controversies of the hour while at the same time constructing a nuanced representation of certain central Christian teachings in a way that responds to Franciscan thought and spirituality. This practice issued in a discourse that would have been apparent to contemporaries—though, in part because of its evident sensitivity to the requirements of orthodoxy, it has escaped recent criticism, which has been more concerned with those who held ecclesiastical and other offices—and so had the power both to promulgate new instructions and to impose sanctions on dissenters.[5] Throughout his lyrics, Ryman offers a considered reading of orthodox theological formulation; this reading stands as alternative to, but does not engage with, discourses of Wycliffite dissent.

Such moderation, practiced in a time of perceived crisis, is virtually a hallmark of Ryman's work. It is an attitude that appears most clearly when a number of his songs and carols are read together, and not scattered, as in Greene's collection, among hundreds of others. The single most important manuscript containing Ryman's lyrics is Cambridge University Library MS Ee.1.12, already mentioned, a small (c. 8″ × 5.5″, or c. 14 cm × 20.2 cm) parchment codex of the late fifteenth century, containing 114 folios, reduced now to 110, which preserves good texts of many of Ryman's English and Latin songs and carols. On folio 80 there appears this colophon, attesting both to Ryman's authorship and to the year 1492: "Explicit liber ympnorum et canticorum quem composuit Frater Iacobus Ryman ordinis Minorum ad laudem omnipotentis dei et sanctissime matris eius Marie omniumque sanctorum anno domini millesimo [c]ccc. [l]xxxxij."[6]

Although Ryman's carols are not limited to folios 11–80v, these form a separate scribal group, and include the six printed here. Greene has considered that the contents of 11–80v are "possibly Ryman's own hand," though the evidence for this conjecture is finally limited to a very few (possibly scribal) corrections.[7] The organization of folios 11–80v, however, is complex, moving from carols concerned with the Annunciation to those concerned with the nativity, then to those concerned with Mary and with Christ's passion and death, and finally to those concerned with the Christian in prayer and in song. These themes interlock and advance but slowly, though it would have been difficult to perform even a small group of

Ryman's carols without encountering and repeating many of them. The progression is gradual, and Ryman's great themes, Mary and the nativity, the Trinity, Christ's love and death, circle and return, forming a kind of leitmotif that runs through his canon.

To further illustrate this practice, I have selected a sequence of six carols to present and examine here. They appear in the manuscript as the songs move away from carols concerned largely with the nativity to those in which Christ and finally the Trinity have more emphasis. This group has a certain unity (they do not by themselves constitute a manuscript booklet, though traces of an earlier one may remain in folios 11–50v), and their cohesion lies in a theological unity that amounts to a kind of devout program. But when we examine Ryman's carols in small groups (as carols often were sung), we can gain an insight into his orthodox and theologically considered beliefs, devout attitudes that are as well revealed in song as anywhere.

I have noted that Greene's anthology of Middle English carols not only deprecated Ryman's art but also scattered his carols throughout its five hundred pages, thereby obscuring the ways in which their themes intersect and reimagine one another. The only other edition of note, that of J. Zupitza, is now more than a century old and difficult of access, though it does publish, if without critical or other comment, the CUL manuscript entire. But particularly when considered together, Ryman's carols appear allusive, thoughtful, melodious, and complete.

Partly to offset the effects of Greene's edition, partly to illustrate how a small number of connected carols can communicate both effectively and in some depth, I present here six carols from MS Ee.1.12, seeking to preserve something of their lyrical mode and intent, their implied musical tone, and even, to a degree at least, their appearance on the manuscript page. I have thus preserved manuscript capitalization, but not word division. I have extended punctuation only when doing so would avoid confusion, but in order to render some sense of the fluency of the hand and the appearance of the manuscript production I have preserved *wt* for *with*, *wtoute* for *withoute*, etc. Those who wish a more heavily edited text have already been served by Greene and Zupitza, whose catalogue numbers I have included, along with those of Julia Boffey and A. S. G. Edwards's *New Index of Middle English Verse*, now universally the *NIMEV*.[8] In any case, there seems to me a good argument for a new edition of Ryman, perhaps one somewhat more heavily edited than this one.

I also have intervened editorially to indicate the burden by placing it in **bold** when it first appears, usually separate from the stanzas that follow, but have *italicized* the first line of the burden when, in numbers 3 to 6, it concludes the stanzas that follow, or when the final line of a stanza is inscribed in the margin so as to prepare for a repetition of the burden.[9]

SIX CAROLS BY JAMES RYMAN, O.F.M.

1. *NIMEV* 67, fols. 41v–42. Greene 71, Zupitza XLII.
In certain of Ryman's carols Greene has indicated a number of scriptural allusions (here, to John 14, in stanza 3, line 2) that he believes the lines either allude to or encode. But except when the allusions are explicit, such identifications should be treated with caution. Like very many members of the fraternal orders, Ryman was deeply studied in the Hebrew scriptures and the New Testament alike, and the language, images, and narratives of these texts frequently informed his own, as did devotional and other religious commonplaces without number—indeed it was often his investment in these sources that produced his best lyrics.

folio 41v
Bothe man & chielde haue myende of þis
How godis sonne of blis
Of marie myelde man become is
To deye for mannys mys

A mayden myelde hath borne a chielde
A chielde of full grete price
And is a moder vndefielde
And quene of paradice

The king of blis his fader is
And Ihesus is his name
folio 42
To bringe mankyende to heven blis
he hathe borne mannes blame

He was and ys and ay shall be
I take recorde of John
Ay thre in personalite
In deite but oon

And in a stalle this chielde was born
Betwene bothe oxe and asse
To save for synne that was forlorn
mankyende as his wille wasse

Whenne he was borne that heuenly king
Of mary quene of blis
Than gloria aungelles did synge
Deo in excelsis

The prophecy of Isay
And prophetes alle & summe
Now ended is thus finally
For god is man become

Nowe laude we god of heven blis
With hert with wille and myende
That of a mayde man bicom is
To blis to bringe mankyende

2. *NIMEV* 1328, fol. 42v. Greene 280, Zupitza XLIII.
Although addressed to the Trinity, this carol moves quickly to an evoca-
tion of Christ and Mary, and then, after an evocation of Christ's passion
(emphasizing his "hert bloode") and ascension, to that reenactment of
his passion, the Eucharist. It thus engages, with evident theological inter-
est, Christ's two natures ("Of whome he toke mortall nature"), while
including too a popular typological identification of Mary with Queen
Hester (Esther), heroine of the Old Testament book of the same name,
and of Christ with her consort, the Persian king Assuere (Ahasuerus),
otherwise Xerxes I (reigned 486–465 BC), with whom she intervened to
save her countrymen from condemnation. Like other of Ryman's carols,
it contains a succession of sung and familiar images that reinforce a
narrative and a teaching already familiar to performers and audience
alike.

folio 42v

My herte is sette alone
On god bothe thre and one

I loue a louer that loueth me well
To alle mankyende whiche is socour
And his name Emanuell
Of alle louers he is the flour

His moder is a virgyne pure
In worde in dede in wille & thought
Of whome he toke mortall nature
To save mankyende that had myswrought

He was dede and beried in sight
And rose ayene on the iijde daye
And steyed to blis by his grete myght
That was and is and shall be ay

He is called king Assuere
Hester his moder callid is
Crowned they be both ij in fere
He king she quene of heven blis

Oure lorde Ihesus of nazareth
That for oure sake shed his hert bloode
And on the Crosse did suffer deth
To vs mote be eternall foode

3. *NIMEV* 3585, fols. 43–43v (not, as *NIMEV* reports, fols. 75v–76).
Greene 53, Zupitza XLIV.
In spite of its conventional language and images, this lyric reveals much
about Ryman's literary method, and it informs and engages the listener by
turning what might have seemed conventional into a teaching that again
links Christ's evident humanity to his place among the "persones thre" of
the Holy Trinity.

folio 43

Ther is a chielde a heuenly childe
I borne this nyght of marie myelde

This child is was and ay shall be
One in godhede in persones thre
ther is a chield &c.

This cheild is named criste Ihesus
That nowe is borne for loue of vs
ther is a chield &c.

Mortall nature this chielde hath take
Of our thraldome vs free to make
ther is a chield &c.

This child is god and man also
Now borne to bringe vs out of wo
ther is a chield.

his father is god of heven blis
And virgyne mary his moder is
ther is a chield

Fro heven to erthe this chielde come is
To suffre dethe for mannys mys
ther is &c.

On good Friday vppon the Roode
To save mankyende he shed his bloode
ther is &c.

folio 43v
This chield was dede and in *graue* laye
And Rose ayene on the thirde daye
ther is &c.

By his grete myght to blis he stide
And sittith on his Faders Right side
ther is &c.

Whenne he shalle come and Iugement make
To blis with hym this chield vs take
ther &c.

4. *NIMEV* 115, fols. 43v–44. Greene 281, Zupitza XLV.

Another of Ryman's more theologically inventive carols, which begins with Adam's sin as having brought about Christ's virgin birth ("As the sonne beame gothe thurgh the glas") and then moves on to his sacrifice and death to save all of humankind, a salvific action that in turn led to the sacrament of the Eucharist. Ryman's aesthetic admits of a certain theological adaptability in the interest of his art, and the carol turns finally to the Trinity in order to celebrate the union, which is at the heart of the carol, of human and divine.

God bothe iij and one
Is oure comforte alone

Adam and eve did geve concent
vnto the feende that vile serpent
Wherfore mankyende to helle was sent
wtout comfort alone

Whenne it therin long tyme hadde layne
Crist goddes sonne came in certayne
To take nature and suffre payne
to comfort it alone

As the sonne beame gothe thurgh the glas
Thurgh virgyne marie he did pas
Taking nature as his wille was
to save mankynde alone

folio 44
That lorde so good vpon the Roode
Suffred vile dethe and shed his bloode
Whoos flesshe and bloode is endeles fode
to feithfull man alone

Now beseche we that king of grace
In blis for to graunte vs a place
And hym to se there face to face
that is both iij. and one

5. *NIMEV* 3332, fols. 44–44v. Greene 61, Zupitza XLVI.

The anti-Semitism present here offers sad evidence that Ryman could be quite uncritical of what he understood to be settled teaching, perhaps particularly when it seemed to have been endorsed by scripture. But the allusion again to the sin of Adam, and perhaps also to the role of "echeone," might possibly allow for a somewhat wider culpability for Christ's crucifixion—a reading, however, that probably escaped both the poet and his audience. Certain of these verses, though not the burden, are echoed, sometimes closely, in a separate carol (*NIMEV* 3467; Greene 62, Zupitza XLVIII: folios 45v–46), suggesting that many of Ryman's carols were often differentiated as much by their (now lost) music as by their (preserved) verses.

The sone of god alone
Hath made vs free echeone

The faders sonne of heven blis
Of a pure [mayd] man bicome is
To forgeve man that did amys
by his mekenes allone

Bothe younge and olde we were forlorn
For synne that Adam did beforne
Till of a mayde this chielde was born
to make vs fre alone

Moder mary and virgyne pure
Clothed hym wt mortall vesture
And closed him in her clausure
of chastite allone

When was xxx.ti winter olde
For xxx. plates he was solde
folio 44v
To the Iewes wikked and bolde
by fals Iudas alone

Vpon his hede a crowne of thorne
The Iewes sett than wt grete scorne

And wt scourg*es* his flesshe they torne
for our trespas alone

The Iewes thanne of wikked moode
Nayled his bodye on the Roode
Wheron he shed his precious blood
To make vs free alone

He was dede and in his graue leyde
And rose ayene as scripture seide
On the iij.de daye and to blis steyde
both god and man alone

Now beseche we this king of grace
That we may haue a dwelling place
And euir to see his glorious face
in heven blis echeone

6. *NIMEV* 2485, fols. 44v–45. Greene 283, Zupitza XLVII.
The five carols just presented effectively lead up to this, one of Ryman's
more theologically considered carols, which is focused on the Trinity. The
Trinity here revealed is a divinity in which its members' substantial unity,
and so their essence, constitute "myght," and the role of humankind be-
comes that of worship and praise. This anticipatory quality in Ryman's
carols has the effect of subordinating some to others, and of highlighting
certain ones for particular attention. As a poet and as a cleric he was aware
of the requirements both of orthodoxy and of performance, a circum-
stance that would have been especially evident when several carols of his
were sung together.

Honoure to the alone
That art bothe iij. and one

O lorde by whome al thing is wrought
And wtoute whom is wrought right nought
folio 45
Wt hert wt myende wt wille and thought
honour to the alone

O whiche haast made bothe day and nyght
The firmament and sterres bright
The sunne and mone to yeve vs light
honour to the alone

O whiche hast take mortall nature
Of moder marie virgyne pure
For to redeme eche creature
honour to the alone

O Fader wtoute begynnyng
O sone of the fader beyng
O holy goost of bothe ij. proceding
honour to the alone

O fader in whome alle strength is pight
O sone also that wisdome hight
O holy goost fro whome alle grace doth light
honour to the alone

O iij. persones in one vnite
Beyng but one god and one light
One in substaunce essens and myght
honour to the alone

O fader o sonne o holigoost
O iij & one of myght*es* moost
Of lest and moost in eu*er*y coost
honour to the alone

Though individually not as lexically complex as many another lyric, Ryman's carols are not as detached from larger matters as they first seem, and it may be useful to consider some of the intellectual, religious, and social constructions that informed them and to which they spoke. It is quite true that direct contemporary allusion hardly exists in these texts, but few if any authors write without some knowledge of the social circumstances of authorship, and Ryman's carols signal not only considered theological attitudes, but also felt responses to two central Christian teachings—the hypostatic ("one substance") union, which indicates how Christ's human and divine natures were united in one person, and the Trinity, a widely acknowledged if imperfectly understood teaching at least since Augustine's *De Trinitate* (AD 399–419). Taken together, Ryman's allusions to these teachings act as complex but evident affirmations both of orthodoxy and of loyalty to the teachings of the established church. Indeed these two widely disseminated doctrines appear so often in Ryman's work that there can be little doubt that their further role was to add to that affirmation a teaching function as well. The Trinity was perhaps the better known of the two and, for all of its complexity, may have been the single most powerful medieval Christian doctrine. In the late medieval period it was widely represented in the visual and verbal arts and communicated in ways no Christian could have escaped. But Ryman's allusions to the Trinity are complemented by others—to Christ's humanity, often represented in the nativity, and by allusions to Mary, and to Christ's passion and death—and, sometimes at least, by the implications of these doctrines for his two natures.[10]

These matters are further complicated by the fact that Ryman's theological representations, even when they are apparent, are sometimes confined by the requirements of metrical convenience, by musical convention, or by the degree of the poet's own imaginative or intellectual inventiveness. But theological representations they are, and as such susceptible to interpretation. Even in the carols printed here, Ryman's references to Christ's human nature are unmistakable. Christ "came in certayne / To take nature and suffer payne" (4.6–7); the poet insists repeatedly, if in different forms, that "A mayden myelde hath borne a chield" (1.1), or that "of a mayde this chielde was born" (5.7), or, in slightly more complicated language, "Moder mary and virgyne pure / Clothed hym with mortall vesture" (5.9–10), or "Mortall nature this child hath take" (3.7; cf. 6.9). The verses thus allude directly to the central Christian teaching that God became man, and that his mother remained a virgin. But Ryman was no Nestorian and took care throughout his carols to encode Christ's divine nature as well as his human. Repeatedly, he insists that the Trinity was "Ay thre in personalite / In deite but oon" (1.11–12), or "One in godhede in persones thre" (3.2), or, even more explicitly, "O iij. persones in one vnite / Beyng but one god and one light / One in substaunce essens and myght" (6.21–23).

Ryman's intention was clearly that his songs should teach and attest as well as delight, and he was particularly attentive to the teachings they represented. Beside his studied and orthodox allusions to the Trinity stands his equally orthodox description of Christ's mission: "To save mankyende that had myswrought" (2.8); "To suffre dethe for mannys mys" (3.17); "Of our thraldome vs fre to make" (3.8); "For synne that Adam did beforne" (5.6); "For to redeme eche creature" (6.11). But somewhat more complicated is his representation of the relationship between Christ's divine and human natures.

Although Ryman's specific theological allusions are articulated in such a way that they avoid controversy, there can be no doubt that, he being a Franciscan, his study of theology would have included the teaching of the great Franciscan philosopher and theologian John Duns Scotus (ca. 1266–1308). Among the most important of Scotus's teachings were those concerning Christ's two natures and those—equally complex, and related—concerning the Trinity. Writing as a poet, Ryman tends to reflect, rather than develop, these teachings, though, as we have seen, specific allusions do occur. But as a general rule his carols are based on a felt poetic responsiveness to devout Christian narrative, not to a studied theological construction, even when they are informed by certain Scotian formulations.

The theological tradition within which Ryman wrote cast further light on his thinking and his art, even though he set himself to reflect, not develop, what he understood to be received theological teaching. Still, in order to understand the theological setting for Ryman's work, it will be useful to go one step further. The relationship between philosophical teaching and literary texts is complex, and often, perhaps usually, it engages larger attitudes rather than specific passages or images. But in a case like this one, it is possible to see the poet responding to teachings of his fellow Franciscan in a way that departed from other, specifically Thomistic, formulations. Although Ryman's citation of theological doctrine is limited, Scotian teaching allowed him effectively to negotiate the relationship between Christ's human and divine natures in a way that permitted his personal inclination toward Christ's humanity to enjoy pride of place. For an analysis of this important theological teaching I am going to turn, if briefly, to Richard Cross's interpretation, which argues, *inter alia*, that the most important and sophisticated exposition in the late-medieval period was that of John Duns Scotus, who turned away from both Thomistic and other scholastic formulations in order to posit a teaching of Christ's human nature that represented Christ as "a whole who includes both a person (the Word of God) and a non-essential substance (the assumed human nature)."[11]

Where Thomas Aquinas had represented that Christ's human nature, in Cross's phrase, "shares in the existence of the divine person," Scotus argued instead that Christ's human nature, set against his divine, was *"like an accident,"* so that his divinity neither diminished nor formulated his human nature.[12] It is of course unlikely that Ryman himself ever made a deliberate choice between the two teachings, but it is worth observing that the one inscribed by his fellow Franciscan accorded better with the focus of his poetry, if only because of the relative significance it accorded Christ's humanity. Orthodox teaching had effectively negotiated between the Monophysite and Nestorian heresies and articulated a position that allowed for one person with two natures in Christ. Yet even so, Cross argues, there is a certain inclination toward Monophysitism in Aquinas, so that it is difficult to see how, in Aquinas, Christ's human nature could *not* be understood as little more than an essential property of his divinity. Scotus, however, redefined the relationship in such a way as to maintain that, since accidents can be understood as individuated from their substance, Christ's individuated human nature retained a unique identity. This position allowed him to argue that it is possible within a substance–accident relationship for a substance to sustain an associated accident without subsuming it. So understood (and greatly to simplify a complex series of arguments), Christ's human nature was not strictly dependent on his divine nature, with which, however, it had the appearance of being accidentally associated.[13]

In theological terms, it may have been a devout reading of Scotus's substance–accident model that allowed Ryman to represent Christ's human person in the wonder-filled but intelligible terms that he employed, while also remaining firmly attached to the idea of a divinity that can be recognized and, to a degree at least, understood. For Ryman, a combination of Christ's inclusion in the Trinity, no less than his often alluded-to nativity, joined together into a controlling insight into a union of divinity and humanity present only in Christ. Thus references to Christ as "this childe" (1.13 and 3.1), who "toke mortall nature. . . . And on the Crosse did suffre deth" (2.7 and 2.19), are set against both specific references to the Trinity, "one in godhede in persones thre" (3.2), while also acknowledging that Christ is, in accord with orthodox teaching, physically present in the

Eucharist, as one "Whoos flesshe and bloode is endeles fode" (4.15). Christ's humanity shares, in one substance, in his divinity, as no other person's ever has or ever shall. But if this probably Scotian insight provides a way of reconceptualizing Ryman's poetics, it is worth stressing too that his carols themselves constitute a reformulation of theological insight into the practical requirements of religious song and personal spirituality. Within the terms of his given medium, poetry, Ryman responded to Scotus's concern for the intelligible integrity of Christ's human nature without discoursing on it, accepting instead a union with his divinity best understood, as he considered, by Christ's participation in the Trinity. No doubt Scotus's extended concern for the substance–accident model in understanding the God–man relationship went well beyond Ryman's poetic purposes, but there is in Ryman's poetry a theological sensitivity that has gone largely unnoticed, no doubt in part because of its studied lack of controversy.[14]

Thus the language in James Ryman's carols gently reflects, rather than develops, such theological positions, and though he is not often credited with religious reflection of any sort, it is probable that, insofar as his theological position can be ascertained, it was more likely to have been Scotian than anything else. In one case, drawing a distinction while also suggesting a relationship between and among "substaunce essens and myght" (6.23) seems to echo, if obliquely, a Scotian sensitivity to God's freedom and power, where "one substaunce" encodes, in a carol "about" the Trinity, Christ's hypostatic union—that is, one "essens" with the Trinity—whose "myght" it shares. In fact the larger issues of Christ's two natures and the Trinity's three persons recur frequently in Ryman's carols, and it would require a certain theological insensitivity *not* to notice with what care the poet has brought them into association. Taken together, they acknowledged both Christ's human nature, about which Ryman wrote easily and often, and his divinity, which he all but identified with the Trinity.

Ryman's theology, though not emphasized in his carols, is unmistakably present in them, and although his allusions do not depend on Scotus's rather more sophisticated teaching, they do illustrate one way in which an understanding of Christ's hypostatic union could be articulated in song, while still allowing, in a composition like a carol, for a degree of poetic wonder. Ryman's carols insist on a certain integrity for Christ's humanity, emphasizing its uniqueness, a circumstance that allows the poet to contemplate Christ and his mother and then move easily to the Trinity and then back again. In a certain way, Soctus's teaching was particularly useful to a poet who wanted to emphasize both his own attachment to the traditionally orthodox formulation concerning the Trinity ("both thre and one") while also keeping a focus on Christ's simple, powerful, and loving humanity, particularly in the nativity.

These connections become more apparent when a certain devotional aspect is allowed to Scotian thought, such as that perceptively alluded to in "Les subtilités de la logique au service du Christ et de la charité," a section of a recent French study that describes the theological impact of Scotus's writing.[15] The reading is not at all insensitive to the practical and homiletic dimensions of Scotus's teaching, and by observing both its sometimes mystical character and the ways in which it responds to the requirements of Christian charity, we can understand how, as a fellow Franciscan, Ryman might utilize the ways in which Christ's human nature depended on and was realized in the Trinity, even in what was essentially a song of praise. The very different genres, poetry and philosophy, in which these teachings are cast make it difficult to develop such connections very far, but what Scotus and Ryman have in common—however obtained—is an orthodox sense of a suffering but divine Christ, and a continuing assurance of God's utterly uninhibited freedom and love. Implicit in Ryman, explicit in Scotus, is a vision of divine freedom that is present along with God's enduring love for all of humankind.[16] Taken together, however, Scotus and Ryman reveal certain common sympathies, though students of Ryman, few though they be, might be more willing to concede that this is so than would students of Scotus. Ryman's poetic delights in a felt and personal spirituality not present in Scotus's austere philosophizing. Still, it is simply not possible to believe that this able Franciscan poet lived in ignorance of the teaching he was both explicitly and implicitly advancing. He may not have incorporated every Scotian nuance, but the larger Scotian and Franciscan ideals are indeed present in his lyrics, and directed purposefully toward his audience.

In the end, it is simply extraordinary that as interesting and important an English poet as James Ryman should be as little known as he is, whether by name or by oeuvre, or that his texts, which constitute about a quarter of the pre-1500 carols extant in English, should not be more studied than they are. Part of the reason for this circumstance may lie in the theological controversies that enveloped and followed his century, part too in an apparent disinclination of students to engage a critical understanding of what is in effect orthodox and, in this case, Franciscan theology. In some cases, at least, this reluctance may be influenced by the circumstance that the way Ryman followed was that of orthodoxy, not rebellion, still less revolution. As modern students of medieval literature, we are inclined to prefer poets who are inclined to object over those who do not, and to assume that it is only in opposition that real thought can be observed. Devout and reflective, James Ryman addressed larger theological constructions in his simple, wonder-filled, but also considered songs and carols. He took care to signal his orthodoxy quite explicitly, even though his medium was usually that of the carol, a genre that, it must be allowed, admits of only limited theological discourse.

In a study that I have already cited, Karl Reichl has argued that the quality of Ryman's work has long been underestimated at least in part because its melody has often been ignored. He perceptively concluded that "we need to be reminded that as songs they acquire an extra dimension and that aesthetic judgments based on texts alone . . . must be viewed with suspicion." David Jeffrey has gone further, insisting that Ryman's poetry shows "a definite rootedness of divine mystery and beauty in the tangibility of Christ's and the Virgin's humanity."[17] Both of these considerations, that of genre and that of explicit theological teaching, must figure in any evaluation of Ryman's work, which, as I have tried to show here, may lead to a higher estimation of his oeuvre than it now enjoys. In this context too it is certainly best to read Ryman's carols, as indeed most carols, in groups, as they were sung, and not singly, as if they were lyrics. Those groups may or may not be as thematically connected as the six presented here, but carols, more than most genres, gain by association, and it is really only in association that we can finally gauge their effect.

I conclude by pointing out that, although Reichl's fine study appears in a Festschrift, as does this one, it is certainly a mistake to think of Ryman as a kind of Festschrift poet, one who is of interest only to scholars, and not all of them. On the contrary, in an explicitly theological context, James Ryman mastered the sung carol, one that enjoyed contemporary popularity, has lasted into our own time, and shows no sign of disappearing. This study has aimed both to call for a critical and academic reconsideration of James Ryman's art and to suggest that our understanding of orthodox poetic practice is still incomplete. Narrow-minded enthusiasts for orthodoxy, then as even now, there certainly were, but there were those too, James Ryman among them, whose theological orthodoxy did not obscure their larger Christian purposes, and whose language and verse offered considered if orthodox formulations that were clearly alternative to those vigorously contesting pronouncements that, then as now, must have seemed everywhere triumphant.

ENABLED AND DISABLED "MYNDES" IN *THE PRICK OF CONSCIENCE*

Moira Fitzgibbons

This essay will argue that *The Prick of Conscience* contributes in important ways to late-medieval discussions of human rationality and thought.[1] The engagement of the unnamed *Conscience*-poet with these issues might seem surprising, given how vividly and adamantly he depicts the wretchedness of the world, the inevitability of death, and the torments of hell. But his audience's innate reason and intellectual potential emerge with their own palpable reality within the poem. These qualities become prominent as a result of the poet's expansive investigation of conscience. Instead of referring simply to penitential self-interrogation, "conscience" functions as part of a rich and interrelated web of human attributes, including "mynde," "skill," "wit," "imaginacioun," and the "kynde" that generates and connects them.

This dimension of *The Prick of Conscience* highlights an important area of inquiry within fourteenth- and fifteenth-century religious writing in England. As defined in the last two decades or so, English vernacular theology of the late Middle Ages is characterized by innovative and ambitious renditions of theological material into Middle English accompanied by thoughtful reflection on the stakes of these translations.[2] While *The Prick of Conscience* participates in all of these practices, it homes in on the fundamental relationship between rationality and belief. Christians' ability to understand complex ideas, to distinguish right from wrong, and to focus on their eternal fates constitutes the *Conscience*-poet's most pressing concern. In attending so carefully to questions of reason and thought, the poem highlights a preoccupation shared by other writers, ranging from Langland to Nicholas Love and beyond.[3] Late-medieval writers needed not just to define what their audiences should learn but also to address the more elemental question of how people think. The poem's consistent yoking of salvation to the capabilities of the mind may help account for its appeal to medieval compilers and audiences; more than 115 manuscripts remain, distributed over a wide geographic range.[4]

As we will see, far from taking rationality for granted, *The Prick of Conscience* characterizes it as both complex and contingent. Potential breakdowns in reason or thought preoccupy the *Conscience*-poet; he invokes madness when describing torments within this world, and suggests that damnation destroys the mental integrity central to human identity.[5] But there are limits to his discussion of this question. Although the *Conscience*-poet refrains from attributing earthly madness to sin, ultimately he proves unwilling to explore the religious, social, and ethical dilemmas raised by this condition. Nowhere does he address how mad people might help or be helped by others, or how they will be judged after their death.[6] Mental soundness is an unstated prerequisite for inclusion in the Christian community that the *Conscience*-poet envisions.

The poet's decisions in this regard highlight questions we might ask of other vernacular works of religious instruction, including (or, perhaps, particularly) those that approach lay instruction in groundbreaking ways. Do writers at times mitigate their blurring of the clergy–laity boundary by reinforcing other kinds of social divisions? Are there cases in which a writer's enthusiastic attention to individual spirituality coexists with an increasingly narrow sense of Christian collaboration and community? Without downplaying the achievements of the *Conscience*-poet or his contemporaries, we should acknowledge that writers can turn their backs on some thorny questions even as they energetically respond to others. A text can advocate greater lay access to religious knowledge while simultaneously failing to acknowledge or engage with certain aspects of human experience. As *The Prick of Conscience* demonstrates, even a dedicated teacher who offers new forms of understanding can still leave some learners by the wayside.

A PERIPHERAL POEM

The Prick of Conscience itself has inhabited a somewhat marginal position within literary studies. Notwithstanding the proliferation of surviving manuscripts and the poem's length (more than 9,600 lines), the text generated little critical commentary during most of the twentieth century, with the invaluable exception of Robert Lewis and Angus McIntosh's *A Descriptive Guide to the Manuscripts of "The Prick of Conscience."* In addition to meticulously categorizing the surviving copies and fragments of the poem, Lewis and McIntosh drew attention to the expansiveness of its content;

they described the poem as "a storehouse of information" that emphasizes "the *understanding* of the great variety of elements in God's universe that leads to self-knowledge."[7] Perhaps because the poem steers clear of conventional literary narrative or characters, however, it continued to play only a small part in "the great spectacle of literature" as defined and studied by scholars.[8] This began to change in the 1990s with the emergence of vernacular theology as a vibrant field of scholarly inquiry. Reinforcing Lewis and McIntosh's assertions, Nicholas Watson included *The Prick of Conscience* within his influential discussions of late-medieval religious writing and culture. To Watson, the poem merits attention both for the wide range of information it provides and for its assumption that lay audience members can, and should, apply this material actively to their own lives.[9] Nicole Rice makes a similar assessment in her study of late-medieval piety: "Even as [the poem] locates the lay reader firmly within the penitential nexus, in need of assistance and frequent recourse to the clerical advisor, *The Prick of Conscience* offers a certain independent literary access to means of 'self-correction.'"[10] As such, the poem functions both as a justification and a resource for lay learning.

Although Watson, Rice, and other scholars have helped make *The Prick of Conscience* a more visible presence within medieval studies, sustained analysis of the poem has remained hard to come by. Part of the problem may be the poem's resistance to straightforward categorization. Howell Chickering, whose analysis of the rhetorical strategies of *The Prick of Conscience* constitutes one of the most thorough explorations of the poem to date, points out the text's deviations from standard didactic material and methods.[11] Apart from a brief recitation of the seven deadly sins, the detailed discussions of elements of the pastoral syllabus found in such texts as *Handlyng Synne*, *Speculum Vitae*, and *Jacob's Well* are nowhere to be found in *The Prick of Conscience*.[12] Chickering contends that the *Conscience*-poet, rather than providing his audience with a thorough introduction to Christian precepts, seeks only to shock his audience into what Augustine would call empty fear, or *timor vanus*. This fear represents a rudimentary understanding of the dangers that await the unrepentant: "Many passages are explicitly designed to stimulate physical fear . . . in the reader or hearer as a first step toward contrition."[13] The main goal of the work, according to Chickering, is attrition, or the initial recognition of sinfulness that begins the process of repentance. "Drede" is essential to this awareness: "When we examine the rhetoric of the poem, we find that his preferred strategies of intensification are consistently deployed to create physical fear and self-abasement in his audience."[14] Characterizing the poem as "unalleviatedly tactile," Chickering suggests that at several points it "must have made a believer's skin actually crawl."[15]

Chickering persuasively highlights efforts of *The Prick of Conscience* to generate visceral fear in its audience. But this dread represents just one aspect of a more comprehensive mindfulness that the *Conscience*-poet wishes to instill in his audience. He appeals to his audience's reason, memories, imagination, and even their curiosity, in addition to their fear. In so doing, he not only allows for give-and-take between himself and his audience but also adds his voice to a larger conversation about human rationality taking place in a wide variety of fourteenth- and early fifteenth-century works. Indeed, the *Conscience*-poet, like Langland in *Piers Plowman*, conveys a sophisticated sense of thought as a complex process involving overlapping faculties. Both writers also demonstrate an uneasy awareness of rationality's precariousness. Precisely because it is such a dynamic entity, an individual's sense of self can dissolve if subjected to internal or external pressures.

NATURAL MINDS

Within the first few lines, the *Conscience*-poet firmly establishes his interest in thought and rationality. No sooner has he praised "Þe myght of þe Fader almyghty" in the first line of *The Prick of Conscience* than he celebrates "Þe witte of þe Son alwytty;" a few lines down, he points out that the triune God "was ay als wys and ful of wytte, / And als myghty als he es yhitte" and that he gained his "myght and wytte" from himself alone (21–23). The poet makes clear that humans enjoy their own portion of this wisdom: He directs his poem to "ilk cristen man and weman / Þat has witte and mynd, and skille can" (197–98). The poet describes several connected facets of thought and makes clear that they are characteristic of women as well as men.[16] "Witte" denotes strong understanding, often in association with the reception and processing of sensory information; "mynde" can refer either to thought in general or memory in particular; "skill" evokes intellectual capability, often the specific qualities of moderation and good judgment.[17] Even as the *Conscience*-poet highlights different facets of rational activity through his use of these terms, he seems less concerned with maintaining firm boundaries between them than in using them for cumulative effect. Whether he refers to "resoun," "mynde," or "witt," the poet's central argument remains the same: Believers must marshal their intellect, memory, and even imagination to remain continually alert to the realities of death and judgment. If his audience can accomplish this, the poet implies, everything else will fall into place.

The prologue goes on to assert that a love of God both depends on and reflects human beings' innate intellectual gifts. Since God has generously created the earth, the *Conscience*-poet writes, "man þat has skille and mynde / Hys creatur [should] worshepe in his kynde, / And noght to be of wers condicion / Þan þe creatours with-outen reson" (59–62). To love God is the appropriate expression of man's nature (his "kynde") and his rationality. The *Conscience*-poet here acknowledges humans' connections with the animal world even while pointing out a crucial distinction: Having been endowed with reason, people have the choice to worship their creator or to disregard him.[18] Before ever bringing up human imperfection, the poet establishes the inherent gifts and abilities given to all people.

The "mynde–kynde" couplet recurs seven times throughout the prologue, each time reinforcing human beings' obligation to focus on their ultimate spiritual fate rather than on worldly preoccupations. Instead of drawing on just one definition of "mynde" to make this argument, the *Conscience*-poet moves fluidly among several of the word's connotations. Construing discernment as the defining attribute of humanity, the poet asserts that God made man the "mast digne creature / Of al other creaturs of kynde: / And gaf hym wytte, skille, and mynde, / For to knaw gude and ille" (74–77). Other references within the prologue highlight "mynde" as memory: "ilk man, bathe lered and lewed, / Suld thynk on þat love þat he man shewed, / And alle þier benefice hald in mynde, / Þat he us dyd til mans kynde, / And love hym and thank him als he can, / And elles es he an unkynd man" (117–22). About a dozen lines down, he uses the couplet once again, this time stating even more explicitly that "mynde" involves both recollection of the past and awareness of events to come: "And what [God] has done and sal do at þe last, / And ilk day dos to man-kynde; / Þis suld ilk man knaw and haf in mynde" (136–38).[19] Eschatological concerns drive the *Conscience*-poet's emphasis on the centrality of active learning, remembering, and judgment to the Christian life and to human identity itself. Interestingly, the *Conscience*-

poet holds off on mentioning the term *conscience* until well into the poem, line 344 of the prologue, by which point he has already done a great deal to link human nature to powers of thought and discernment. In so doing, he indicates that his text should serve as something more than a manual for examinations of conscience. Instead, *The Prick of Conscience* argues more broadly that an awareness of last things represents the highest fulfillment of human beings' potential abilities.

Toward this end, the *Conscience*-poet reminds his audience of the intrinsic sinfulness of humanity in a postlapsarian world. His "mynde–kynde" references become correspondingly more negative as he moves through his text's major subject areas, which include the wretchedness of our worldly selves, the dangers of the world, the terror of bodily death, the pains of purgatory, the horrors of the last judgment, the pains of hell, and—somewhat incongruously, but in a discussion longer than all but one of the other sections—the joys of heaven. The final "mynde–kynde" couplet within the prologue, as well as the two in the first full book of the poem, makes clear that people need to understand their innate flaws: Each man should "haf mynde / And knawe þe wrechednes of [his] kynde" (428–29). Within the rest of the main body of the poem, the couplet emerges sporadically, with varied meanings. One instance in book 2 makes a positive comparison between the constellations and humanity: "Yhit þe bodys of þe world in þair kynde, / Shewes us for bisens to haf in mynde, / How we suld serve God in our kynde here, / Als þai do þar, on þair manere" (1026–29). Two subsequent references in book 3 assert that it is only natural for people to fear death and to love God.[20] The *Conscience*-poet then seems to set the couplet aside, using it only in book 4 when describing the nature of the devil.[21]

While the devil's "kynde" is clearly abominable, the conclusion's two uses of the "mynde–kynde" couplet acknowledge the complexities involved in human nature. As the *Conscience*-poet begins the final section of his poem, he states that "Now haf I here als I first undir-toke / Fulfulled þe seven partes of þis boke, / Þat er titeld byfor to have in mynde, / Þe first es of þe wrechednes of mans kynde" (9535–36), echoing statements at the end of the prologue. But the poet's final "mynde–kynde" couplet returns to the more positive possibilities raised at the very beginning of the poem. Understanding the book's subject matter will "make a man knawe and halde in mynde / What he es here of his awen kynde, / And what he sal be, if he avyse him wele, / And whar he es, for to knaw and fele" (9561–64). The "chiastic restatement" within specific passages of the poem identified by Chickering seems to be at work in the *Conscience*-poet's introductory and concluding use of this couplet as well; "mynde–kynde" passages move from humanity's exalted qualities to its debasement and back again.[22] The *Conscience*-poet's return to a positive usage of the couplet indicates his commitment to something other than constant admonition. However wretched, human "kynde" entails the possibility of salvation through self-awareness and discernment.

Exploring the "mynde–kynde" framework of *The Prick of Conscience* not only demonstrates the positive aspects of the poet's view of humanity but also illuminates common ground between the poem and other literature of the period. Specifically, the *Conscience*-poet's vocabulary and several of his preoccupations recall key aspects of *Piers Plowman*. He does not make use of personification, of course; "conscience," "mynde" and "kynde" do not walk the earth, as do Consience, Resoun, and Kynde Wytt in Langland's text.[23] Nevertheless, the poet does seem to share Langland's interest in the connections between conscience and reason, "wytt," and other faculties. Moreover, both Langland and the *Conscience*-poet engage with the term "kynde" when posing questions related to religious knowledge. To what extent is it inborn rather than acquired? Does our spiritual fate hinge completely on our ability to learn?[24] While neither writer offers simple answers to these questions, both the *Conscience*-poet and Langland insist that the mind's natural abilities represent only a starting point; individuals need to pursue religious knowledge actively and persistently. As Andrew Galloway has argued, Langland uses the term "kyndenesse" to highlight both the social and the spiritual aspects of this process: Within *Piers Plowman* the term conflates "the language of kinship, nature, and gratitude."[25] A similar definition underlies the *Conscience*-poet's statement, quoted above, that an "unkynd man" is one who refuses to love and thank God for the blessings he gave humanity. The passage suggests that the most "natural" Christian relationship with God involves a spirit of thoughtful loyalty rather than terrified obeisance.

TALKING BOOKS

Unlike Langland, however, the *Conscience*-poet refrains from describing specific kinds of people in great detail; focused on death and judgment, he cannot make time for unscrupulous friars or hard-working farmers.[26] But neither can he completely ignore one earthly distinction—that between the "lered" and the "lewed." He asserts in his prologue that he has written the work in English to alert "laude men þat er unkunnand" to "sere maters" they do not yet know about (337–38). Throughout the work, he refers more frequently to those who will hear his work than to those who will read it (though the discussion below will explore ways in which he blurs this distinction). Perhaps the most telling indication of the audience he anticipates is provided by the conclusion of the prologue, which carefully explains how prologues function: "Ga we now til þat part þat first es, / Þat spekes of mans wrechednes; / For all þat byfor es wryten to luk, / Es bot als an entré of þis buk" (366–69). In addition to helping his audience understand heaven, hell, and their own flaws, he must introduce his listeners to book culture itself.

How best to do this? A key dimension of the *Conscience*-poet's responses to this question involves consistent bridging of the gap between oral and written modes of communication. Instead of presenting clerical knowledge as a privileged domain accessible only to the lettered, the *Conscience*-poet elides the distinction between written and oral sources of information.[27] This strategy provides key support for his overarching emphasis on the responsibilities of the active Christian "mynde": He thinks everyone in his audience has the potential to make strong judgments if only he can manage to educate them in an accessible way.

Some writers of the period underscore the association of the "lered" with books. In his edition of the roughly contemporary poem *Speculum Vitae*, Ralph Hanna makes note of "a very great number (perhaps defensible, given the announced programme of vernacularizing clerical subject matter) of books telling and clerks reading."[28] As Hanna suggests, such passages offer insight into the relationship the poet sees among his own writing, his sources, and his audience. The *Speculum*-poet, for example, not only alludes to clerical knowledge through such tag lines as "als clerkes wate wele" (4959) but also includes phrases highlighting priests' access to written authorities: "Als clerkes in Haly Writte may se" (4946), "Als clerkes in boke can rede" (3601), "Als clerkes may fynde in boke and fele" (2074), and so on.[29] The *Speculum*-poet extends this privilege to contemplatives, who read "of Haly Wrytte þat clerkes lokes, / Þat es wryten in dyuers bokes" (2203–4), but for the most part upholds the different methods of learning available to the "lewed," who "can na manere of clergy" (82–3), and to the clergy, who "can bathe se and rede / In sere bokes of Haly Writte / How þai sal lif, if þai loke itt" (86–88).

The Prick of Conscience contains its own references to clerical knowledge and access, particularly when specialized knowledge is under consideration: It attributes information about the positioning of the stars, for example, to "clerkes . . . þat er wise and sleghe" (7570). Other examples are used along the same lines as those found in *Speculum Vitae*: "als clerkes wate" (2635), "als clerkes can se" (2854), "als clerkes in bukes bers witnes" (730), and so forth.[30] In other instances, however, the *Conscience*-poet blurs the distinction between lay and clerical knowledge. He regularly refers to information that "men" (as opposed to just clerics) might find in books: "Here may men se, als þe buke wittenes, / And understand what purgatori es" (2784–85); "Als in þe psalme men may written se" (5753); "Als docturs says of haly writ, / In bukes thurgh whilk men may knaw it" (2278–9). Moreover, phrases like "als a buke shewes us" (2520) and "als þe boke us leres" (8105) conflate the position of the poet with that of his audience in the learning process.[31] One gets the sense that the *Conscience*-poet seeks not simply to transmit information but to persuade his audiences of the indispensability of written sources to the fates of their individual souls.

In keeping with this practice, the *Conscience*-poet takes pains to highlight the common ground between texts and speech. His use of the verb "speken" provides him with a useful way to do this. Like most of his contemporaries, the *Conscience*-poet typically uses forms of the verb "seien" when quoting written authorities.[32] But in several instances he brings these sources closer to actual speech, as in his discussion of purgatory:

Als I shewed byfor openly,
Spekes Innocent and Austyn
In bukes, whar þair maters er sen;
And Raymund spekes of þe same
In a boke, þat es called his name;
And Thomas Alqwyn spekes alswa
Of þis mater, and of other ma
In a boke, þe whilk made he,
Þat hat Veritas Theologie.
(3943–51)

Although almost synonymous with "seien," "speken" evokes the physical articulation of words more strongly than does the former verb.[33] By depicting figures such as Augustine as talkers, the *Conscience*-poet implies that these authorities should circulate freely in contemporary discussions of religion rather than remaining within the pages of a book.

The *Conscience*-poet makes clear that his own work contributes to both written and spoken forms of conversation. He frequently uses "speken" when referring to his own work, often in transitions between one section and another: "Here es þe thred parte of þis buke spedde / Þat spekes of þe dede, als I haf redde" (2682–83). The interplay between writing and speech remains at the forefront of his references to the poem: He notes that the sixth part of his work "specialy spekes, als writen es, / Of þe paynes of helle þat er endeles" (6410–13). Similarly, when discussing the endless death suffered by the condemned, he characterizes the poem as both a text and a speaker:

Of þis dede may men rede and luke
Ynoghe, in þe sexte part of þis buke.
Þat spekes of þe payns of helle;
Þarfor here-on I wille na langer duelle,
Bot of bodily dede I wille spek mare.
(1758–62)

The poem combines the benefits of both oral and textual delivery: It can be visually encountered and consulted by readers in the sequence they prefer, even as it "spekes" itself and will be read aloud to others. Given these lines, the poet's reference to what he himself "wille spek" implicitly links his composition process to both the convenience of written texts and the immediacy of speech. Through his willingness to afford legitimacy to both modes of communication, the *Conscience*-poet implies that his audience can and should engage with theological sources. While these passages at times become a bit unwieldy, the *Conscience*-poet functions here and in similar passages as a patient and committed guide to unfamiliar academic discourse.[34]

In addition to making written authorities talk, the *Conscience*-poet proves willing to elaborate on ways they might differ from one another. As part of several discussions, the poet includes ideas that "som clerkes" have about the material under consideration and allows for dissension among sources. When describing the demise of the Antichrist, for example, the

Conscience-poet points out that "Some clerkes yhit says alswa, / Þat Saynt Michael sal hym sla. . . . And þe boke says, alswa, þat he, / Thurgh þe gast of Goddes mouthe slayn sal be" (4605–10). Although the poet shuts down this discussion without extensive speculation—"Bot how swa it be þis es certayn, / Thurgh Goddes myght þar sal he be slayn" (4611–12)—he does so only after having provided his audience with insight into the grounds for theological debate.[35] A fuller discussion comes when the *Conscience*-poet quotes "Rabby Mosyses," whom he calls a "gret philosiphir . . . Þat thurgh witt mykelle couth se" (7656–58). Although he provides a thorough account of the rabbi's measurements of the heavens, the poet ends on an uncertain note: "Raby Moyses says alle þis, / Þat er noght alle my wordes bot his; / Bot whether alle þis be soth or noght, / God wate, þat alle thyng has wroght" (7685–88). Although these lines lack the playfulness of "Thise been the cokkes wordes, and nat myne," the *Conscience*-poet does encourage his audience to recognize the limitations of earthly information and interpretation.[36]

This necessitates critical engagement here on earth, a practice that the *Conscience*-poet seems to validate in his audience. In his discussion of the itching caused by vermin who attack the damned in hell, the poet interrupts himself partway through:

> Bot yhit may men say here ogayne,
> Ffor men may in som boke wryten se
> Þat after þe gret dome þat last salle be,
> Na quyk creature salle lyf an,
> Bot anely aungelle, develle and man,
> 'How suld in helle þan or ourwhare elles.
> Any vermyn lyf als men telles,
> Or any other best þat moght dere?'
> To þis may men gyf answere
> On þis manere, wha-swa kan;
> Þe vermyn þat salle be þan,
> Als I understand, noght elles es
> Bot devels in vermyn lyknes . . . .
> (6978–90)

These lice, he argues, are more "to drede" than standard-issue vermin (7002). Even as the physical pains of hell emerge starkly here, the intellectual pleasure of debate is also opened to the audience. Elsewhere he anticipates from his audience a query—"Bot now may þou ask me and lere / A questyon" (8297–98)—that he clearly regards as welcome and to which he replies with a discussion of how St. Anselm "answers to þis" (8303). In keeping with his discussions, in his prologue and beyond, of the rational "mynde" as the basis for salvation, the *Conscience*-poet characterizes his audience as critical thinkers and participants in a dialogue, whether they are reading his poem or hearing it.

WIDE-RANGING POSSIBILITIES

This openness to questioning gives way to an almost playful tone when the *Conscience*-poet turns to the joys of heaven. In this section, he proves willing to stretch the boundaries of both his "mynde–kynde" discussions and the "dialogic" form of learning he supports. In this section the poet acknowledges his own presence and interpretive activity more fully than previously, and invites his audience to take part in imaginative activity. Generating this decision is the fact that heaven's glories cannot be accounted for through rational thought. Pointing out that "We fynd wryten þat [heaven] es fayre and bryght," the poet points out that no one, even a "wyse clerk," can "descryve it ryght" (8869–71). Given this limitation, the poet states that "Yhit wille I ymagyn, on myne awen hede, / For to gyf it a descripcion; / Ffor I have þare-to, gret affeccyon" (8873–75). The homely phrase "myne awen hede" takes evocations of "mynde" to a much more material and individual level than seen before, as does the poet's reference to his own emotion.

Throughout the section, through phrases like "Yhit I lyken, als I ymagyn in my thoght" (9065), he continues to emphasize the role his subjective imagination plays in his vision of heaven.[37] That at least one writer found this musing inappropriate is suggested by *Pore Caitif*, which draws on several portions of *The Prick of Conscience*. When the *Caitif*-compiler describes heaven, he goes out of his way to point out that he will include "no þing of myn owne heed."[38] But the *Conscience*-poet allows for a speculative spirit when considering the finer points of the afterlife, on his audience's part as well as his own. At the conclusion of this discussion, he makes clear that anyone can attempt to understand heaven through imaginative analogy: " Þus may a man þat kan and wille, / Alle þe ceté of heven lyken bi skylle" (9194–95). In addition to exercising their reason, judgment, and powers of literacy, the *Conscience*-poet's audience can creatively engage their "myndes" in generating images of paradise.[39]

One subgroup of *Prick of Conscience* manuscripts highlights this possibility by changing the work's title. As Lewis and McIntosh indicate, six manuscripts contain passages that call the work *The Key of Knowing* rather than *The Prick of Conscience* (and a seventh seems to belong to the same grouping, although it does not use this title).[40] This different title is indicated by colophons and also within the text itself, as in this passage from the conclusion of Bodleian Library MS Digby 87:

> In þese are fele materis drawen
> Oute of fele bokys þat ben vnknawyn
> To leued men namely of engeland
> Þat con nouth buth engelis vnderstand
> Þer fore þis tretis draue j wold
> In engelys þe qwyche may ben cald
> Be certeyn skyl kye of knowyng
> Þat may seruen to ryth openyng
> Specialy of þese thynges seuene
> Þat 3e herd me be forn neuen
> Þat schuld ben opned and no sperd
> To maken to ben of synne offerd
> And to maken hem self þus and god to knowe
> And to meknesse & loue & dred him to drawe
> Ffor men may se and here 3our þis kay
> Þa that ben and is and schal ben ay . . .
>
> (132v–133r)

According to the title used within the majority of *Prick of Conscience* manuscripts, the treatise itself functions as a "prik," or stimulus, that will create a more "tendre" conscience in those willing to take it to heart.[41] By replacing the prick with a key and substituting knowing for conscience, this subgroup of manuscripts underscores the need for believers to look outward as well as inward. The poem opens up new areas of knowledge for its audience, in order to enable believers to flee sin, understand themselves, and worship God. I would argue that this revision represents an extension of ideas found throughout the more commonly seen rendition of the poem, rather than a departure from them. In both the "key of knowing" sub-group and in the more widespread version, the poem links the conscience and a productive fear of God to the expansion of the audience's intellectual horizons and mental efforts. When steered in the right direction, learning, remembering, discerning, and even imagining lead to salvation.

UNTHINKABLE "WODENES"

But what fate awaits those whose powers of reasoning and thought are com-promised in some way? The closest the *Conscience*-poet comes to addressing this question is in his discussion of purgatory; children too young to under-stand sin, he asserts, must experience purgatory but are permitted to do so "[al]s a foul þat flyes smertly" (3323). Nowhere, however, does he consider the posthumous fate of grown individuals who lack the "inwit" necessary to make moral judgments. This omission makes sense in light of his emphasis on judgment: The last thing he wants to do is open up potential loopholes or exceptions. Moreover, madness presents the *Conscience*-poet with a vexing question: How can rationality function as the defining attribute of humanity if some people clearly lack it? We might expect the poet, then, to refrain from bringing up madness at all. In fact, as we shall see, he frequently invokes the "wode" when describing the suffering of the dying or the damned, even while refusing to address directly their status as believers or community members. Madness seems to provide him with a concrete way to depict the enormity of damnation. People's failure to use their reason properly and to avoid sin amounts to the rejection of their "kynde"; as such, it should be punished not just with suffering but with the dissolution of identity itself.

In effect, the *Conscience*-poet tries to have it both ways. He wants to set forth an innovative understanding of hell as the utter destruction of a per-son's sense of self. At the same time, he insists that every individual shares the same responsibility to exercise reason and avoid sin. Referring to people whose reason has failed them—who have, in effect, already lost their sense of self—helps make the first element of his argument more vivid but under-cuts the second idea. So he alludes to madness while remaining silent about the spiritual status of actual mad people. In the broadest sense, then, *The Prick of Conscience* reminds us that positive approaches to lay rationality and intellectual potential do not inoculate a text against inconsistency or obtuseness.

The failure of *The Prick of Conscience* to engage fully with its own references to madness should not be regarded as inevitable, given the wide range of medieval approaches to the issue. Although Penelope Doob argues that some writers of the period characterize madness as "both the most appropriate punishment for sin as well as its most fitting emblem," she also sheds light on the more positive ramifications of the "wildness" shown by such figures as John the Baptist and of the tests of mental strength endured by Job and many saints.[42] Moreover, some writers stress the possibility that the mad enjoy "special access to God and God's truth," as Derek Pearsall has put it.[43] That madness reflects interplay between the material and psychological worlds is assumed within *De proprietatibus rerum*, which emphasizes the negative effects of humoral "smoke" on the brain and subsequently on behavior.[44] Medieval legal theory often also approached madness in nonpunitive ways, as several contributors to Wendy Turner's anthology *Madness in Medieval Law and Custom* have demonstrated.[45]

Writers of the period additionally acknowledge that the boundaries between sanity and madness are not always clear-cut. *Book to a Mother*, for example, uses the term "wodenes" when referring to God's righteous wrath when judging sinners, and it calls Judgment Day the "day of woodnes" itself.[46] It also points out that in some cases good people are misconstrued as mad: Jesus' own cousins, the author writes, "helden him wod" because he was so eager to teach others about spiritual matters.[47] St. Bridget faces a similar problem in her experience: "Diuers folk saide þat she was wode" when she changes her clothing to reflect her new identity as a widow and pilgrim.[48] These texts are quick to point out that the accusations are mistaken, but they do acknowledge the difficulty society has in determining the boundary between fervent religiosity and madness. Remorse can lead to similar ambiguity, as *The Cloud of Unknowing* makes clear: Although it favorably comments on those who go "ni wood for sorow" when they perceive their own sinfulness, the text also warns people not to desire "to vnbe" as a result: That would constitute "deuelles woodnes & despite vnto God."[49]

Similarly, although Margery Kempe stoutly defends herself against those who think she is possessed by a "wikkyd spiryt," she admits at times to fearing that she is experiencing the "illusyons & deceytys of hir gostly enmys" rather than divine interaction.[50] Kempe suggests that she conquered these doubts less through her own efforts than through the comforting explanations that eventually came to her via God's grace: "aftyr hir turbele & hir gret fere it xuld ben schewyd vn-to hir sowle how þe felynges xuld ben vndyrstondyn."[51] Conversations with sympathetic clergy also provided reassurance in some instances; for example, Jesus tells her that his "spyrit xal speke" through the friar he recommends to her as a counselor.[52] For Kempe as for other late-medieval religious writers, understanding the boundary separating inspiration from madness requires careful consultation with one's conscience and with spiritual guides. But at times the division appears impossible to resolve: *Piers Plowman*'s description of "lunatyk lollares and lepares" is so heavily weighted with qualifiers ("as hit semeth," "as it were," and so on) that it remains unclear to both the dreamer and the reader exactly how "wode" these individuals are, if indeed they are mad at all.[53]

For its part, the *Prick of Conscience* steers well clear of this uncertainty. One could argue that this is in keeping with "the giddy either–or structure of the entire work," as Chickering has characterized it.[54] But as shown above, the *Conscience*-poet encourages his audience to engage in dialogue and to think about the complexities of a functioning mind. It is only when dysfunction enters the picture that he shuts down potential inquiry. He wants to urge Christians to use their inherent reason to gain salvation, not to interrogate how perception and consensus shape definitions of reason or madness in the first place. As a result, the rational "mynde" emerges in all its wondrous complexity while madness hovers on the periphery, associated only with deviance and suffering.

Some of the *Conscience*-poet's more straightforward uses of the term *wode* involve references to animals who display the viciousness associated with rabies.[55] The eighth pain of hell, he writes, brings on attacks by dragons, snakes, and "wode bestes grysely and grym" (6902). Stressing the "wode" nature of these beasts multiple times, the poet links them to the vermin-infested bed described by a prophet to Nebuchadnezzar, himself a well-known victim of temporary insanity.[56] Elsewhere the *Conscience*-poet specifies that the animals in question are actually devils. These can appear at the time of death: the poet writes that in typical cases devils gather around a man "[a]ls wode lyons" who "raumpe on hym, and skoul, and stare" (2224–45). They appear in much the same manner to souls in purgatory, though in this case they act more like lions of this world: "Als wode lyons to wayt þair pray, / And to ravisshe it with þam away" (2908–9). Devils take on a variety of animal guises in the poet's summary of hell-pains in the conclusion to the poem as a whole. Among other gnawing animals that the damned will encounter are "wode wolfes, lyones, and beres felle, / Þat sal noght be elles, bot devels of helle, /In liknes of hydus bestes and vermyne"(9449–51). Such terms are common: Trevisa's Middle English translation of Bartholomew, for example, alludes to the "venemous woodnes" of the devil.[57] In these instances, the madness in question signifies the victim's complete loss of control: Evil spirits will be not only violent but also beyond the reach of human intervention.

Animals also emerge in *The Prick of Conscience* not as instruments of torture but as emblems of irrationality. As quoted above, the prologue asserts that those who refuse to love God demonstrate that they are "of wers condicion / Þan þe creatours with-outen reson" (61–62). A bit later in the introduction, the *Conscience*-poet reiterates that those who refuse to know themselves or "lere for to knaw" God's law are living "als an unskylwys best" (166). The association of irrationality and ignorance with animals is a common one: Nicholas Love reminds his audience in *The Mirror of the Blessed Life of Jesus Christ* of the need to deal patiently with people "þat semen to vs as vnresonable & bestiale in maneres & in lyuyng."[58] Similarly, Trevisa's translation of Bartholomew notes that too much wine can quench the "light of resoun" and replace it with "bestial madnesse." A more nuanced view emerges later in the treatise, however, with the acknowledgment that animals do have "redynesse of witte" in many areas.[59] The *Conscience*-poet, however, manifests no interest in blurring the boundary between animal and human intelligence.[60] Reason is a defining quality of humanity—but if people fail to apply their rationality to behaving virtuously and learning assiduously about the faith, they risk losing this essential gift.

Madness within some religious texts emerges as an earthly punishment, sometimes visited even on the innocent: Mirk's *Festial*, for example, tells of a woman whose children roam "as mased bestes al ȝent þe contre" as punishment for her own habit of cursing them.[61] The *Conscience*-poet, however, presents sinners as engaged in a vicious circle of obstinacy and irrationality, with consequences that become clear primarily in the afterlife. Intellectual and moral weakness lead to results that are more debilitating. If a person believes in God and refuses to act accordingly, "[i]t semes þat he es wittles, / Or over mykel hardend in wikkednes" (9602–6). Excessive preoccupation with worldly things also suggests that a person is "noght witty" (1094). When considering people who refuse to fear the possibility of damnation, the *Conscience*-poet in his condemnation becomes even more severe: "it semes þat swilk men er wode,/For þai hald gud thing evell and evell gude" (1607–8). Instead of simply indicating a lack of intelligence, madness here results from sheer willfulness. Similar references to stubbornness crop up in other religious poems, in reference to sins both small and great. *Handlyng Synne* tells of a cleric who yearns to own a dead knight's fancy cloak: "þe clerk was wode algate / To were a cloth aȝens hys state."[62] Within *Speculum Vitae*, "wodenes" emerges as a specific branch of unfaithfulness (itself a branch of the sin of pride) associated with the heedlessness of youth.[63] Within *The Prick of Conscience*, however, references to madness seem to indicate problems more fundamental than relatively contained moments of anger or impulsiveness. Whoever privileges earthly existence, the *Conscience*-poet suggests, "es outher clomsed, or wode; / Or it es a signe of suspecyon / Þat he es in way of dampnacyon" (1652–53). Implying a suspension of thought brought about by a physical problem, such as excessive exposure to cold, "clomsed" shares with "wode" the idea of a combined moral, corporeal, and intellectual malfunctioning.[64] Those who resist understanding and fearing God risk losing their reason altogether. Even as the *Conscience*-poet invites his audience to regard themselves as participants in a Christian textual community, he insists that any worldly preoccupation puts the mind itself at risk.

Having described the profound irrationality of people who refuse to look beyond earthly things, the *Conscience*-poet makes clear that an eleventh-hour resumption of sanity—that is, concern for the soul's state— will not be possible for most people. Indeed, he asserts that the transition to death is such a struggle that it brings on a kind of madness in many individuals. The poet carefully spells out the loss of mental control often involved in death: "Þe ded fra a man his mynd reves / And na kyndely witte with hym leves, / For þan sal he fele swilk payn and drede, / Þat he ne may thynk of na mysdede, / Bot of his payn and of noght elles" (2002–6). While this struggle affects all people during their death throes, it strikes a particular blow to those who have failed to direct their thoughts toward God:

[When death comes] Þan sal he be in swylk drede sette,
Þat he sal God and hymself forget,
And þat es skylle for he wil noght,

Whyles he has hele, haf God in thoght,
Þarfor he sal þan his mynde tyne. . . .

(2026–36)

Mindfulness of God during life will presumably soften this blow; the suffering involved in death may well still lead to madness, but the need for last-minute mental clarity is less urgent for those who have spent their life suitably aware and repentant. The *Conscience*-poet will not leave the subject without reiterating that bodily death also entails mental disintegration: "For when ded here assayles a man / He may noght thynk wele on God þan, / For þe dede hys mynde away þan brekes" (2076–78). The *Conscience*-poet needs to emphasize this point because of an obvious ramification of divine mercy: Why should people preoccupy themselves with sin during their lifetimes if they plan to make a full confession on their deathbeds? It should be said, however, that other writers turn to bodily factors that will prevent this from happening: Both Robert Mannyng and John Mirk depict devils' making it physically impossible for delinquent sinners to express repentance in the last moments of their lives.[65] For the *Conscience*-poet, I would argue, the prospect of losing one's mind at death functions more broadly as a reminder that the "mynde" is a vulnerable component of human identity as well as a potentially powerful one. If an individual has not cultivated his mind's rationality and fear of God, he or she will fall victim at death to raw terror and madness.

The sights and sounds of fiends produce a similar effect. At several points in the poem, the *Conscience*-poet notes that the sight of devils is enough to drive people insane: "For if [devils] had swa large powere, / In swilk forme to shew þam here, / Out of witte þan þai shuld men flay, / Swa orrible and swa foul er þai" (2314–16). Indeed, he writes a few lines later, the vision of a devil always involves the risk that a person "for ferdnes of þat sight / Shuld dighe, or at þe leste tyn his witt" (2321–22). Such discussions emerge in many other religious works: Mirk's *Festial*, for example, notes that St. Gowdelac was made "so sore afryght" by his vision of hell "þat he had nygh lost hys wytte" and that a Jewish man shown a similar vision by the Blessed Virgin "was nygh out hys wytte for ferde."[66] *The Prick of Conscience* takes matters a step further, however, by reminding its audience that physical strength is no match for the horrors of this encounter. As mentioned above, the *Conscience*-poet uses a "mynde–kynde" couplet to highlight humanity's universal vulnerability to terror at the hands of devils: "For swa hardy es na man, ne swa balde / In þis werld, nouther yhung ne alde, / If he myght right consayve in mynde, / How grysely a devel es in his kynde. . . . [He] suld wax wode for ferde and be wittles" (6855–64). This horror marks the limits of both the mind's imaginative abilities and its resilience. Sound effects rather than sights produce the same result. Describing the cacophony of hell, the *Conscience*-poet asserts that it would cause "alle þe men lyfand þat herd it, / To ga wode for ferd and tyne þair witt" (7344–45).

Like the transition from life to death, an encounter with a devil takes place within temporal limits; in each case, the madness brought on by the experience is not necessarily permanent. When the *Conscience*-poet begins to describe the unending hell-pains experienced by the damned, however, his references to madness change. In three separate passages, the *Conscience*-poet not only describes the general danger of losing one's mind but also compares the behavior of the damned to the actions of earthly mad people. He implies that both the condemned and the mad experience the same terrible paradox: They lose their sense of themselves as individuals and of conventional societal boundaries and simultaneously are more removed from other people than ever before. The pain of hunger, for example, will lead sufferers to eat the dead: "For þai sal gett nan other meete; / For hungre þai sal be als brayne-wode, / Bot þe dede sal be þair fode" (6706–7). This reference clearly links hell-pains to the experience of madness as a mental and physical condition. Similarly, when the wicked enter an oven of fire, they are so compressed that they add to one another's misery: "And nane of þam salle other eese, / Bot ever fyght togyder and stryfe, / Als þai war wode men of þis lyfe" (7375–77). This condition pervades hell: As various pains come to the damned, they "salle ilk ane on other stare and gryn, / Als wode men dose here, and makes gret dyn" (7426–27).[67]

What should we make of this emphasis on a behavior seen in " þis lyfe" and "here"? In many ways, it seems to signal that hell involves a complete breakdown of community. Despite their terrible loudness, the damned will be unable to communicate with one another; instead of being able to "eese" one another, they will consume one another's remains. This situation parallels the *Conscience*-poet's description of the eleventh day of the Last Judgment, in which "men sal com out / Of caves, and holes and wend about, / Als wode men, þat na witt can; / And nane sal spek til other þan" (4798–4801).[68] For the poet, then, earthly madness precludes collaboration or any form of communication—a profound contrast to the community of speakers, readers, and learners his own text establishes.[69]

In keeping with this idea, the *Conscience*-poet emphasizes the mental anguish experienced in hell: "[The damned] sal thynk on nathyng elles, / Bot on þair payns, als som clerkes telles, / And on þair syn þat þai here wroght, / Swa salle payns and sorow troble þair thoght" (7322–25). Any mental soundness left unharmed by horrific sights and physical pains will be exclusively occupied in regret. In emphasizing this aspect of damnation, the poet departs from discussions of hell that are typical of the exemplary tradition. For the most part, these tell of living people who receive earthly confirmation that sinners are suffering horrible punishments in hell; usually little is said concerning the interior life of the damned.[70] The writer of *Book to a Mother* does describe a process of realization taking place amid the torment: People in hell "knowlechen now þat þei were wode whanne þei wende þat þe lif of Cristes simple folk hadde be but wodnesse, but to late."[71] Even this intellectual transformation is denied by the *Conscience*-poet, who instead stresses something close to oblivion. The damned will not "have witt, ne knaw, ne fele / Na dede þat ever was done wele, / Bot on þair payns salle be alle þair thoght / And on þair syns þat þai had wroght" (8365–72). If the mind is not lost entirely, it nonetheless becomes unable to steer itself in a more salutary direction. This loss of control emerges in marked contrast to the experience of the saved, who enjoy the instant fulfillment of their thoughts: "And what-swa þai wille think in thoght, / Alle salle be at þair wille þare wroght" (8493–94). Reinforcing this idea are the *Conscience*-poet's flights of fancy when describing heaven; as he candidly admits, paradise is a subject on which he gives himself permission to speculate freely.

The Prick of Conscience uses madness to underscore that hell involves not merely physical suffering but also complete isolation and a devastating loss of agency. But where does this leave earthly people who experience madness? In some ways, the *Conscience*-poet's approach is less punitive than that found in other texts. *The Prick of Conscience* does not endorse confinement of the mad, as does St. Bridget in the Middle English *Liber Celestis*; she approvingly quotes God's statement that a pagan man, "as a man oute of minde," should be "bunden and closed in dirke places."[72] On the other hand, even admonitory texts at times do more than *The Prick of Conscience* to keep even the "wode" part of the community. When relating the life of St. Bartholomew, for example, Mirk tells of a fiend in India who makes people

"croke, seke, halt, and blynd, defe, and dombe, and mony oþer wayes seke"
so that he might then heal them.[73] Once Bartholomew arrives at the temple
inhabited by the devil, however, the fiend can no longer "cure" his victims,
and the strength and reliability of Bartholomew's healing powers quickly
become apparent. When he hears the crying of "a wodde man þat had a fend
wythyn hym," Bartholomew quickly dispatches of the devil. According to
Mirk, word of Bartholomew's prowess quickly reaches the local king, whose
daughter was "wode and bowndyn wyth chaynes, for harm þat scho wold do
to hom þat scho myght euer rechyn. And when þe kyng herd of þys wode
man, how he was helut, anon he send to Bartholomew, prayng hym to come
to hele hys doghtyr; and so he dyd." The miracle leads not just to the health
of the daughter but to the conversion of the king and his countrymen.

Mirk's narrative highlights the urgency of madness as a problem: It
reduces a presumably powerful king to pursuing any rumor of a possible
cure for his daughter. It also draws attention to the wide-ranging implica-
tions of the problem: The daughter's chains attest to the danger that she
poses to others in the community as well as to herself.[74] Precisely because
of these complications, madness serves as a useful test case for would-be
healers. Unlike the fiend in the temple, who apparently meets with success
only when treating the physical problems listed by Mirk, Bartholomew has
the authentic divine support needed to cure the "wode."

The Book of Margery Kempe echoes Mirk's presentation of madness as
a particularly grueling test for sufferer, family members, and potential
healers alike. Indeed, *The Book* places Margery in a situation similar in
many ways to that of St. Bartholomew. As in the *Festial*, Margery encoun-
ters a madwoman's male relative—this time a husband—whose own suf-
fering is immediately apparent: She sees him "wryngyng hys handys &
schewyng tokenys of gret heuynes." In this case, childbirth has brought
on the malady: The husband reports that "hys wyfe was newly delyueryd
of a childe & sche was owt hir mende." Like the woman healed by St.
Bartholomew, the woman is "bowndyn handys and feet wyth chenys of
yron þat sche xulde smytyn no-body."[75] Margery, however, is able to calm
and comfort the woman until her day of purification, when she recovers.

Both *The Festial* and *The Book of Margery Kempe*, then, present madness
as a torment for the sufferer and her family, a danger to the community as
a whole, and a conduit for the curing power of God.[76] By depicting "wode"
individuals within a larger social context, these narratives at least maintain

the place of the mad within the Christian community. Langland makes this argument even more forcefully. Although the nature of the madness of the "lunatyk lollares" is unclear, he asserts unambiguously that "We shoulde haue hem to house and helpe hem when they come."[77] By contrast, the *Conscience*-poet refrains from directly addressing madness, instead using it strategically to threaten his audience. Most people possess the ability to avoid this fate if they embrace the fear and love of God to which their reason directs them. Those without this fundamental rationality, however, function as opaque symbols of suffering rather than as fellow humans. Even as he facilitates the emergence of a wide-ranging Christian community of learning, the *Conscience*-poet bars some individuals from entering it.

More remains to be said about the ways medieval writers address madness in their discussions of moral accountability and about disparate definitions of "mynde" and rationality emerging within religious works of the period. It also seems important to recognize that late-medieval works of vernacular theology do not always set forth a version of Christian community that is fully accessible to everyone. The teaching strategies of *The Prick of Conscience*, and the limitations of those efforts, might even spur us to reflect on our own pedagogy as a social practice. Like the *Conscience*-poet, we provide information about unfamiliar textual traditions, encourage new forms of dialogue with the past, and urge our listeners to develop their powers of recollection, discernment, and analysis. But how successfully do we engage with the many different "myndes" we encounter? Whom might we unwittingly relegate to the margins of the communities we create in our classrooms, through the discussions we bypass as well as the ones we initiate? The more we acknowledge the wide range of our students' abilities, experiences, and forms of literacy, the more complex it becomes to uphold a form of intellectualism that is both rigorous and humane. But if *The Prick of Conscience* exemplifies this problem, it might also provide us with a potential response. However jarring some of the *Conscience*-poet's ideas might be, the state of perpetual and uncomfortable mindfulness he recommends might remain useful for us as we take it upon ourselves to teach.

THE IDEA OF PUBLIC POETRY IN LYDGATEAN RELIGIOUS VERSE: AUTHORITY AND THE COMMON VOICE IN DEVOTIONAL LITERATURE

John T. Sebastian

Recent analyses of the verse and prose writings of John Lydgate have turned to Anne Middleton's well-known idea of Ricardian "public poetry" to describe the role of the Lancastrian laureate in shaping response to social debates conducted in the public sphere.[1] Public poetry, in Middleton's formulation, is above all that which speaks in a common voice on behalf of the common good.[2] Although Lydgate's credibility as a spokesman for the masses has had to contend with his status as what we might call a "Westminster-insider" and representative of the institutional church, several scholars have nevertheless found Middleton's concept productive for reappraising Lydgate's relations to his patrons and the ways in which those relations are reflected in his poetry. Thus Scott-Morgan Straker, in calling into question Lydgate's presumed subservience to a Lancastrian political agenda, has remarked that "it is a fundamental misunderstanding of the nature of Lydgate to assert his complicity in his patrons' self-interested and aggressive agendas, because such an assertion overlooks his willingness to criticize those agendas." Straker instead proposes a realignment of "Lydgate's illocutionary acts with the public poetry that Anne Middleton situates in the late fourteenth century" and asserts that Lydgate's laureate productions strike a careful balance between promoting Lancastrian causes, on the one hand, and critiquing political authority, on the other.[3] Similarly invoking Middleton, C. David Benson has identified a "civic Lydgate" who writes the "idea and experience of the city, especially London" but in doing so avoids naive or propagandistic idealization by at least hinting at the city's shortcomings.[4]

This representation of Lydgate's public voice in the service of a common good has not gone unchallenged, however, with some scholars suggesting that Lydgate's ventriloquization of the "voice of public poetry" aims ultimately not at the common good but rather toward the interests only of society's most powerful ranks. In discussing a range of Lydgate's secular productions, from the classicizing political prose of the *Serpent of Division* through the entertainments staged before royal and civic elites, Maura Nolan argues for a severe delimiting of Lydgate's public audiences and states that "what transforms this group of readers and viewers into a 'public,' however, is the way in which these texts combine didacticism—moral exhortation and pedagogical instruction—with a clear sense that their audience *represents* the only public that matters: the ruling elite."[5] Claire Sponsler in her study of the mummings and disguisings likewise questions how public Lydgate's public voice might really have been. Noting that these civic productions served as private entertainments for coterie audiences and that they were unlikely to have circulated much beyond these original audiences even in manuscript form, Sponsler contends that such texts rarely engage concerns or ideologies that extend beyond those of the urban elite. For Sponsler, Lydgate's contribution to the shaping of public culture, at least in London, was limited. She concludes that, to find a genuinely public voice "and a broadly public culture to which it is linked, we may, paradoxically, have to look to other of Lydgate's writings, those that are private, religious, and located outside London, rather than those created and performed within the city."[6]

In this essay, I seize on Sponsler's paradox by extending the search for Lydgate's public voice to his religious poems and asking: What happens if we read Middle English devotional literature as public poetry? For Middleton, the voice of public poetry is emphatically nonreligious and nonclerical,[7] yet this definition is premised on the common assumption that the categories *private* and *religious* are coterminous and mutually opposed to the *public*. But in Lydgate's day, as in our own, devotional practice was not a strictly private affair. This was especially true from the 1380s on, as Wycliffite ideas threatened the authority not only of the church but also of a new political dynasty plagued by questions about its own legitimacy, a seemingly endless war with France, and the accession of an infant monarch on the premature death of Henry V in 1422. Both church and state responded to the crisis of heresy in strikingly public ways, beginning with the Blackfriars Council of 1382, which first set about defining the threat. In his compelling revisionist account of the "invention of Lollardy," Andrew Cole has recently observed that the bishops at the council, under the leadership of Archbishop William Courtenay, "constructed Wycliffism as a cohesive body of heretical thought and practice in order to render religious dissent as *publicly* visible, legally troublesome, conceptually easy to understand, and equally easy to fear,"[8] while the public burning of the suspected Lollard preacher William Sawtre in the run-up to Parliament's promulgation of the statute *De heretico comburendo* in 1401 and the subsequent execution of the layman John Badby in 1410 functioned as cautionary spectacles for other, would-be reformers. The literature of the period likewise attests to the conspicuously public nature of the official response to heresy, as, for example, in the numerous show trials recounted by Margery Kempe in her spiritual autobiography. Matters of personal devotion were hotly contested in the fifteenth century, and public discourse, including public poetry, readily admitted of religious subjects.

If devotional poetry *is* public poetry in the fifteenth century, then what can we gain from reading it in this way? In this essay I consider two of John Lydgate's lesser-known poems, the pseudo-autobiographical *Testament* and a brief verse meditation on the joys and sorrows of the Virgin, that represent Lydgate's intervention in an ongoing debate about the spiritual legitimacy of meditation on devotional images. During Lydgate's career as a writer, Wycliffite iconoclasts challenged the enduringly popular peda-gogical commonplace that understood images as "books for the illiterate" and indirectly sanctioned the proliferation of religious painting, sculpture, and even drama.[9] It is clear from Lydgate's poetry that he was an unwaver-ing supporter of traditional teachings about the inherent instructional value of religious art, yet he chose to advance his position through ver-nacular writings—that is, on the very ground on which Wyclif's followers had made their stand, and without the polemical tone that characterized both sides of the contest. In each of the poems discussed below, the speaker advocates, without polemic, a form of moderate Christianity that steers a middle course between the demands of a sometimes seemingly inflexible orthodoxy and the very real need for vernacular forms of piety.

The poetic speaker who gives voice to Lydgate's argument on behalf of images is, furthermore, an exemplary rather than an authoritative figure, one who models good Christian devotion for the reader rather than taking cover in a facile didacticism. By refusing to justify his claims merely by appealing to authority, Lydgate's speaker becomes the nexus of a community joined together in mutual devotion around a unifying religious icon. This community's shared faith stands in sharp relief against the religiously riven landscape of late-medieval England. Lydgate deemphasizes authority in these poems in two related ways that are characteristic of his public devotional poetics. First, like Chaucer, he multiplies the number of voices competing for the reader's attention. The absence of a clearly established hierarchy among multiple speaking voices, or, for that matter, between the speaker and the audience he interpellates, results in the undermining of any notion in these poems of univocal authority in favor of the claim made by all the voices for a truly common and public form of devotion that could bridge the gaps between *lerned* and *lewed*, clerical and lay, orthodox and Lollard.[10] Lydgate thus speaks through a cacophony of intertwined voices no less complex or slippery than those of Langland, Gower, and Chaucer in responding to social crisis. Second, Lydgate combines traditional literary forms into novel hybrids, in which competing registers converge to produce insights deeper than those available to any single mode of discourse. For Middleton, poetry exhibits its "publicness" not only through its attempt to offer solutions to social crises but also through the voice that mediates those crises. Lydgate experiments with new forms of poetry suited to the spirit of compromise that infuses his response to the religious unrest of his time and place. His efforts to mitigate the extremism of both orthodox and reformist ideologies result in poetry that is conspicuous for its authoritative instability and generic hybridity, and yet it is precisely and paradoxically this instability and hybridity that serve to unify his readers through their mutual desire for a measured and communal response to social upheaval.[11]

THE TESTAMENT

Given not only the relative lateness of its composition but also the intimacy and privacy of its pseudo-autobiographical content, *The Testament* may seem an unlikely starting point for a discussion of public poetry. And yet, in its undermining of various forms of literary and spiritual authority in favor of a communal form of Christian faith embodied by the universal brotherhood centered on the image of a suffering Christ that is invoked in the poem's conclusion, it is exemplary of Lydgate's poetics.[12] The text is divided into five parts that alternate between rhyme royal (seven-line) and eight-line stanzas. An account of the spiritual turning points in the life of a monk now in his twilight years, the poem combines recollections of the subject's wild youth in the best tradition of St. Augustine's *Confesssiones* with prayers to Christ and meditations on the passion to form an extremely innovative hybrid form. In adhering to the conventions of hagiography and spiritual biography, the fourth section of the poem overemphasizes youthful indiscretions, including perhaps some invented solely for the occasion of the poem, that undermine the speaker's claims to authority. The narrator's musings are replete with animal imagery as he recalls being subject to untamable passions, which "did my brydell lede" (622), and rebelling against authority. He recites a litany of trespasses and excesses, including truancy, fruit-thievery (a flimsily disguised nod to Augustine), impiety, and all-around disobedience. The latter, he reports, haunted him even after his entry into a community of Benedictines, whose habit he purports to have worn "only outward as be apparence" (692) but whose rule he found stifling:

> To folowe that charge sauoured but fullyte,
> Saue be a maner counterfete pretence,
> But in effecte ther was none existence:
> Like the image of Pygmalyon,
> Shewed lyfly and was made but of ston.
> (693–97)[13]

The narrator concludes his gratuitous reminiscing by recalling perhaps his most grievous misdeed, his failure to be mindful of what Christ endured to guarantee salvation for the ersatz monk:

> Of all vertu and pacience I was bare,
> Of rekles youthe list non hede to take
> What Cryst Iesu suffred for my sake.
> (737–39)

The aged speaker ascribes his indifference to the tendencies of "rekles youthe" and to a former self distinct from his present state of being. Failure is characteristic of Lydgate's public devotional voice, and the tendency to fail here and elsewhere serves to unite persona and audience in a shared struggle for spiritual perfection, a struggle that resists easy resolution and to which high-minded pronouncements by figures of authority cloaked in counterfeit habits are poorly suited.

The senescent monk's reacquaintance with his youthful alter ego also conjures, seemingly unbidden, a distant but deeply affecting memory of his encounter as a teenager with the depiction of a crucifix hanging from a wall of the monastery's cloister:

> Wythinne .xv. holdyng my passage,
> Myd of a closyter, depicte vpon a wall,
> I savgh a crucifyx, whos woundes were not smalle,
> With this [word] "vide," wrete there besyde,
> "Behold my mekenesse, O child, and leve thy pryde."

> The which word, whan I dyd vndirstond,
> In my last age takyng the sentence,
> Theron remembryng, my penne I toke in honde,
> Gan to wryte with humble reuerence,
> On this word, "vide," with humble diligence,
> In remembraunce of Crystes passioun,
> This litel dite, this compilacioun.

> (740–53)

The narrator does not remark explicitly on what effect the image may have had on him when he was fifteen years old, but it is clear that age has finally allowed him to comprehend the full meaning of "vide" that had escaped him in his youth. The dying Christ paradoxically represents birth into true life and starkly contrasts the earlier image of Pygmalion, which "shewed lyfly" but was made of lifeless stone. In the final stages of his life, the monk finally acquires genuine spiritual sight, allowing him to pierce the veil of his false habit and his own hypocrisy to achieve self-understanding.[14]

The speaker takes pen in hand to explicate this *sentence* in the fifth and final section of *The Testament*, which he describes as a "litel dite" or "compilacioun" and which takes the form of an interpolated lyric in the widespread tradition of verses spoken by Christ from the cross. In a moment of ekphrastic fantasy, Lydgate's Christ directly addresses the monk-speaker along with the poem's reader, repeatedly urging them to behold not only the scene of the crucifixion hung on the cloister wall but also the greater history of his suffering, as it were, diachronically:

Behold the paynemes of whom that I was take,
Behold the cordes with whiche þat I was bounde,
Behold the armoures which made my herte to quake,
Beholde the gardeyn in which þat I was founde,
Behold how Iudas took xxx^{ti} pens rounde,
Beholde his tresoun, beholde his couetyse,
Behold how I with [many a] mortall wounde,
Was like a lambe offred in sacrifice.

(762–69)

The image of Christ on the cross becomes a stage across which the entire passion sequence, from Jesus' capture to his inevitable death, plays out. By beholding the scene set before him, the speaker, in contrast to the pagans, armorers, and Judas himself, finally comprehends the full meaning of Jesus' sacrifice and of the word "vide." Yet the final stanzas of *The Testament* offer this narrative as a reminder no longer to the poem's subject but rather to its audience of the universal need for repentance and the saving power of Christ's sacrificial blood.[15] We are likewise reminded, if more subtly, of the instrumentality of prolonged meditation on devotional images for scaling the heights of spiritual truth.

Despite its length, autobiographical character, and invocation of familiar literary tropes, *The Testament* has received surprisingly little critical treatment. What has been written about *The Testament* has tended to focus on this concluding scene and the memorable device of the speaking image.[16] Among recent critics, Jennifer Bryan in particular has addressed the question of voice in *The Testament*, which she interprets as "an exemplary narrative, suitable for other readers." The poem, she continues, "is a tool Lydgate uses to act on himself and others, and part of its lesson is about the way readers change themselves through the processes of meditation and desire, taking up various voices in turn—conventional ones, personal ones—to transform memory and inclination."[17] Bryan stops short of developing her idea about these interchangeable speakers into a more general theory of voicing in the text, yet it is precisely this sliding subjectivity in the poem that marks *The Testament* as "public" in the Middletonian sense— that is, as a poem "defined by a constant relation of speaker to audience within an ideally conceived world community, a relation which has become the poetic subject."[18]

At the conclusion of *The Testament*, the poem shifts mode from narrative to lyric when Christ on the cross displaces the monk-persona as the poem's authoritative voice. The narrator takes his place alongside the poem's reader as the recipient of Christ's repeated command to "behold." The call to repentance issued from the cross thus interpellates the narrator himself and through him the reader, both of whom Christ entreats to turn away from the pride and sinfulness exhibited by the unruly young monk of the preceding section. Speaking voices and reading audiences rapidly dissolve into and out of one another as the poem careens toward its salvific conclusion. The effect of this play of voices is a decentering of the authority of the narrating figure associated with Lydgate the monk-poet in favor of the experience of the reader himself. The narrator is depicted as fragmented, the various parts of his self at war with one another. The reader, by contrast, is invited to join his heart in unity with Christ's "and late hem neuer parte in no wyse" (871), to learn from the narrator's experience, and to achieve the kind of genuine spiritual wholeness that eluded the narrator until the period of his senescence.

Anne Middleton identifies the mode of Ricardian public poetry as "didactic," "tonally vivid," and "often structurally unstable," all of which characterics are in evidence in John Lydgate's *Testament*.[19] The life narrated by multiple voices in *The Testament* thus functions as a cautionary tale, a negative exemplum. The fuguelike poem eventually comes to rest with Christ summoning the reader/spectator to "turne home ageyn" (866) and to take his place as part of a perfected community in which all are brothers in the blood of Christ outpoured:

Tarye no lenger toward thyn herytage;
Hast on thy weye and be of ryght good chere.
Go eche day onward on thy pylgrymage;
Thynke howe short tyme thou hast abyden here.
Thy place is bygged aboue the sterres clere,
Noon erthly palys wrought in so statly wyse.
Kome on, my frend, my brother most entere!
For the I offered my blood in sacryfice!

(890–97)

This vision of a utopian community united in love through the blood of the cross contrasts sharply with the image of unruly monastic life presented elsewhere in the poem as well as with the divisiveness of contemporary English religious politics. By the end of *The Testament*, Lydgate has thoroughly dismantled any notion of the cloister as a privileged space, with the only remaining trace of the monk-persona found in Christ's address to his "brother most entere" in the penultimate line of the poem. The true addressee of Christ's exhortation is revealed to be the poem's reader, who is instructed in the plainspoken diction of friendship and brotherly love to learn from the young wanton and to meditate on the full meaning of Christ's suffering as the first step to reforming a wayward will. The publicness of *The Testament* thus resides in its ability to produce a universal brotherhood of Christian believers united in the blood of Christ. Lydgate accomplishes this through the exemplary figure of an uncertain narrator often at odds with himself in a poem that combines narrative reflection with devotional lyric into a unique, hybrid literary form. Rather than destabilizing meaning, however, the poem's competing voices finally resolve harmoniously in an explication of the word *vide*. The voice of Christ, no longer distinguishable from that of the poet, exhorts both the poem's own narrator and his audience to see Christ's mercy, issued forth in the blood of his sacrifice, as an invitation to abandon conflict and "turne home ageyn."

THE FIFTEEN JOYS AND SORROWS OF MARY

Evidence of a distinctively public poetics can also be found in Lydgate's *Fifteen Joys and Sorrows of Mary*. This verse meditation on a well-known theme in devotional art and literature resembles *The Testament* not only in its ekphrastic turn to another set of popular devotional images but also in its fascinating mingling of voices and styles for the purpose of downplaying authority in favor of a communal resolution to spiritual tensions. This poem offers a stanza-by-stanza treatment of each of the joys and woes of the Virgin and opens with a brief but remarkable prologue voiced by another spiritually troubled figure. In the tradition of Chaucerian dream-vision narrative, Lydgate's protagonist seeks solace in reading in order to escape his otherwise undisclosed difficulties:

> Atween mydnyght and the fressh morwe gray
> Nat yore ago, in herte ful pensiff,
> Of thoughtful sihes my peyne to put away,

Caused by the trouble of this vnstabil liff,
Vnclosyd a book, that was contemplatiff;
Of fortune turnyng the book, I fond
A meditacioun which first cam to myn hond,

Tofor which was sett out in picture
Of Marie an ymage ful notable,
Lyke a pyte depeynt was the figure
With weepyng eyen, and cheer most lamentable;
Thouh the proporcioun by crafft was agreable,
Hir look down cast with teerys al bereyned,
Of hertly sorwe so soore she was constreyned.
(1–14)[20]

The restless narrator, seeking some respite from his uneasiness, opens a book of spiritual contemplation by chance onto a *pietà*, the popular image of Mary holding Jesus' lifeless body. Beneath the "pyte," a favorite image of Lydgate in his devotional poetry, appears a series of rubrics outlining the individual joys and woes experienced by Mary according to medieval tradition. Spiritual reading offers him some solace, and in the concluding stanza of the prologue he is depicted as eager to make that consolation more widely available:

Folwyng the ordre, as the picture stood,
By and by in that hooly place,
To beholde it did myn herte good;
Of affeccioun turnyd nat my face,
But of entent, leiser cauht and space,
Took a penne, and wroot in my manere
The said balladys, as they stondyn heere.
(29–35)

Like the narrator of the fourth part of *The Testament* on recalling a depiction of the crucifixion mounted to a cloister wall, Lydgate's speaker here, moved by a devotional image, takes pen in hand and translates the image into text so that readers without access to this particular book "that was contemplatiff" might nevertheless derive some spiritual consolation from it secondhand. The prologue concludes with the narrator seeking to translate his experience of devout meditation on the *pietà* and spiritual reading into poetry, with his own verses, written "in my maneere," standing in place of the book that comforted him. These stanzas trade the intimacy of the prologue's speaker for the authoritative voice of the absent manuscript. As he does elsewhere in his devotional poetry, Lydgate shifts modes, in this case from spiritual narrative to direct and prayerful address to the Virgin Mary, who is exhorted, for instance, to recall the boundlessness of her joy or the depth of her sorrow and to protect her "servauntis."

Whether the "I" of the prologue is to be identified with the first-person speaker of the "balladys" is unclear and seems unlikely; the narrator observes a second image depicted beside that of the Virgin, that of a figure who knelt "deuoutly on his knees" (25) and recited one Pater Noster and ten Aves "at th'ende of ech ballade" (27). The poem casts the kneeling figure as the speaker of the "balladys." Thus, while the experience of the speaker of the prologue is depicted as exemplary, a model for imitation by other devout insomniacs who may find that reflection on the extremes of Mary's joy and woe help them achieve greater perspective on "the trouble of this vnstabil liff," the sleepless narrator is hardly a representative of authority in the poem. He chooses his book haphazardly, opens to the *pietà* by chance, and mimics what he discovers there. The didactic authority of *The Fifteen Joys and Sorrows of Mary* is vested in an illustrated figure who speaks from the pages of an inaccessible manuscript, while the author's own persona reveals himself to be no better equipped than his own perhaps accidental reader to navigate the shoals of spiritual life. The poem thus inculcates an appreciation for a common devotional practice grounded in meditation on religious images and the reading of sacred texts within a community that includes a narrator who disavows any privileged claim to authority over his readers. The interchangeability of real and fictive readers, however, recalls again Anne Middleton, who argues that

the "I" of public poetry presents himself as, like his audience, a layman of good will, one worker among others, with a talent to be used for the common good. It is his task to find the common voice to speak for all, but to claim no privileged position, no special revelation from God or the Muses, no transcendent status for the result, and little in the way of special gifts beyond a good ear. The "I" is otherwise like "you" and includes himself and his poetic endeavor in the world's work.[21]

In John Lydgate's devotional poetry the authority of the speaking voice is ultimately displaced by the shared experiences of the pious communities that the poems invoke and address. In the two poems discussed here, Lydgate refuses to assume the mantle of clerical and didactic authority in speaking to his audiences, opting instead for a voice that is conspicuously vernacular, plainspoken (despite his prevailing reputation for prolixity, aureation, and unwieldy syntax), and practical.[22] These poems do indeed speak in a common voice on behalf of that community. They feature narrators and speakers whose devotional practices are put on public display in order to shape the religious behavior of their readers. And while some spiritual failure on the part of the narrator distinguishes both of these poems—failure to "behold" fully Christ's suffering in *The Testament* and to find solace within himself in *The Fifteen Joys and Sorrows of Mary*—it is precisely through the imperfections of his personas that Lydgate's readers can identify with the poet.

This mutuality is evident in the conclusion of *The Fifteen Joys and Sorrows of Mary* when the narrator finally explains the purpose for which these meditations on key events from the life for the Virgin were originally set down:

> Off humble entent that we good heed may take
> During our liff with gret devocioun
> What Crist Iesu suffryd for our sake,
> Thy deere sone—deth, peyne, and passioun—
> And for we shulde haue eek compassioun
> With the, pryncesse, that boughtist his deeth ful deere.
> For that entent they been rehersyd heere.
>
> (288–94)

The "we" of these lines includes both narrator and reader, whose collective tribulations are further subsumed into the suffering of Christ and whose experiences become the occasion for increased sympathy with, and indeed empathy for, Mary. Recollection of the physical anguish of Jesus and the emotional torment of Mary brings the narrator and his fellow sufferers together at the foot of the Cross, where their pain is sublimated into a form of *imitatio Christi et Mariae*. Once again multiplicity and hybridity ultimately give way to unity in the cross, the final authority in this as in others among Lydgate's devotional poems.[23]

The Testament and *The Fifteen Joys and Sorrows of Mary* aspire to envision an ideal community united by a common, practical devotion opposed to the fractiousness of contentious disputes over rarefied theological concepts that were raging in Lydgate's England.[24] As Andrew Cole and Shannon Gayk have recently observed, Lydgate's intervention in these debates negotiates the extremes of orthodoxy's rigorous theology on the one hand and Wycliffite anti-authoritarianism on the other. Cole comments that Lydgate "never indulges in the kind of polemic that characterizes the efforts of his religious contemporaries, Roger Dymmok or Thomas Netter, both of whom produce works in the service of church and state."[25] While it is true, as Cole further observes, that Lydgate is certainly capable of full-throated anti-Lollard invective,[26] it is also clear that Lydgate's participation in this contest of religious ideas is more restrained, and while he ultimately comes down on the side of orthodoxy, he does so by appropriating the common, popular, vernacular voice synonymous with Lollardy but also with public poetry.

Gayk, in turn, argues that by "translating Latinate, pre-Bernardine devotional practices and hermeneutics into vernacular poetry, Lydgate simultaneously authorizes the vernacular as a mode of theological instruction and reasserts the importance of clerical mediation of lay spirituality." She continues: "Precisely because he translates monastic hermeneutics into vernacular religious verse, Lydgate's authorization of religious writing in English is fundamentally different from both Lollard assertions of lay spiritual autonomy and orthodox assumptions that the vernacular is unsuited for more complex or abstract theology."[27] In the best tradition of public poetry, then, Lydgate speaks for the common English citizen in an exemplary voice that models a lay, vernacular, and eminently practical devotion as an alternative to competing and extreme forms of ideology.

Viewed from the vantage point of Anne Middleton's concept of public poetry, John Lydgate's devotional verse is shown to be not " 'about' contemporary events or abuses, whether viewed concretely or at a distance"; likewise "it is rarely occasional or topical, and it is indifferent on the whole to comprehensive rational systems of thought or of poetic structure."[28] Instead it addresses matters of public interest through an array of public voices with no real claims to authority in unstable and hybrid genres. The idea of "public poetry" thus attunes us to the complexities of voice in Lydgate's writing and reveals the fifteen-year-old rapscallion of part 4 of *The Testament* to be no less fascinating than his better-known predecessor personas,

Geoffrey and Long Will. It sheds light on the formal instability and play evident in these poems, as competing genres and modes of address ricochet off of one another in the course of decentering authorities and staking claims for a common set of devotional practices available to all Christians, clerical and lay, orthodox and reformist, seeking spiritual consolation. Finally, the idea of "public poetry" enables us to begin the process of recuperating the neglected spiritual writing of John Lydgate free of the critical assumption that, in order for it to be effective, didactic religious poetry must be transparent and self-interpreting (else how can one guarantee that the correct message has gotten across?). In this brief meditation on the public voice of two of these poems, I hope to have taken a first step toward recovering this body of writing for critical interpretation, a project that will require the attentions of not a few sleepless scholars seeking solace in devotional poetry.

NATURE'S *YERDE* AND WARD: AUTHORITY AND CHOICE IN CHAUCER'S *PARLIAMENT OF FOWLS*

Nick Havely

At the end of the debate in Chaucer's *Parliament of Fowls*, as Nature struggles to control the increasingly raucous voices, she turns to the creature she (like some noble hawking lady) holds "on hir honde": the female eagle ("formel").[1] Throughout all the "noble dispute," the "noise," and the variety of "verdicts" that have attended the three tercel eagles' competitive pledges of love for her, the formel has remained silent, expressing her feelings only through a surreal avian blush.[2] Now, however, as the still center on whom the pressures of time and desire converge, she is faced with Nature's "conclusyon" and the burden of choice: "that she hir selfe shal have hir eleccion" (*PF* 621). Her own voice is thus heard for the first and last time in the poem, and her decision is not to make a decision and to reject "as yet" the act of "serving" in love that has meant so much to her male suitors (648–53).

In her refusal or postponement of the service of Venus and Cupid, the formel shows some affinity with Boccaccio's Emilia in the *Teseida* and Chaucer's Emily in the *Knight's Tale*.[3] She also shares some features with another female object of desire in Chaucer: the *Book of the Duchess*'s White, who is pursued by the aristocratic Man in Black, initially rejects him, then grants him "mercy" "another yere."[4] Her voice and position are more broadly characteristic, too, of the woman's role within the cult and discourse of "courtly love," defined as "an arena in which negotiations can take place, even if we almost always hear only the male side of the argument."[5]

The formel's decision or lack of it has been seen as reflecting on other "unresolved" aspects of the *Parliament*—on "the narrator's own amused or troubled indecisiveness," for example, or the poem's response to contemporary philosophic concerns with "choice in general and the faculty of will that engages in it."[6] My main argument here is that, when addressing the problems of the formel's response to Nature, we may find it helpful not only to place them in such philosophical contexts but also to locate them within the framework of a particular contemporary social and legal practice—namely, wardship. Wardship obviously involved the main issues of authority and choice that are in play at this point of the *Parliament*; it was a practice whose significance in other medieval English texts, especially romances, has recently been the subject of some important research; and that research could well be relevant also to the reading of Chaucer.[7]

A key phrase that, in my view, points towards this social and legal context is the one through which the formel herself defines her subordinate status in relation to Nature's authority. This phrase forms part of her very first spoken assertion, as she responds "with dredeful vois" to the request to choose between her three suitors, prefacing her own request with a formal acknowledgment of Nature's supreme power over her:

My ryghtful lady, goddesse of Nature—
Sooth ys that I am ever under youre yerde
(*PF* 640)

The phrase "under youre yerde," with the attendant image of Nature's rod or sceptre, has attracted relatively little attention from commentators. *Yerde* was used in fourteenth-century English as a term for "sceptre" and hence "an emblem of authority, office or power."[8] As used by the formel here, it thus vividly reinforces the "royal" authority of Chaucer's Nature, who is introduced first as a "quene" (298) and is subsequently said to convene and preside as a "noble emperesse" over the assembly of birds (319). It is significant for the present argument that, of the participants in the assembly, it is only the formel who explicitly acknowledges this authority in the form of her address, speaking to Nature as "my ryghtful lady" and "Almyghty quene" (639, 647). The formel's formality here, moreover, underlines the parallel between her position and that of a noble ward in relation to a guardian—a parallel to which we shall return later in this essay

First, however, we need to identify more precisely how the powers of the formel's "guardian" are imagined. What are the literary and linguistic contexts for the *yerde* with which she and Chaucer invest Nature? The regality (or viceregality) of Nature as "vyker of th'almyghty lorde" had been stressed in a twelfth-century Latin text named in the *Parliament*—Alanus of Lille's *De planctu naturae*—as well as in the later *Roman de la Rose*.

Alanus indeed introduces his personification with a lengthy description of her crown.[9] As an image of her philoprogenitive force, the rod of power with which the formel endows Nature in the *Parliament* has affinities with the productive "hammers" that are associated with Nature in both the earlier texts, and the noun *yerd/yard* itself of course has a phallic sense in both Middle and Early Modern English.[10]

De planctu naturae provides a further related context and a likely source for Nature's *yerde* in the *Parliament*, together with a possible reason for the formel's use of the term. In Prose 8 of Alanus's text, Natura, together with her support team of Hymen, Truth, Temperance, Generosity, and Humility, seeks to bring humanity to order within the bonds of marriage. This involves a formal decision to chastise and cast out recalcitrant elements. In order to put that judgment into effect, Nature resolves to enlist the aid of Genius and does so by means of a proclamatory letter. Both the letter and the account of the deliberations that produce it describe the implementing of Nature's judgment and power as the wielding of a "*rod* of excommunication" (*virga excommunicationis*).[11] The formel's recognition or pledge that "I am ever under youre yerde" can thus be seen as an allusion to the way in which Nature's jurisdiction has been imagined in *De planctu*—and as the eagle's somewhat apprehensive acknowledgment of the dangers of trying to thwart the almighty queen's power. The imperative of Nature's *yerd* in the *Parliament* could thus be seen as the equivalent of the formel's biological clock. Moreover, the Latin term *virga*, which Alanus thus uses to describe both Nature's generative potency and the exercise of her divinely sanctioned authority, covers a semantic range very similar to that of *yerd* in Middle English. Among the particularly relevant uses of the word are those that refer to symbolic rods or staffs of office and the phrase *sub virga*, denoting the status of those under "tutelage [or] guardianship."[12] We shall shortly investigate some of the applications and contexts of this phrase and of the equivalent expression, *desous la verge*, in law French; meanwhile it is worth noting that "under youre yerde" in the *Parliament* parallels both of these as an acknowledgment of subjection to a higher authority.

"Under youre yerde" is used in other Chaucerian texts to convey such subjection in several different ways. At the very beginning of his considered response to the Host's gruff order to "telle us som myrie tale," the Clerk duly recognizes that

> Hooste . . . I am under youre yerde;
> Ye han of us as now the governance,
> And therfore wol I do yow obeisance,
> As fer as resoun axeth, hardily.
>
> (*CT* 4[E].22–25)

Specifically, the Clerk is acknowledging the reminder a few lines earlier (10–11) of his "assente" to the rules of the pilgrimage "pley," and hence to the Host's power to impose those rules; although, as might be expected, the wording of the acknowledgment includes a proviso ("as fer as resoun axeth") that will allow for some leeway in interpreting the latter's command for a "myrie tale."

In the context of another power structure—that of Chaucer's *Troilus and Criseyde*—the phrase carries considerable resonance at a decisive stage in the development of the Trojan love affair. At the center of the scene in Deiphebus's house, which constitutes Chaucer's most substantial departure so far from the narrative of the *Filostrato*, we find Troilus proffering his *servise* to Criseyde in the following terms:

> As to my lady right and chief resort,
> With al my wit and al my diligence;
> And I to han, right as yow list confort,
> Under yowre yerde, egal to myn offence,
> As deth, if that I breke youre defence.
>
> (*Troilus* 3.134–37)

Criseyde's *yerde* quite clearly symbolizes the power she is thus given by Troilus to reward or punish him, according to the merits or faults of his *servise*; as such, it is perhaps an image that she will evoke when the game has progressed much further and she is playfully threatening to chastise him for his *childissh* jealousy.[13] In his affirmation of Criseyde's authority here, Troilus seems to be setting out quasi-contractual terms for his surrender of power—hence his use of *agreen* (131) and repeated forms: *And I to . . .; And that . . .; And I to . . .; And . . . to serve; And . . . Receyven*.[14] Use of such legalistic language seems to reflect what Charles Muscatine describes as "the boyishly literal completeness of Troilus's devotion to the ideal," and it is evident again when he seeks to scrutinize the *text* of mercy as *writen* in the expression of Criseyde's eyes; here, as Richard F. Green points out, "when Chaucer came to describe Troilus's attempts to divine his lady's true feelings for him, he . . . turned to the image of a written contract."[15] Troilus's eager efforts to endow a passionate, clandestine, and vulnerable relationship with documentary stability and permanence are of course not without their ironies, and D. W. Robertson was quick to notice the further "amusing inversion" through which Criseyde's request for Troilus's lordship and protection has been met with his determination to place himself beneath her *yerde*.[16] Robertson was also aware of the fact (not registered by the poem's modern editors) that the phrase *under yowre yerde* reflects the Latin legal phrase *sub virga*, which was, as he notes, "conventionally used to describe the condition of children, or, occasionally, of wives."[17] His own eagerness to relate this "inversion" to the somber vision of disrupted medieval (and male) hierarchies, however, seems to have prevented him from seeing more precisely how the playfully subversive use of legal language continues to operate in this context.[18]

In a somewhat less exalted urban context, Chaucer's "Shipman's Tale" also describes the position of subordination and dependency by use of the term *under the yerde*. In this tale, which makes much so much play with the terms of trade and *taillynge*, a more hard-nosed clandestine affair is negotiated between a merchant's status-conscious wife and his "cousin," the worldly monk Daun John. Here, however, neither of the prospective lovers is put in Troilus's subordinate situation, since both the mercantile Wife and the Monk are quite evenly matched in their dealings on the sexual futures market. Instead, the phrase is applied to the young girl who accompanies the Wife as she meets the Monk in the Merchant's garden and is thereby witness to the initiation of those dealings:

> A mayde child cam in hire compaignye,
> Which as hir list she may governe and gye,
> For yet under the yerde was the mayde.
> (*CT* 7 [B²]. 1285–87)

The precise position of this *mayde child* in the narrative of the tale and in the household is uncertain. She remains silent and without any recorded reaction during this encounter between her mistress and the Monk, and she has no further role to play—except perhaps as participant in the household's universal rejoicing at Daun John's return during the Merchant's absence (1500–1502). But her presence as witness to the initial bargain between her elders raises some interesting questions about relationships in the household, which, in view of the tale's specificity about mercantile lifestyle, are worth considering.

We have no way of knowing what exact form of relationship is being imagined between the Wife and her *mayde child*; but the term *under the yerde* (along with *governe and gye* in the previous line) suggests several possibilities. Since the equivalent Latin term (*sub virga*) could apply to the status of infants as well as of wives, it is possible that the girl is, as Peter Beidler has recently argued, the Wife's daughter; however, the conspiracy she is about to become privy to might thus have tragic rather than comic potential for conflicting loyalty.[19] Alternatively, she might be seen as in a position of familial service with the Merchant and his wife. As the Riverside editors note, quoting evidence from the Merchant Tailors' *Minutes* of the mid-fifteenth century, a merchant of standing would expect to have "an honest mayde chyld to wayte upon my wyf" during any kind of excursion.[20] Service within such a family could, as Barbara Hanawalt points out, be of formative and educational value for young Londoners in this period, enabling them to acquire "polished manners and knowledge of the world."[21] Hanawalt also shows how this kind of service could be combined with an extremely well-documented social function of the urban merchant family at this time: that of fostering and guardianship.[22] There is ample evidence from the records of late-fourteenth-century London and Bristol that the majority of wards in the care of city families became so at a young age (below twelve) and that the city authorities took their custodial responsibilities and those of the appointed guardians very seriously.[23] The duties of care in such a relationship are outlined in the will of a Canterbury widow who uses very similar phraseology to Chaucer's when entrusting her daughter to the care of a male friend with the condition that she be not married "unto the tyme that she be of reasonable age of years for to have discretion and understanding to govern and rule heresilf in such things as longith to womanhode."[24] The way in which the Shipman's Wife governs and rules the girl under her guardianship (whether as ward, servant, or daughter) is not of course to be taken as a civic model; indeed, in its suggestive fabliau mode it could be seen as complementing the Physician's much more ponderous and somber admonition to aristocratic *maystresses* who have "lordes doghtres . . . in governaunce."[25]

With such models of authority, subordination, and custodianship in mind, we can proceed to consider further the nature and possible implications of the *governaunce* that Dame Nature in Chaucer's earlier poem exercises over her young and marriageable *doghter*, the female eagle, and then to investigate the parallels between Nature's tutelage of the formel and the social and legal practices of feudal wardship. In the scene that we began with, at the end of the *Parliament*, the formel's respectful mode of address to her *ryghtful lady* and her recognition of being *ever under youre yerde* can (especially if we bear in mind the potency of the *virga* in Alanus's *De planctu*) be seen quite generally as a way of representing the subjection of all sublunary creatures to the law of Nature while, as the formel puts it, "lyf may dure" (642). In the *Parliament*, Nature's role—especially in the case of those creatures regarded as "primates" (the noble eagles)—is also at times envisaged as parental.[26] She emphasizes how she has *formed* the tercel eagle as the epitome of her procreative craft (396–98) and gives him precedence as her *sone* (406). Her relationship with the formel as her *doghter* (the mode of address she uses in 448) has also been presented in close, even intimate terms: The female eagle, like the male, is described as the noblest *amonge hir werkes* (373–74); she treats her with a demonstrative affection (377–78) that has been described as "delicate homoeroticism" and she responds to her signs of distress with ready maternal reassurance (447–48).[27] Yet the formel's formal language of submission to her *ryghtful lady* and *almyghty quene* also evokes other social and legal contexts.

Such contexts are suggested as soon as Nature makes her appearance as *quene* and *noble goddesse* presiding over those who wait on her words and "judgment" (*dome*, 308).[28] Legal and parliamentary vocabulary underwrites her authority during the course and conduct of the ensuing debate. As J. A. W. Bennett noted, she "is no arbitrary monarch: she governs 'by statute' and 'rightful ordenaunce,'" constitutional terms that were being distinguished from each other at the time of the poem; and as Derek Brewer explains further: "Nature's *statute* has the sacred character of law . . . her *ordenaunce* is a particular act or decision within the scope of the statute."[29] Nature opens the proceedings like the Chancellor giving the reasons for the calling of a Parliament (382–29); as the debate unfolds and intensifies, other terms—*delyvered, pledynge, juge, remedye, assented, presente, accepteth*—evoke legal and parliamentary procedure.[30]

At points, of course, such authoritative procedure is evoked mainly in order to be subverted, and one of the most striking ways through which (in 494–504) the lower fowl register their impatience with the tendency of their betters' *cursed pledynge* is, as Marion Turner argues, "the mockery of legal discourses, reminiscent of Bakhtin's description of carnivalesque language parodying formal discourses."[31] Indeed, following this outbreak, the "noyse of foules for to ben delyvered" becomes so vocal and dominant that the "fool" cuckoo claims the *auctorite* to speak for the common good and even to help dissolve (*delyveren*) the assembly (506–8). In the face of the "murmour of the lewednesse behynde," and in order to preserve some semblance of proper procedure, Nature then seems constrained to accept a form of wider consultation, while the force of the challenge to her own authority may perhaps reflect, as David Aers suggests, a contemporary "loss of plebeian respect for traditional elites."[32] However, as Bennett notes, Chaucer's Nature has reserved and will exercise an authority that is comparable to that of the Plantagenet monarch in parliament: the right to have "the final decision and the power of dismissing the assembly he had summoned of his own accord."[33] This quasi-regal authority is, as we have seen, explicitly recognized in the opening words of the formel's speech at the end of the *Parliament*, and it informs a relationship, between her and the *almyghty quene*, that in some ways resembles that of guardianship.

The possibility that Nature's role is being imagined both as a quasi-maternal one but as a kind of guardianship is reinforced not only by her regal role and the vocabulary through which this is described (as we have seen) but also by the formel's use of the phrase *under youre yerde*. The Latin and French equivalent terms *sub virga* and *suz/desous la verge* had long been used in legal parlance to describe one person's subordination to the authority of another. In the first half of the thirteenth century, Henry de Bracton, author of the English legal treatise *De legibus et consuetudinibus Angliae* (The Laws and Customs of England) discusses the situation of persons who "are in the wardship or tutelage [*custodia sive tutela*] of lords" or "in the care [*in curatione*] of relatives and friends." Bracton uses the phrase *sub virga*, giving "wives and others" (*uxores etcetera*) as a further example of this condition.[34] The phrase is also applied earlier than Bracton to the legal incapacity of those under tutelage and guardianship, as outlined by the *Leges Regis Henrici Primi*.[35] Its French equivalent, *suz* or *desuz sa verge*, seems to have been in common usage by the later thirteenth century: It is used, for instance, in cases of 1275 and 1304, where a husband's responsibility for getting his wife to court, or hers for a deed of gift, are in question.[36] In 1292 also, the validity of the will of a London woman, Christiana La

Flaoners, who had left a tenement "to be sold for paying her debts and for pious uses for the good of her soul and the soul of William her former husband," was challenged on the grounds that not only did she hold the tenement only for life but she also "had a husband at the time of making the testament, and so [was] *sub virga*." And, as we have seen, the Middle English term (*under the yerde*) that translates this is applied in the urban world of Chaucer's *Shipman's Tale* to the *mayde child* who is the Merchant's servant and/or ward. However, the formel's *gentil* status in the *Parliament* and the quasi-regal role that Nature exercises there suggest that a rather more exalted legal and social context is being evoked—one in which the rights and interests of aristocratic heirs and guardians are involved. Hence, for an appropriate form of guardianship to compare in the case of the *Parliament*, we shall need to look beyond the world of the Shipman's urban wardship and "burgage tenure" to that of more specifically *feudal* wardship.[37]

Wardship was a long-established and important fact of English medieval aristocratic life. As S. F. C. Milsom makes clear, the "prerogative wardship" exercised by the king over the minor heirs of landholders was not a special creation of royal power but a survival from what had been the norm.[38] "Under wardship," as Scott L. Waugh explains, "the king retained custody of the lands until the heir came of age, twenty-one for males, fourteen or marriage for women, and he also gained the right to marry the heir to whomever he chose, as long as the heir consented and the marriage did not disparage the heir."[39] We shall turn to the question of consent shortly, but we should first consider how royal power over wards was exercised in the century or so before Chaucer and what was the position of unmarried female heiresses at this time.

With regard to wardship, the Crown continued to pursue two main objectives during the late thirteenth and fourteenth centuries: that of patronage and rewarding loyal followers through advantageous marriages, and that of achieving "the smooth descent of property" and "stable continuity between generations by ensuring, insofar as it was possible, that legitimate heirs would inherit and marry."[40] It was not only male monarchs such as Henry III or the first two Edwards who were involved in this pursuit; at least one powerful queen, Edward I's wife Eleanor of Castile, shared her husband's authority "in the process, critical to effective lordship, of distributing wealth through wardships and marriages," and she is known to have passed on wardships to "favoured squires, yeomen and serjeants."[41]

In Chaucer's time, prerogative wardship over lands and persons was still a means by which English kings exercised patronage and acquired income, although attitudes toward the practice were changing. For example, the huge inheritance of the earldom of March fell into the Crown's hands twice in the later fourteenth century, and in 1381 the king was "under pressure from some of the nobility not to grant it out to courtiers who might exploit it."[42] There had been previous petitions of a similar nature, and in this case, it seems, the interests of the estate prevailed. Royal wardship and its proper conduct was thus a live issue at the time of the composition of the *Parliament of Fowls*.

The position of unmarried female heirs under such wardship was in principle restricted and could be particularly problematic. Back in the late twelfth century, *Glanvill* had insisted that

> If a woman or women are left as heirs of anyone, they stay in ward [*in custodia*] to their lords. If they are under age they will be in wardship until they come of age, and when they have come of age their lord is bound to marry them off. . . . Even if they are of full age, still they shall remain in ward to their lords until they are married on the lords' advice and direction, because by the law and custom of the realm no woman who is heir to land may be married without the direction or consent of the lord.[43]

In the thirteenth century Bracton, when discussing the marriage of heirs, recognized the principle that, while male heirs "of full age" might arrange things for themselves, a female heir "though she is of full age . . . may not marry without the consent of the chief lord to whom the marriage is known to belong, for the reason given a little above, lest the lord be compelled [to take the homage of his chief enemy or other unsuitable person]."[44] The position of the unmarried female heir is thus seen to be fraught with considerable danger to the system. As Noël James Menuge explains the nature of the threat and its consequences: "The putative autonomy of the heiress puts feudal/patriarchal authority under pressure because of her ability to marry an 'unsuitable person'. . . . She cannot hope to increase her family's holdings, . . . nor can she really hope to retain her own. Therefore her marriage must be contained."[45]

There is a further possible analogy here with the situation at the end of the *Parliament of Fowls*. Like the unmarried heiress within the nexus of feudal relationships, the formel eagle unsettles the framework of social and philosophical assumptions that appear to govern the world of the poem. Unwittingly, she becomes the cause of noble rivalry, potential violence, and increasingly noisy dissension. More consciously, she delays her choice, thereby posing a significant threat to the smooth running of Nature's system.

The formel's problematic situation may also reflect on the range of choice in marriage that was available to noble wards, male or female. Addressing the constraints on choice for feudal wards in medieval England, Sue Sheridan Walker has argued that with regard to coercion and "forfeiture" (fines, often very substantial, for marriage without the guardian's consent), there is

> nothing in the surviving evidence to show that the heiress was treated differently from the heir. Heirs of both sexes married contrary to the guardian's wishes [and thus paid the fine], heirs of both sexes were kidnapped. If the smaller number of pleas of forfeiture against heiresses meant they were more docile about first marriages, they amply made up for such docility when as widows they freely remarried.[46]

Basic principles concerning freedom of choice in marriage had of course been articulated by the church in the mid-twelfth century. Gratian's *Concordia discordantium canonum* of ca. 1140, known as the *Decretum*, opposes coercion with the argument that "forced marriages generally have bad outcomes" (*inuitae nupthae solent malos prouentus habere*).[47] The principle that *in matrimonio animus debet gaudere plena libertate* was commonplace in canon law; it was considered "evident that no woman should be coupled to anyone except by her free will," that the "power of choice was equally that of man and of woman," and that the age of consent should be twelve for girls and fourteen for boys.[48] The canon-law principle of freedom also seems to have been accepted in English law and applied, for example by Bracton, to the situation of "an heir within age [i.e., still under guardianship], male or female . . . since marital unions ought to be freely contracted" (*cum libera debant esse coniugia*).[49]

However, the statement by Bracton forms a parenthesis in a sentence that is chiefly concerned with the provision of compensation for the guardian in such circumstances (the "forfeiture" referred to above), and the true nature and extent of the "freedom" exercised especially by female feudal wards seems rather circumscribed. For example, Walker's conclusions about wards of both genders who "supported by the canon law, . . . married as they wished—subject to the payment of the feudal marriage tax" are, as James Menuge points out, "drawn from marriage-fine evidence, and while this evidence may demonstrate a limited figure of wards marrying where they chose, it does not . . . represent a norm."[50] The *Prerogativa Regis* of the early fourteenth century (given as Statute of 17 Edward II) provides for thoroughgoing forfeiture of "Lands and Tenements" in the case of women who "hold of the King in Chief any Inheritance" and who choose to "marry themselves without the King's Licence [*sine licencia Regis*]."[51] A slightly earlier passage in the same statute deals with the strictly limited options available to a female royal ward who had been betrothed by her late parent or ancestor: On attaining majority she might choose (*eligat*) either to honor that agreement or to take a husband of the king's choosing—a statement that, Waugh comments, "summarizes the relation between consent and choice. It envisions only a very narrow range of personal choice between alternatives selected by the family or lord under special circumstances."[52] Nor was the doctrine of consent in canon law without its provisos and circumscriptions: For example, as J. T. Noonan makes clear, Gratian himself "assumed that parents would arrange their children's marriages; and, once that assumption was made, the social and psychological factors *restricting* choice were substantial [emphasis added]."[53]

This social and legal context should be borne in mind when we consider two key and complicating features of Nature's treatment of her *doghter* at the end of the *Parliament of Fowls*. On the one hand, Nature has clearly recognized the general principle of free consent as applicable to females of all species: "That she agree to his eleccioun" (407–10).[54] Indeed, in concluding the debate she subsequently grants what appears to be free choice to the formel: "That she hir selfe shal have hir eleccion / Of whom hir lyste" (621–22). On the other hand, it is quite clear that the range of choice on offer is, in practice, limited to one or other of the three current noble suitors, and Nature, acting as the formel's guardian and the voice of courtly and aristocratic *Reson*, is hardly making a secret of her own preference for her *doghter*:

But—as for counseylle, for to chese a make—
Yf I were Reson, than wolde y
Counseylle yow the royal tercel take—
As seyde the tercelet ful skillfully—
As for the gentileste and most worthy,

Whiche I have wroght so wel to my plesaunce
That to yow hyt ought to ben a suffisaunce.

(*PF* 631–37)

Nature, of course, is *not* Reason (although Jean de Meun's *Raison* clearly supports her procreative goals), and Elaine Tuttle Hansen has pointed out the irrationality of her attempt here to reconcile "historically competing matrimonial codes [the feudal and the courtly] that appear to differ fundamentally in their strategies for containing female desire and their concomitant construction of female subjectivity."[55] Nonetheless, despite (or perhaps because of) such irrationality, there can be no mistaking the pressure being exerted by Nature's velvet glove upon the creature she still holds *on hir honde*. The repetition in this stanza of "reasonable," if hypothetical, *counseylle* and the conclusion that all this "ought to be good enough for you" (*to yow hyt ought to ben a suffisaunce*) clearly suggest to me the kind of guidance that a noble guardian bent on advantageous matchmaking might have proffered "in your (i.e., my) best interests." Nature's coercive tactics are of course rather more refined than the 'force and fear' that operated upon some female wards such as Golboru in the romance of *Havelok the Dane*, or in a number of documented legal cases.[56] A more appropriate analogy to her marital strategy might perhaps be the busy matchmaking activities of another powerful queen, Eleanor of Castile, since these, as Waugh argues, "provide a striking demonstration of how wardship and marriage could advance the interests of both wards and guardians and cement relations between curial families."[57] In this context then it seems that Chaucer's female eagle is placing herself in a somewhat risky position by rejecting the advice of the *almyghty quene* who is acting as her guardian and is proposing a match that could certainly not in the legal or any other sense be considered "disparaging."[58]

How, then, in relation to such contexts and traditions, should we read the formel's final decision or indecision? Her negotiation of the problem spans three stanzas (ll. 638–54), and it reflects a combination of caution and resolution. She has plainly registered the force of Nature's *counseylle* in the previous stanza, and, as we have seen, she submissively recognizes Nature's regal and guardian-like authority, particularly through phrases such as *under youre yerde* and *Almyghty quene*. Conversely, her resolution in postponing a decision is also strongly and increasingly in evidence:

Almyghty quene, unto this yere be doon,
I aske respite for to avysen me,
And after that to have my choyse al fre.
Thys al and some that I wol speke and seye;
Ye gete no more, al though ye do me deye.

I wolle noght serven Venus ne Cupide,
For sothe, as yet, by no maner wey.

(PF 647–53)

Her determination is here underlined by phrases such as "*Thys al and some*," "*Ye gete no more*," "*I wolle noght*," and "*by no maner wey*." She thus, as some critics have recognized, implicitly begins to challenge Nature's assumptions as well as those of the masculine hierarchy that is pressing her toward the kind of choice it has in mind.[59]

The choice that the formel herself has in mind and has committed Nature to *graunte* (643–45) is just as carefully formulated here. It not only requests a year's delay; it also has to be "completely free" (*al fre*) and requires the recognition that she will not serve Venus or Cupid "for sothe, as yet, by no maner wey" (652–53).[60] It has been frequently assumed that the formel's words here "pledg[e] her to a deferred submission"; that "she is contracted to relinquish the power that she has temporarily seized"; even that she "utterly accepts that she will marry" and in a year's time her "broken bow will join the extensive collection of such trophies which hang 'in dispit of Dyane the chaste.'"[61] But *as yet* (653) does not yet mean *yes*. If I say I will not do something *yet*, it of course concedes the possibility (even the likelihood) that I *may* do it in the future, but it does not amount to a "pledge," "contract" or "utter acceptance" that I *will* do it. The formel's language here can thus be seen as strikingly "non-performative."[62] The issues it addresses—those of choice, consent, and response to authoritative pressure and advice—are akin to those that Chaucer would also explore (or was already exploring) in Book 2 of the *Troilus*, through the portrayal and speech of another problematic object of desire: Criseyde.

The formel's careful sequence of provisos here is thus crucial both to her negotiations with her guardian, Nature, and to the range of uncertainties at the end of the poem: the "unresolved" aspects of the *Parliament* with which this essay began. Her indeterminate status has been seen as in some ways comparable to (and distinct from) the inconclusive position of the narrator, resolved only to continue harvesting what the *olde bokes* yield *fro yere to yere* (23–24). It can also be seen in the context of the kinds of social issues and practices with which this volume and Penn Szittya's critical work have been concerned. The formel's capacity to unsettle the assumptions of the power structure within which she is situated can be compared with that of the "putative autonomy of the heiress," able to put "feudal/patriarchal authority under pressure because of her ability to marry an 'unsuitable person.'"[63] The ability of both the female eagle and the feudal ward to act in such a way is and was of course severely constrained. But the possibility that the former may choose not to follow Nature's *counseylle* is allowed for in the poem, just as in some cases, although not as the general norm, the latter might successfully have gone against her guardian's wishes.[64]

In the end both the poem and the social and legal contexts that have been outlined here reflect the demands of established interests, codes, and authorities and the (albeit circumscribed) opportunities for the individual will and choice to negotiate those demands. And in the end, although we may be somewhat more confident about the eventual direction of the formel's choice than we are about the value and outcome of the dreamer's further reading, we cannot predict it with any certainty. For now, as Chaucer's *quene* says, wryly but authoritatively, about her *doghter*'s decision not (as yet) to decide:

> Now, syn it may noon other weyes betide,
> . . . here is no more to sey.

FABULOUS WOMEN, FABLES OF PATRONAGE:
METHAM'S *AMORYUS AND CLEOPES*
AND BL MS ADDITIONAL 10304

Kara Doyle

In *Chaucer and His Readers*, Seth Lerer refers to Chaucer's "fables of patronage: fictional accounts of power relationships that, in allegorical or figurative ways, tell stories of the commission and reception of literature."[1] The fables of patronage created by Chaucer cast a long shadow in the fifteenth century, Lerer demonstrates, as male poets, patrons, and manuscript compilers fashioned themselves and their relationships with one another by reworking Chaucer's tropes. Just as Lerer explores the implications of Chaucer's fables of patronage for male poets and patrons, we might well ask what impact Chaucer's fables of female patronage might have had on fifteenth-century English poets dealing with female patrons. Does Chaucer's shadow fall as heavily across these interactions?

In the *Legend of Good Women*, Chaucer most directly confronts the uneasy power struggle between poet and patron, as an angry God of Love takes the poet-narrator to task for his previous works and requests a new text with very narrow specifications. The *Legend* is a late entry in Chaucer's career-long exploration of the interaction between poet, *auctor*, and audience, in which he wonders about the tension between his respect for classical *auctores*, his self-definition as maker, and the demands or potential response of his living audiences. As in the *Hous of Fame* and *Troilus and Criseyde*, this tension reaches a peak of urgency when it involves the representation of classical heroines—Dido, Criseyde—and the response of the women in the audience. Thus, although in the *Prologue to the Legend of Good Women* Chaucer presents us with an angry male patron bent on humbling and punishing a male poet-narrator, he complicates the picture considerably by involving women much more deeply than in the *Hous of Fame* and *Troilus and Criseyde*. Alceste is not merely a female reader who might be offended by the portrayal of Criseyde; because she helps define the narrator's assigned project, she stands as co-patron with the God of Love.

Moreover, having mercifully interceded on the narrator's behalf, she is to be honored by being featured in the work herself, as the heroine of the final story in the collection. Alceste is simultaneously the female audience of past texts, the female patron of the present text, and the female protagonist in the as-yet-unwritten final legend.

This unique threefold role poses some fascinating questions. Chaucer, in the *Legend of Good Women*, is not merely asking what impact the power of a patron might have on the poet's choice of *matere* and *sentence*. He is asking what impact the patron's and the poet's choices of *matere* and *sentence* might have on women, and what difference it makes when the patron is female. He is asking whether, in such a situation, the medieval maker's loyalties should lie more with the male *auctores* or with the female patron-audience. And he is asking what relationship a poet may implicitly set up between female figures from antiquity and female patrons, especially when the work's purpose is to please, to praise, or to canonize the female patron.

It can certainly be argued that the power of these questions is implicitly undermined by the irony of the treatment of individual heroines in the *Legend of Good Women* and by the fact that the female patron in this case, Alceste, is herself already a literary figure. Even if we assume that Alceste was originally a stand-in for Queen Anne, the allegorical portrayal of Alceste as a marguerite (a re-vision of de Lorris and de Meun's Rose) treats Anne as a symbol, rather than as a living patron, and thus puts her at a double remove from the proceedings. It is hard not to suspect Chaucer of having been influenced, to at least some degree, by Boccaccio's dismissive and condescending treatment of his female patron, Andrea Acciauoli, in *De mulieribus claris*. It is very clear that both Boccaccio and Chaucer, despite ostensibly putting their pens at the service of their female patrons, retain ultimate control over the *matere* and *sentence* of their works. Boccaccio's dismissive and Chaucer's fictionalizing treatments of female patronage mean that ultimately in these texts it is the poets, not the patrons, who try to shape attitudes about women. Moreover, or perhaps as a result, their texts end by reifying present attitudes about women rather than challenging them.

However, Chaucer's having even jokingly posed these questions about the impact of female patronage makes it possible for Chaucer's fifteenth-century English successors to explore those questions further and makes Chaucer's works a potential model for how these successors might interact with their own, living female patrons. Increasingly, in the century after

Chaucer's death, English literary patrons actually *were* female. Female literary patronage was not newly invented in fifteenth-century England, of course; the work of June Hall McCash, Carol Meale, and many other scholars documents the numerous female patrons in earlier centuries who commissioned literary works or had works dedicated to them.[2] But a significant percentage of the major authors and known scribes of the English fifteenth century (at the very least, Osbern Bokenham, John Capgrave, Thomas Hoccleve, John Shirley, John Lydgate, and probably also Richard Roos) openly dedicated texts to historical women, copied or translated texts for women, or wrote with the interests of their female patrons in mind. These authors and scribes, coming after Chaucer and Boccaccio, had to work out how closely to follow the relationships their predecessors modeled between male poet and female patron.

The two mid-fifteenth-century British poets whose work I will examine here, John Metham and the anonymous Middle English translator of part of Boccaccio's *De mulieribus claris*, were part of this fifteenth-century wave of female patronage. Of particular interest in this essay is the way their consciousness of an actual female patron reverses the power dynamic between patron and author. Their acknowledged source authors, Chaucer and Boccaccio, set up exemplary women from the past in order to shape ideas about women in the medieval present, and they treat the female patron as a convenient fiction. Conversely, in the work of John Metham and the anonymous Middle English translator of Boccaccio, their consciousness of the presence of female patrons of literature changes the significance of the lives of women from classical antiquity. The female patrons of these texts, Katherine Stapleton and an unspecified "prynces," are patrons in the sense that their financial (and presumably literary) support is being solicited, not in the sense that they actively sought out the writers and told them to write these specific texts (as does Chaucer's God of Love). Thus, when I speak of female patronage I will be discussing mainly the impact of these women's presence as the intended audience. But unlike in Chaucer and Boccaccio's texts, theirs is not necessarily a passive or powerless presence. A patron who is the dedicatee rather than the commissioner of a text, whether male or female, still exerts a kind of gravitational pull on the project. In the case of these two literary projects, the presence of the female patrons as the intended audience makes both Metham and the translator of Boccaccio think carefully and sincerely (rather than ironically) about what to write, about what fourteenth-century canonical texts to draw on, and about how the female patrons they hope to please might react to the way those texts represent women. This results in a revision of Chaucer and Boccaccio. In these texts, the power to challenge the literary tradition shifts from vernacular author/translators such as Chaucer and Boccaccio to female patrons. In navigating the tension between respect for the source text and the demands of the female patron, these fifteenth-century authors choose the road Chaucer and Boccaccio did *not* travel: They treat the power of the female audience as a real force to be reckoned with. These texts demonstrate that in some cases, medieval female patrons of literature could indirectly revise the meaning of the lives of women from classical antiquity; and in so doing, their patronage opened up possibilities for revising and rethinking the fourteenth-century canon.

NOT DEAD YET: KATHERINE STAPLETON AND JOHN METHAM

The first example, John Metham's fifteenth-century Middle English romance *Amoryus and Cleopes*, explores ideas about female goodness as expressed in both Chaucer's *Troilus and Criseyde* and the *Legend of Good Women*.[3] A brief plot summary may be helpful, since the text is not widely known: Amoryus, a pagan knight, and Cleopes, a pagan maiden, meet and fall in love; though their first meeting is in public, at a temple service, we later learn that they are the children of neighbors. When Amoryus must fight a serpent, the highly educated Cleopes teaches him about serpents and prepares him to defeat his opponent. Later, the two of them decide to elope; they agree to meet outside the city walls, but Cleopes is frightened away from the meeting place by a lion, who bloodies the cloth she leaves behind and gives Amoryus the impression that she has died. He commits suicide; Cleopes returns to find him dying and kills herself. A local hermit, through his prayers, saves the souls of the lovers and resurrects them; they convert to Christianity, return to their city, overthrow the pagan gods, convert the town, and then marry and live happily as Christians until death.

Metham dedicated this romance to Katherine Stapleton, wife of Sir Miles Stapleton (and cousin to William de la Pole, the third husband of Geoffrey Chaucer's granddaughter Alice Chaucer). The very end of the poem mentions Miles and Katherine Stapleton; in particular, the poet hopes that Katherine will be remembered as a model woman by her descendants as yet unborn. Metham's description of Katherine slides uneasily between his authorial obligation to praise a living female patron and his authorial ambition to have his text serve as a memorial or monument to Katherine in the future. As a result, during the description Katherine (rather like Chaucer's Alceste) moves back and forth across the line between female audience and member of the canon of classical "good" women. The dedication begins by highlighting Katherine's traditional feminine virtues, such as nurturing and helping those in trouble:

> And fore that thei—the qwyche be nowe onborne—
> Qwan this lady ys pasyd, schal rede this story,
> That thei for her schal pray on evyn and morne,
> I alle the storyis that I endyght, I wryte this memory:
> That be here lyve thus sche was namyd communly
> Modyr of norture, in her behavyng usyng alle gentylnes,
> Ever redy to help them that were in troubyl and hevynes.
>
> (2157–63)

As he begins this stanza, Metham makes clear that all of his texts intend both to praise his female patron and also to memorialize her, using multiple verbs in the past tense, even though she has not yet died. The second stanza of the encomium continues and expands his focus on traditional feminine virtues, emphasizing Katherine's demureness and her almsgiving, with a nod to her beauty as well:

> So beuteus eke and so benyngn, that yche creature
> Here gretly magnyfyid, commendyng her womanhede
> In alle her behavyngs, ireprehensybyl and demure;
> And most to commende that of thoughte: sche toke gret heede
> To the necessyteys of the pore, relevynge them at every nede.
> Of her beute and vertuys, here I sese; for yt ys so,
> I hem declare in Crysaunt, and odyr places mo.
>
> (2164–2170)

Metham here aligns the purpose of this text with the purpose of other works ("Crysaunt, and odyr places mo"): praise of the living patron. Yet, as in the first stanza, the past-tense verbs in this passage, such as "magnyfyid" and "toke," continue to generate the idea of Katherine as having already died, preparing us for the final stanza of the encomium, which compares

Katherine directly to the long-dead women of classical antiquity, particularly those named in Chaucer's works:

> As yf I the trwthe schuld here wryght,
> As gret a style I schuld make in every degré
> As Chauncerys of qwene Eleyne or Cresseyd doth endyght,
> Or of Polyxchene, Grysyld, or Penelopé.
> As beuteus, as womanly, as pacyent as thei were wunt to be,
> Thys lady was, qwan I endytyd this story,
> Floryschyng the sevyn and twenty yere of the sext Kyng Henry.
>
> (2171–77)

Memorializing Katherine as if she were dead, Metham places her in the canon of famous women of antiquity. Yet, despite the "was" in the penultimate line, the specific date and the term "floryschyng" in the final line of the encomium reassure the audience that Katherine is still alive as Metham finishes his work. Like Chaucer's Alceste, Katherine both inhabits the world of the women who read about good women and is herself one of those legendary good women.

Metham's premature epitaph, its many literary allusions, and its assumptions about the audience's familiarity with the classicizing work of Chaucer and Lydgate, also raise questions about the projected relationship between Katherine, the female patron, and the women of antiquity to whom she is being compared. Metham indirectly compliments the literary sophistication of his patron. He assumes that Katherine and her descendants (not to mention the rest of Metham's audience) will be familiar with quite a lot of Chaucer: There are allusions here to *Troilus and Criseyde*, the *Legend of Good Women*, and the *Canterbury Tales*. He may also assume some familiarity with Lydgate's *Troy Book*, given the references to Trojan stories (Helen and Polyxena) not found in existing Chaucer texts. These assumptions, however, raise a number of questions about the relationship Metham envisioned between his patron and the female figures named in the text. What does Metham mean by placing Katherine Stapleton in the same canon of female excellence as Criseyde, Helen, Polyxena, Griselda, and Penelope? What hermeneutic gymnastics would result in lumping the unfaithful Criseyde, the faithful Penelope, and the face that launched a thousand ships together as examples of women who were "beauteous" and "pacyent"? We should also note that Cleopes' romantic fidelity, and the Christian conversion for which she is praised, bear little or no relation to the everyday "feminine" practices that Metham has just been praising in Katherine, such as nurturing and almsgiving. Nor do they have anything to do with the traditional feminine beauty and patience that Metham here highlights by alluding to Chaucer and Lydgate. Then, too, the encomium significantly fails to connect Katherine with the heroine of the romance Metham is dedicating to her. Why isn't Cleopes on this list of exemplary women? If she is less than exemplary, why did he choose to dedicate her particular story to Katherine Stapleton? Is there any implied comparison between Katherine and Cleopes, or not? In short, how can this romance, and its memorialization of a "classical" female protagonist, function as a celebration or memorialization of Metham's patron?

For answers to at least some of these questions, it is worth looking in detail at the way Metham uses Cleopes to rethink Chaucer's handling of female behavior in *Troilus and Criseyde* and the *Legend of Good Women*. As I shall show, by revisiting the actions of Criseyde and Thisbe (and passing over the ambiguity and irony in Chaucer's portrayal of Criseyde), Metham re-imagines Chaucer's canon so that his female patron has no reason to object to being classed with Chaucer's women, or to the way texts in general treat women. Although he envisions his literary work functioning more or less like an epitaph on a tombstone, and although he envisions future generations treating Katherine like a classical exemplar, her living presence obviously has a powerful impact on his work. In contrast to Chaucer, whose ironic, intertextual treatment in the *Legend of Good Women* casts doubt on whether the fictional female character can have any relation to the lives of real women, Metham's dedication validates his praise of a real woman's qualities by comparing her to re-imagined Chaucerian classical exemplars.

Metham's romance, especially the scene in which the protagonists fall in love, is quite clearly influenced by and responding to the early courtship scenes in *Troilus and Criseyde*, as Stephen Page has demonstrated.[4] However, Metham does not merely imitate Chaucer's structures and themes; he interrogates and alters them. In particular, he seems anxious to refute the essentialist ideas about male and female fickleness that rear their ugly heads twice in Book 5 of *Troilus and Criseyde*: first when Criseyde fears that "wommen moost wol haten [her] of alle" because they will feel that in leaving Troilus for Diomede she has done "deshonour" to all women

(5.1063, 1066); and later as the narrator struggles to control the female audience's reaction to the tale:

Bysechyng every lady bright of hewe,
And every gentil womman, what she be,
That al be that Criseyde was untrewe,
That for that gilt she be nat wroth with me.
Ye may hir gilt in other bokes se;
And gladlier I wol write, yif yow leste,
Penelopëes trouthe and good Alceste.

N'y say nat this al oonly for thise men,
But moost for wommen that bitraised be
Thorough false folk—God yeve hem sorwe, amen!—
That with hire grete wit and subtilte
Bitraise yow.

(5.1772–83)

In response to these concerns about fidelity, Metham reimagines—and significantly alters—the role of the love object as originally played by Chaucer's Criseyde.

The biggest change Metham makes is to give Cleopes subjectivity and agency from the start. Eliminating the role of Pandarus, Metham creates a heroine who falls in love with Amoryus almost as quickly as he falls for her.[5] When he walks past her as if on his way to worship at the altar, she notices him glance at her:

But qwy he so her beheld sche knwe noght veryly,
Save for because of hys godely chere,
Sche dempt that he her lovyd in frendly maner.

(769–71)

Cleopes's awareness and interpretation of Amoryus's interest is a far cry from the account of Criseyde's "somdel deignous" look in Book 2 of *Troilus and Criseyde*; it gives Cleopes a subjectivity that is denied to Criseyde until Book 2. Next, Cleopes realizes who Amoryus is, remembers his good reputation, and wonders whether he is attracted to her:

And wyth that, sche gan remembyr hys manhed and fame
That in ryfe was, and eke hys amyabyl stature.

"O" quod sche, "thys ys Amoryus for certen; this ys the same
That so manful ys in bateyl and so lovely to yche creature.
O Venus!" quod sche, "deme I noght aryte that this wurthy weryour
Schuld cast a love to me that fostryd hath be among most beuteuus
Of all Rome? for certyn yt ys noght thus,
But for sum odyr cause he dothe me behold?"

(772–79)

There are certainly overtones here of Criseyde's soliloquy in *Troilus and Criseyde* 2.689–812, which outlines her careful consideration of Troilus's attractions and his attraction to her. Like Criseyde, Cleopes acknowledges her status among the beauties of the city and is attracted by the knowledge of Amoryus's skill in battle. Like Criseyde, Cleopes puzzles over the sincerity of her love interest's attraction to her. Metham is using Cleopes to reenvision how Criseyde's courtship might have begun.

Metham also makes Cleopes's role more active by compressing the courtship. Chaucer creates suspense about the love object's feelings by making Criseyde's soliloquy conclude vaguely. Unlike Chaucer, Metham refuses to maintain any suspense about Cleopes's feelings. Amoryus's intentions become clearer to Cleopes as the passage continues:

And as sche this gan revolve in her mende to and fro,
He come forby at her; bak and forth hys cours gan hold,
And sche anone gan consydyr hys stature as he gan goo,
Comendyng hys semlyness; and sone the delectabyl woo
Of lovys fyre had perced here hert that her ful cure
Was hym to love before yche erthely creature.

(780–85)

In a mere sixteen lines (769–785), Metham's Cleopes moves from ignorance to awareness to interpretation to "the delectabyl woo / of lovys fyre." The audience familiar with *Troilus and Criseyde*, whose skepticism the narrator struggled to control in Book 2, might be expected to ask, "This was a sodeyn love; how might it be / That she so lightly loved [Amoryus] / Right for the first syghte, ye, parde?" But in contrast to Chaucer, Metham needs to address no such qualms about his audience condemning Cleopes for falling in love so fast, because he has not evoked the misogynist assumptions about female faithlessness that Chaucer plants in the audience's minds in Books 1 and 2 of *Troilus and Criseyde*. At no time in this section of the romance does Metham undermine the portrayal of Cleopes's affection by veiling it from us as Chaucer does in Book 2; nor does Metham, as Chaucer does, hint darkly in his opening stanzas that there might be "sorwe," irony, or indiscretion lurking in the lovers' future. On the whole, Cleopes's path to love differs significantly from that of Criseyde, who in the temple merely glances at Troilus a bit defiantly (as if to say, "What, may I nat stonden here?"), into whose psyche Chaucer does not allow us until Pandarus has begun to influence her thinking, and who must be subjected to an additional book and a half of manipulation and blackmail before she accepts Troilus as a lover. Metham has effectively rewritten Chaucer's plot so that the Criseyde-figure, Cleopes, takes an active role as lover, rather than the passive role Chaucer created, and so that she may be held blameless in returning the love of the Troilus figure.

While Metham is clearly responding to Chaucer's *Troilus and Criseyde*, he is also thinking through and about the *Legend of Good Women* in his romance, particularly the story of Thisbe. Metham is effectively combining Chaucer's two texts, reducing the plethora of classical women being celebrated to one figure who behaves consistently. Collapsing a group of disparate lives into the story of one heroine, Metham removes (and this indirectly highlights) the problems and ironies raised by Chaucer's treatment of female fidelity.

When Metham's Cleopes, like Thisbe, kills herself as a gesture of fidelity, she signals her membership in the canon of faithful women celebrated (however ironically or dismissively) by both Chaucer and Boccaccio. But Metham gives his audience no reason to reject her as a model. Throughout the romance, Metham emphasizes the lovers' fidelity to one another by making each of them repeatedly worry about being perceived as "unkynde"— the epithet Chaucer attaches to Criseyde in the proem to Book 4 of *Troilus and Criseyde*: "For how Criseyde Troilus forsook— / Or at the leeste, how that she was unkynde— / Moot hennesforth been matere of my book" (*TC* 4.15–17).[6] This emphasis is particularly visible in part 3 of *Amoryes and Cleopes*, which contains the elopement and suicide episode. Both Amoryus and Cleopes explicitly decide to kill themselves in order to avoid being "onkend." As Amoryus puts it,

> I must wyth sorowful hert ende
> Owre love begunne; for sche for me hath bought yt dere,
> And Y as dere yt schal yeld that I onkend
> Never schal be found in bodé ner mend.
>
> (1703–6)

Likewise, Cleopes wishes to avoid untrouth: ". . . yt must nedys be / That I schal dye, for I knowe never more to se / Hym lyvyng ayen, that for my sake ded ys, / I wer to onkend aftyr to lyve, iwys" (1747–50).[7] At the end of the story, her fidelity is reiterated on her tombstone: "And be hys syde, Cleopes, hys lady dere, / Byryid is—exsampyl to alle women, fer, and nere, / Of trwelove, stedfastenes, and curtesy" (2097–99). Metham's emphasis reimagines Chaucer's portrayal of female infidelity in *Troilus and Criseyde*—and, moreover, female fidelity in the *Legend of Good Women*.

As Page points out, by the time Metham was writing his romance in the late 1440s, Metham could have had access to several Middle English versions of the story of Piramus and Thisbe: Gower's *Confessio Amantis*, Chaucer's *Legend of Good Women*, and Stephen Scrope's translation of Christine de Pisan's *Epistre Othéa*. Metham's retelling of the story connects most closely to Chaucer's explanation of the double suicide and his emphasis on fidelity. Neither Scrope's nor Gower's Thisbe constructs her suicide as a gesture of fidelity. In contrast, in Chaucer's version of the story, fidelity plays a much stronger role. It surfaces twice, first in Thisbe's motivation for leaving her hiding place and returning to the meeting place—

> Now Tisbe, which that wiste nat of this,
> But sittynge in hire drede, she thoughte thus:
> "If it so falle that my Piramus
> Be comen hider, and may me not fynde,
> He may me holde fals and ek unkynde."
>
> (853–857)

and again when she delineates her own suicide as a token of all women's ability to be faithful:

> "But God forbede but a woman can
> Ben as trewe in lovynge as a man!
> And for my part, I shal anon it kythe."

And with that word his swerd she tok as swythe,
That warm was of hir loves blod, and hot,
And to the herte she herselven smot.
(910–915)

Metham responds specifically to each of these Chaucerian moments. In making *both* Amoryus and Cleopes speak about being "onkend" before suicide, he recalls Thisbe's fear that her absence will be misinterpreted, but he expands that concern about fidelity to include Amoryus. Moreover, he makes Amoryus interpret the bloody kerchief as a sign not merely of Cleopes's death but also of her loyalty:

O most trosty, most trw, most lovyng!
Cursyd be that owre that we gan trete of this metyng.
For this ys trwth, experyens schewyth yt opynly;
And be this blody kerchyf I yt deme
That for very trw love sche keme hydyr ryght erly
Me to abyde—alas, for sqweme!
(1665–1670)

Metham's repetition of "trwe" in these six lines emphasizes, indeed, perhaps overemphasizes, the fidelity of the Thisbe figure. As he used Cleopes in part 1 to recuperate Chaucer's Criseyde, in part 3 of the romance he uses her to evoke and expand on the fidelity of Chaucer's Thisbe (and, by extension, of all women, since the *Legend of Good Women* claims to support the claims of the female sex).

The question then arises: Why does Metham dedicate to Katherine Stapleton a romance in which he chooses to reimagine Chaucer's Criseyde and Thisbe so as to emphasize female fidelity? It would be tempting to speculate about the state of the marriage between Katherine and her husband Miles, but probably not very fruitful. However, two possible literary explanations occur. First, like his fellow fifteenth-century authors Lydgate and Henryson, Metham may have felt inclined to respond to Chaucer's ambiguous portraits of female virtue by providing clearer, unambiguous, unironic portraits.[8] Second, unlike Chaucer, Metham wrote for a real female patron, rather than for a fictive one drawn from classical mythology. Though, as we saw in the encomium, fidelity is not among the qualities for which he directly lauds Katherine Stapleton, it seems plausible that her presence in the intended audience inspired Metham to make the female figure in his romance less ambiguously positive than those she might have found when reading Chaucer's *Troilus and Criseyde* and *Legend of Good Women*.

It could also be said that Metham effectively turns his patron, Katherine Stapleton, into a second Alceste, by looking forward to the day when her descendants will read this text and its encomium as a memorial. Reimagining Chaucer's canon of good women, Metham inscribes his female patron within that canon, just as Alceste, the narrator's patron, is designated as the final heroine in the *Legend of Good Women*. Just as Chaucer's narrator in the *Legend of Good Women* must revise his source texts in order to accommodate the commands given by Alceste, so Metham must alter Chaucer's canon, and the meaning of the female figures in it, bridging the gap between *Troilus and Criseyde* and the *Legend of Good Women*, in order to place Katherine Stapleton inside it. The main difference is that Chaucer, not having an actual female patron, feels free to treat that process of alteration ironically in the *Legend of Good Women*. Ultimately, Chaucer remains more loyal to the male *auctores* than to any female patron or audience. Conversely, Metham's loyalty to or admiration for Chaucer's work (signaled in his references to Chaucer's heroines) is outweighed here by his desire to honor his patron by writing her into Chaucer's canon. As much as Metham might want to memorialize her and treat her as already dead, Katherine's living presence and her role as patron effectively alter his representation of Chaucer's classical female figures.

THE "PRYNCES" AND THE POET: BL MS ADDITIONAL 10304

Metham's audience-friendly solution to the tension between fidelity to source text and responsibility to female audience is also employed by the author of our second example, British Library MS Additional 10304, a mid-fifteenth-century Middle English translation of about twenty lives from Boccaccio's *Concerning Famous Women*.[9] Just as Metham felt free to challenge his source text by revising away the misogynist ambiguities Chaucer built into *Troilus and Criseyde* and the *Legend of Good Women*, so this translator deliberately alters Boccaccio's emphasis so as to present more clearly positive portraits of famous women. And like Metham, he does so precisely because he hopes for female patronage.

The translator's agenda is visible from the start. Like Boccaccio, he begins by noting that many lives of famous men have been composed by "writerss olde," and then immediately goes on to introduce Boccaccio's text and himself as translator:

An odyre [bok] he wrote vnto the laude and fame
Of ladyes noble, in prayse of all wymen;
But for the rareness few folke do it ken

The whiche boke I haue had in purpose,
If I in Englysshe cowde it clere expresse,
To haue translatyd. But euer I dydd suppose,
Without grrete ayde of sum noble pryncess
All in veyne shuld be my besyness;
For poetys ben of litell reputacion,
That of estatys haue no sustentacion.

(19–28)

Because of the translator's financial dependence on the aid of "sum noble pryncess," he knows that his poetic aspirations may leave him impoverished, so he is clearly constructing this canon of good women on spec, as it were. Likewise, in the final stanza in the manuscript, the translator pauses for his female audience's approval (and perhaps further funding):

If it fortune to be acceptable
And plese the herers, forth I wyll procede
To the residue of ladyes notable;
But fyrste of all, to se howe this shall spede,
I will take counsell, er it go on brede,
Leste that I eyre the bareyn se-banke
And gete me more of laboure than of thanke.

(1779–1785)

Following the examples of both his Italian Latin source, Boccaccio, and his famous Middle English predecessor, Chaucer, this translator chooses material that he thinks will be somehow appropriate: He chooses to honor a (potential) female patron by memorializing the women of antiquity. The translator's subordination of his artistic choices (and the value of his labor) to the approval of the female audience revises away Boccaccio's egotism in the dedication to *De mulieribus claris*, where Boccaccio chooses as dedicatee Andrea Acciauoli rather than Queen Johanna of Naples, because he fears that Johanna's light would outshine his own. Not only does the Middle English translator seek to please the women in his audience, but he also seeks their protection and support against possible criticism:

> Neuer the less with all my dilygence,
> Thof all I make full rude interpretacion,
> I shall intende brevely in sentence
> Of this boke to make a translacion,
> All ladyes beseechynge with humyliacion.
> To kepe this werke from sclaunder and envy;
> For som wyll allwey construe frowardly.
>
> (29–35)

The translator has not named an individual female patron, preferring instead only to speak of an anonymous "prynces" and to seek the protection of his female readers as a group. His desire to construct a position of patronage for every female member of his audience contains echoes of the position Chaucer's narrator sketches out for himself at the end of *Troilus and Criseyde*, where he fears the misinterpretation of his work and seeks the approval of the women in his audience, and in the prologue to the *Legend of Good Women*, where Alceste's intercession on behalf of the narrator provides protection from the hostile reaction of the audience (represented by the God of Love). But unlike Chaucer, the translator does not fictionalize his patron; and unlike Boccaccio, he does not treat her dismissively. Instead, like Metham, he acknowledges the potential power of a historical female patron.

Like Metham, too, this translator feels free to reimagine the lives of women in his source material (though in this case, because Boccaccio is directly credited with the work being translated, the potential effect is to recuperate Boccaccio, perhaps inadvertently, by making him seem far less misogynist). The Middle English translator frequently revises Boccaccio's stories so that the portraits of women are as exemplary and unobjectionable as possible. Many of these revisions consist of omitting Boccaccio's misogynist commentary. For instance, in the story of Ops, Boccaccio includes a long rant on the foolishness of the men who turned Ops into a goddess and worshiped a woman who had died, turned to dust, and been damned to hell—a rant that effectively lowers Ops in status. The Middle

English translator omits this passage. Similarly, he also omits Boccaccio's final sentence in his life of Pallas Minerva, which lessens the achievements of Minerva by agreeing with authors who think the deeds of many were attributed mistakenly all to this one woman.[10] In each case, the Middle English translator in Additional 10304 has eliminated material that Boccaccio used to encourage the reader to condemn or think less of the woman whose deeds he has just described.

The translator's pattern of improving Boccaccio's portraits of women is most clearly visible in the story of Semiramis. He includes only the positive parts of her tale: the story of how, newly widowed, she at first disguised herself as her young son to guide the country and then later ruled in her own right, conquering even more countries and cities than did her husband. He also describes her actions in terms that are more positive than Boccaccio's. Where Boccaccio's version describes her plan to disguise herself as "a colossal trick plotted with feminine cunning,"[11] the anonymous translator abstains from making essentialist remarks, instead emphasizing Semiramis' courage, her cleverness, and her wisdom:

> Afterward the kyng Ninus dydd dy,
> That many cuntreys by myght hadd subiugate,
> Lefte hir allon, a wydowe all desolate.
> LV
> The prynce not able the lond for-to governe,
> Semyramys, of hert and wytt right stronge,
> All the nacyons, with armys stowte and stronge,
> That hir husbond, owdyr be right or wronge,
> Hadd subduyd, yeres and dayes longe
> By sotell craft and wyse, as ye shall here,
> Rewled forthe, as thow his son she were.
>
> (376–85)

The syntax of lines 380–85, in particular, neatly establishes Semiramis's achievements as parallel to her husband's deeds. On first reading, it is not clear whether the phrase "yeres and dayes longe / By sotell craft and wyse" modifies the activities of her husband in subduing "all the nacyons" or the activities of Semiramis as she "rewled forthe." This linguistic ambiguity essentially takes her activity in maintaining his kingdom and elevates it to parity with his activity in creating and subduing it.

But the translator does not settle for merely subtle challenges to Boccaccio's treatment of Semiramis. He boldly celebrates Semiramis's role as individual ruler, particularly through the story of how, hearing the news of Babylon's rebellion, Semiramis went to battle with her hair half braided, and how, to commemorate her victory, a statue was commissioned showing her with her hair half done. After describing the statue, both Boccaccio and the translator lament the loss of further records about Semiramis's deeds:

LXVII

Odyr cytees newe she mad also
And didd grete actys of magnanymyte.
But John Bochas remembereth no mo;
For he seithe: "Oblyvyous antiquyte
Hir odyr dedys saue thies, that wryten be,
Hath worn awey without memoryall,
As many mo daily it doth and shall."

(463–69)

In Boccaccio, a long passage follows describing how Semiramis undid all of her good actions by committing incest with her own son—an act that the Middle English translator completely omits from his profile of Semiramis. Through this omission, the Middle English translator has implicitly recategorized Semiramis's incest as one of the deeds that are "wornawey" by "oblyvyons antiquite." This transforms Boccaccio's lament about the inaccuracy of historical records into a strong assertion that whatever is written is what exists. The Middle English translator, in Chaucerian fashion, thus highlights both the power of the author and the power of the translator. However, he also transforms the memorialization of Semiramis, and in doing so he acknowledges the power of the female patron much more strongly than do either Chaucer or Boccaccio. Instead of ending his account with racy gossip about Semiramis's unbridled sexuality, as Boccaccio does, the Middle English translator ends with the image of the brass statue of Semiramis with one side of her hair braided, rushing off to defend her kingdom in battle successfully—a figure who crosses the gender divide. For the unnamed "prynces" in the intended audience, she serves as a positive role model, indeed.

More important, however, is that the translator's alterations also implicitly acknowledge the power of the female patron, both the "prynces" and the female audience whose approval and support he seeks. Like Metham, this translator rejects his source text's misogyny or irony; he wants there to be a straightforward relationship between the female reader and the memorialized female figure from antiquity. In doing so, he credits his female patron and audience with a high level of perception. The fifteenth-century audience's lack of appreciation for irony was once lamented by Paul Strohm, who noted that fifteenth-century Chaucer scribes had a tendency to recopy only the least ironic, most exemplary *Canterbury Tales*.[12] From the changes made by Metham and the translator of Additional 10304, it would be tempting to concur with Strohm that fifteenth-century readers simply do not appreciate complex irony in the forms in which Boccaccio and Chaucer bequeathed it to them. But I suggest that it is more likely that Metham and the anonymous translator of 10304 were a bit uneasy about the ironic way in which Boccaccio and Chaucer commented on female behavior. Why would they revise away this irony, unless they perceived it, understood its ramifications, and moreover expected their very real female readers and patrons to grasp and be displeased by it?

THE SHADOW OF THE PAST

Both of these fifteenth-century poets honor historical women by creating permanent, "physical" monuments to women of antiquity. The translator of Boccaccio in Additional 10304 ends the story of Semiramis with a description of Semiramis's bronze statue, freezing her in transition from female to male pursuit, commemorating her ability to bridge the gender gap, perhaps as an example or a salute to the "prynces" whose patronage he seeks. Likewise, Metham closes his romance with a monument, a description of the tomb and epitaph of Amoryus and Cleopes:

"Flowre of knyghthod, to the world a memorial
Of trosty love, Syr Amoryus resstyth here,
Defensor of the cuntré, keper of pes contynwalle;
And be hys syde, Cleopes, hys lady dere,
Byryid ys—exsampyl to alle women, fer and nere,
Of trwelove, stedfastenes, and curtesy;
Upon hos soulys almyghty God have mercy."
(2094–2100)

This tombstone treats each protagonist as an individual monument and exemplar. Amoryus is a "memorial / Of trosty love," a (now dead) testament to the fact that male fidelity in love can coexist with knightly virtue; Cleopes serves as a model of feminine "trwelove, stedfastenes, and curtesy" for medieval female readers. *Amoryus and Cleopes*, likewise, presents Katherine's (premature) epitaph. Moreover, Metham wants *all* of his texts to serve as monuments to Katherine Stapleton, inspiring her descendents to remember her as a paragon of medieval female virtues. Such monuments, whether in bronze, in marble, or in parchment, immobilize the past in the process of making it exemplary.

And yet the female patrons of these poets, because still living, had the power to change the way women of the past were re-presented in texts. As Metham and the Middle English translator of Boccaccio commemorate their female patrons by celebrating and memorializing the women of antiquity, their respect for living women revises the meaning of the lives of women from classical antiquity. This respect had the potential to loosen the stranglehold of the essentialist misogyny propounded by Chaucer, Boccaccio, and the long line of classical *auctores* and medieval authors before (and after) them. Instead of serving solely to inherit negative female traits such as fickleness and weakness, as in Boccaccio, instead of being treated ironically as hapless victim of the male-authored literary tradition, as in Chaucer, the later medieval female patron has some power to prompt a revision of the literary tradition, creating, if only for one brief moment, a new canon of what Virginia Woolf once called "mothers to think back through."[13] Alceste, I think, would have been pleased.

This freedom to reimagine the literary tradition has implications not merely for fifteenth-century female patrons but also for the way we think about the relationship between Chaucer and his fifteenth-century successors. Not all fifteenth-century poets, it would seem, enjoyed the privileged social and intellectual position that made Lydgate's imitations of Chaucerian irony and misogyny acceptable despite his documented interaction with female patrons. And though most of them acknowledged the long shadow of Chaucer's influence, not all of them defined themselves as unworthy sons of father Chaucer. Neither Chaucer's vision of the past, nor Boccaccio's, is set in stone, as it turns out. The bronze can be recast. A new tomb may be designed. Can it be entirely coincidental that we see this sense of artistic liberty at work in texts meant to honor historical female patrons?

DOWEL, THE PROVERBIAL, AND THE VERNACULAR: SOME VERSIONS OF PASTORALIA

Anne Middleton

The small bright feature that prompts this essay is the English dictum "do well and have well," with which the Priest "construes" the text of the Pardon in English.[1] While this moment has proved pivotal both to the ensuing formal unfolding of the poem and to the course of its critical history, I do not attempt here to traverse again either of the two large, ancient, and well-plowed topical fields (the "dowel triad" and the "pardon scene") it has opened to critical industry, but rather begin with a more limited object: the early history, formal and registral consequences, and literary implications of the English locution itself. The exercise provides a small-aperture view through which some larger questions of rhetorical propriety latent in the scene, and in the poem generally, may be reexamined, particularly by those for whom the poem offers a supremely complex instance of "vernacular theology."[2]

Universally categorized as "proverbial" by earlier medieval users of this adage, the Priest's somewhat perfunctory "translation" of Truth's message becomes the catalyst for the narrative, dialogic, and figurative development of the poem's difficult third vision, which in turn establishes the modes of representation that govern the remainder of the poem. As the pursuit of Dowel turns gradually from an attempt to determine the minimally necessary and sufficient "legal" requisites for salvation—the poetic persona's implicit notion of his aim at the outset of his quest—to imaginative self-knowledge and penitent self-scrutiny as the key requisites for the pursuit of perfection, the dialogic process of the vision also examines the register and rhetorical techniques that support this spiritual reorientation. The third vision explores the pastoral figurative arts appropriate to those who, like Piers, are "lerned a litel," and their relation to the arts of "poetes." Medieval attestations of the formulation "do well and have well" contemporary with the poem imply that the "proverbial" was a ubiquitous register

of vernacular didactic idiom recognizable as such; earlier occurrences—
including a hitherto unnoticed example offering a trenchant commentary
on the scope and limits of this rhetorical gambit—indicate how and why
this notionally "popular" sententious idiom becomes in Langland's hands
an opportunity for advertent reflection on the character of pastoral didac-
ticism, to which his own poetic project is an uneasily aspiring cousin.[3]

A caveat of my own is in order here. This essay is severely constrained
in demonstrative and referential scope by the modest length limits proper
to its genre. As a tribute to its honoree, whose work on the rhetorical as
well as ideational genealogy of the poet's art remains seminal for subse-
quent scholarship on the poem, the contribution to knowledge this essay
intends must remain here largely proleptic of work still to appear. Some of
it will be accomplished by those with stronger specialist expertise than
mine in some of the discursive constituents of this supremely difficult
poem, while a few claims proposed summarily here will receive more de-
tailed substantiation in my forthcoming volume 3 of the Penn Commen-
tary on the poem. Yet the broader general bearing of the patterns I identify
in what many readers consider the most difficult segment of the poem
warrants synthetic consideration in an essay—in the original sense of that
term, as a trial effort to assess what their concerted testimony reveals about
the poem generally. By historically convening, and rewarding, the cumula-
tive attention of many minds, Langland's poem is a very medieval intellec-
tual object; this small genealogical exercise is meant to encourage vigorous
continuation of its living tradition.

––––––––

Dowel leads most of its formally dispositive half-life in the poem within
the confines of Vision 3. Following its waking preface, in which the
dreamer challenges two friars who offer him guidance to Dowel, the term
is immediately amplified into three degrees in the opening encounter of
the ensuing dream, by Thouht, "a muche man . . . lik to myselue" (B.8.70).
This gradational *divisio* of the term is most prominent as an expository
device, and as a term in the *ordinatio* of the poem, in the A version, reced-
ing gradually from marked expository interest in successive dreams of the
long versions.[4] In the early years of its reception, the "degrees" of Dowel
was a sufficiently distinctive device that brief allusion to it served as short-
hand to indicate readers' designs to align Piers with their cause. Despite
at least two generations of effort, however, the term itself has resisted

attempts to assign it a durable meaning across the course of the poem and has offered little broader purchase on its poetic form. It is the Priest's English paraphrase of the Pardon that introduces the term *Dowel* into the poem, as it is his formulation, identical in all versions, that elicits Piers's catalytic "tene." For medieval readers it was not the term itself, whether single or in its "degrees," but the whole gnomic dictum—"do well and have well"—that made the Priest's dictum recognizable and eminently repeatable.[5]

SOURCES, ANALOGUES, AND MODELS
FOR LANGLAND'S "DOWEL" DICTUM

The proverbial character of this sententious formulation is what nearly all other earlier and contemporary medieval users explicitly note about it, and in doing so they offer accurate testimony of native speakers about how sayings of this general form are still framed grammatically and construed. Consisting of paired verb phrases joined by a loose (more often absent) copula, such sayings are normally understood by English speakers as expressing a relationship of cause to consequence, in which the first member functions as an "if" clause, the second a "then" clause: "Marry in haste, repent at leisure" frames the single assertion that *if* you marry in haste, *then* you will certainly have plenty of time thereafter to regret having done so. That English speakers have recently become less alert to this syntactic convention of "proverbial" idiom is suggested by the common misunderstanding of the familiar medical aphorism "Feed a cold, starve a fever" as a mnemonic specifying remedies for two different ailments rather than as traditional Hippocratic wisdom concerning the "if . . . then" causal relation between two symptoms of the common cold.[6] Similarly "do well and have well" is understood by all who repeat it in the medieval centuries to express a secure and unspeculative causal relation between good deeds and reward. Dismantling the claim that this relation is in every case one of direct cause to certain effect will prove to be the task of the third visionary episode—an expository task both precarious and urgent, since its English version enters the poem with the imprimatur of ecclesiastical authority, as equivalent to the key claim of the creed: if you do well (i.e., perform "good deeds"), you will invariably "have well"—that is, attain reward in heaven for deeds considered meritorious on earth.

The collocation "do well and have well" provokes not only Piers and the "pensif" dreamer but also early readers, from the moment of the poem's initial circulation. Two contemporary invocations of it that register awareness of Langland's use of the dictum are among our earliest testimonies for the reception of the poem; significantly, both are in texts that purport to record spoken discourse. In a sermon preached to the clergy in convocation before the Good Parliament (May 18, 1376), Thomas Brinton, bishop of Rochester, retells the fable of the rodents who bell the cat and ends with with the same anodyne formulation, calling it a proverbial usage: "proverbialiter solet dici, Benefac et bene habe."[7] Brinton's audience on that occasion consisted of ecclesiastical lords who are also Latin adepts, requiring neither beast fables nor familiar "sayings" to engage their attention (though as gestures, both *captationes benevolentiae* may have evoked appreciation as rhetorical felicities; in Langland's poem both, despite their putatively "folkish" provenance, invoke the schoolish common referential repertory that convenes their audience as *literati*). Both inclusions mark Brinton's idiom as summoning the heterogeneous speech scene of the community of the realm, of which the parliamentary occasion is metonymic: as a speech community it is not so much monolingually vernacular as knowingly multilingual in competence and registral awareness. The same dictum, though partially rather than fully explicit in its wording, also underlies the exhortation to "do wel" in two of the 1381 rebel "letters": that of "jakke carter" in Knighton's *Chronicle*, and the message ascribed to John Ball in the chronicle of Thomas Walsingham.[8] In both letters, the appearance of "do wel and betre" in close proximity to the name of Piers the Plowman marks the phrase as appropriation of the poem; its use as an injunction to continue what has been begun establishes that the allusion intends the same "if–then" causal relation of effort to result as the "do well" dictum, and articulates it as a received truth.

In these two late-fourteenth-century examples, "do well and have well" is marked as "proverbial" by its syntactic form: it has the idiomatic shape of a "wise saying" in English. Green has shown that the "rebel letters" as reported by Knighton and Walsingham are pervaded by similar formulaic pairings, typical of oral commonplace, and favored by medieval preachers for framing memorable saws: He notes in them several analogues to the "Sayings of the Four Philosophers," variously attested in the *Speculum Christiani* and in the Auchinleck MS, and cites additional examples gathered by

Siegfried Wenzel. Though "do well and have well" is not among the rebel "sayings" found in these assemblages of pastoral pungency (as Green notes, "confirmation, if any were needed, that this is a conscious Langlandian allusion")—nor does the saying, as we shall see, originate with Langland— its language of utterance is universally understood to be English, whatever the language of record in which it is attested: couched in the idiomatic form thought best for ready recall by the notionally "lewed," it claims the common ground of incontestable and generally accepted knowledge. These were the rhetorical characteristics of both proverbs and parables, as expounded by early scriptural commentators; its use by the Priest here in an assertion of pastoral authority has a manifest illocutionary force: it signals an attempt to contain challenge rather than invite reflection, to claim discursive control of a linguistically heterogeneous occasion, to convene auditors rather than literate interpreters, and (like the invocation of Piers in the "rebel letters") to keep the plowman rusticated amid bodily (and "merely" vernacular) rather than "clergial" enterprises.[9] The speech-scene in which the Priest intervenes is thus the most prominent of several depictions in the poem of uneasy relations between the pastoral arts of guidance and governance and the capacities and purposes of their wide range of intended beneficiaries—not always, as earlier interpreters tended to assume, to the discredit of the notionally "lewed" party to the exchange, as Piers's resolution in response to the Priest's intervention demonstrates. Such dramatized or narrated encounters are legion in the poem, and their tone varies widely, from the satiric to the plangent, from the imperfect understanding of the "Omnia probate" that Conscience imputes to Mede, to Patience's response to Hawkyn's lament at his inability to keep his garment clean while engaged in his worldly occupation of producing bread for the commune. Yet as language historians have by now discredited the top-down or trifunctional models of insular language use and register once common in early literary histories, so such pervasive dialogic misfires and cross-purposes in the poem testify to the character of the challenges to which the pastoral arts must be answerable.

Ralph Hanna has noted that "the only earlier [i.e., anterior to Bishop Brinton's well-known] use of the English proverb I know appears in BL MS Egerton 613, fol. 5 (s. xiii med.) in a mainly Anglo-Norman (but in fact trilingual) tract for nuns, where it is cited in a similar context of eternal reward for (and divine sustenance in) avoiding sin." The manuscript is a collection of mostly short texts in prose and verse; the item in which the dictum occurs is a work in rhythmic prose, of SW Midlands dialect provenance.[10] The strongest filiations of its contents are with *Ancrene Wisse* and other texts for eremitic or cloistered contemplatives long associated with it; the text in which the "dowel" adage occurs is pervaded by the richly metaphoric discourse of its Anselmian and Bernardine antecedents and proceeds partly in the rhythmic prose that within the thirteenth century would become, as in late Old English, a recognizable register for works of spiritual guidance.[11] Hill remarks (496 and n. 63) the "native origins" of this "proverb," evidenced by its formal similarity to Old English *sententiae* and the awkwardly unidiomatic and unmemorable character of its French and Latin equivalents. In this context, she suggests, the "dowel" dictum functions along with other English inclusions as "part of [its] semantic and stylistic structure," and undergoes a figurative translation in its immediate generic environment. As in the underlying Latin meditative tradition, the "well-doing" urged upon the user of the text entails not simply the avoidance of sin, or works of active charity in the world, but the patience and inner fortitude requisite for spiritual understanding, and for the pursuit of "perfection" as the *melior pars* for those who elect to turn their attention to goods not of this world.

The registral interplay sustained within this trilingual text offers in miniature the formal and idiomatic ingredients of the encounter that ends the second vision of *Piers*. While to the Priest, Truth's message as paraphrased in English offers nothing of substance to guide the folk, the humiliated but inspired Piers construes it much as the users of the Egerton text are invited to do, as a spur to turn from busy "swynke" to patient labors of the soul. (This spiritual remedy is again commended in the "patient poverty sermon" that under Scripture's guidance assimilates Trajan's deed to Christian spiritual example after that speaker's irruption into the third vision, and yet again in the "slogans" Patience offers Hawkyn Activa Vita in the fourth.) After tearing the text asunder in AB, Piers frames this resolution by the "ensaumple" of the "foweles in the firmament" who possess by divine provision what suffices for their "fyndyng"—a foretaste of the similarly humbled recognition the dreamer undergoes in the latter half of the inner dream of Vision 3, prompted by the same similitude "seen" in the mirror of nature: the harmonious spectacle of birds building nests and rearing their kind. With the AB example of the untutored birds, Piers antici-

pates a key topic of the poem's third dream, proposed first by Wit and ampli-
fied in its final dialogue by Ymaginatif: the creator's distinctive provisions
for humankind as his sole animal creation made in his image. As glossed
by Ymaginatif, the panorama of avian proprieties presented by the second
of the two "mirror" displays of Vision 3 illustrates the spiritual utility of the
soul's image-making power, and the capacity of the "clergial" arts, properly
understood and practiced, to sustain it. In sum, the English dictum in the
Egerton 613 treatise is marked as proverbial to situate it within the kind of
discursive contest to which the denouement of Langland's second vision
subjects it: as a watchword for the devout who have taken the same resolution
as Piers. Insofar as the Egerton text is a pastoral treatise for a community of
religious, the aphorism has an evocative power that it lacks in both of the
fourteenth-century occurrences prompted by Langland's poem; insofar as
it is also advertently rooted in meditative exposition for such a community,
the dictum is offered for the same "translation" it undergoes in the course
of Langland's third visionary episode.

THE PASTORAL ARTS OF WILLIAM DE MONTIBUS

Some decades earlier than this multilingual setting of "do well and have
well," the dictum appears in the *Similitudinarium* of William de Montibus
(d. 1213), as a defining example of a pastoral adage that is memorable but
inadequate to its purpose. Scholars of the poem have not heretofore noted
this occurrence, but more trenchantly than any of the foregoing examples
it offers thoughtful testimony to the constituents of pastoral craft, and the
ethos of pastoral art, that undergirds Langland's poetics.

Disposed under headings that indicate their roles in pastoral practice
(*Proverbia, Similitudinarium, Distinctiones Theologice, Numerale*), and
including (*Tropi*) an account of the grammatical, logical, and rhetorical
principles indispensable to the correct understanding of the scriptures, the
several parts of William's massive oeuvre were meant to transform the
intellectual riches of the schools into compositional resources for every
kind of spiritual guidance; together they constitute an orderly suite of the
skills and arts he considered fundamental to pastoral care. As William
understood it, this enterprise entails the use of figurative discourse as what
Mary Carruthers terms a "craft of thought" for the reflective reader or
hearer, not simply as a rhetorical arsenal for the preacher's persuasive

"saying": enlisting both "kynde" and "clergie" in a single spiritual endeavor, it informs the orientation and usages commended by Ymaginatif in the last dialogue of Langland's third vision.[12] Predating the Fourth Lateran Council and the arrival in England of the mendicant orders, William's works remained a seminal resource for later *summae confessorum*, informing pastoral instruction of the laity well into Langland's lifetime and beyond. William assembled them, however, chiefly to inform the spiritual guidance of various categories of religious, among them such communities as the one for which MS Egerton 613 was made, and for which he himself composed pastoral letters: literate religious women.[13]

William's citation of the "do well and have well" dictum illustrates the principled and efficient use of figurative tropes that makes his works much more than a suite of florilegia. Under the headword "preaching," the adage does illustrative double duty, making a deft formal point about the use of similitude while also providing admonition on the limits of "sound-bite" dicta in pastoral teaching. William sets forth the purpose of the *Similitudinarium* in its prologue: "For explaining an argument in any kind of discourse we have collected similitudes whencesoever God gives them, knowing that examples and similitudes lend credence to arguments raised and elucidate authorities and reasons." Describing this "compendium of images, metaphors, similes, and examples" as "the largest systematic collection of these that has been identified," Goering adds that "in his *Proverbia* William created an alphabetical repository of authorities; in his *Distinctiones* he did the same for 'reasons' or arguments" (304). In William's usage, similitudes "can be distinguished from *exempla* in that the latter are drawn from human history and the former from the world of nature" (305); he illustrates the distinction with the virgin birth, of which no other historical example can be found, though it has a likeness in nature (*sicut flos uitis odorem*). After illustrating the general program of the *Similitudinarium* by presenting in full its first ten items, Goering lists the topical headings of its remaining entries, which, as he notes, vary in amplitude: "Many are quite brief, and read like *bon mots* from the schools. Other entries are more discursive"—a point he illustrates (305–6) with the citation that I take to be Langland's ultimate "pre-text" for "do wel and haue wel":

> Preaching: . . . Some say that the sum of all preaching is this: "Do good and it will be well with you." But this is as if one said to a traveller seek-

ing directions: "Always follow the right road and you will reach your destination." Does this suffice? Again, some say: "I know the sum of all preaching: avoid evil and do good." This is as if he said: "I have learned the whole of physic and all of medicine: avoid illness and preserve your health." Is it enough to say this?[14]

Here, I think, we have the "original" (and skeptical) prompt for the pivotal dictum of the Pardon episode—along with a succinct formulation of the ethos of pastoral "craft" that underwrites both William's broader enterprise and Langland's distinctive inflections of it. In this similitude William gives a miniature rationale for all the others: without compelling figuration and analogy well expounded by the instructor, the gnomically memorable is insufficient to instill knowledge of, or sustain desire for, the good, and may lead to error.[15]

The poet's deep and wide local debts to the *summae confessorum*, and the likelihood of multiple mediated access to William's works by the poet and his "fit audience," need little additional documentation at this point in *Piers Plowman* studies. William's use of the "dowel" dictum is more productively regarded, however, not as a newfound "source" for another of the poet's "citations" but rather as illuminating commentary *avant la lettre* on the poet's pivotal deployment of it. The similitude in which he frames it presents a purposefully surprising analogy, of a kind repeatedly staged in Langland's poem. By setting it in the poem as the catalytic dictum that brings the second vision to a close, and then developing William's critique into an extended rationale for the several modes of figurative invention deployed in the third, Langland develops both its ethical and formal implications. Between the austerely universal propositional form of the doctrinal postulates in which Truth's "content" is most uncompromisingly expressed (the logical operators "every," "all," "nemo" are characteristic markers of such "philosophical" statements, and the dreamer's conspicuous use of these in dialogue from the beginning of his quest for Dowel demonstrates his facility with this authoritative register of the literate magisterium), and the vernacular canniness of the "dowel" dictum, with its absent causal copula, lies the terrain explored in the "inward journey" of Vision 3.

The poet's setting of the adage develops both the ethical and formal implications of William's critique. William uses it to articulate an applied ethos for pastoral rhetoric: however its beneficiaries may be defined by design or occasion, neither the "lewed" laity nor the variously "lettred" in pursuit of gospel-enjoined perfection can be adequately nourished by such bare slogans as the "dowel" dictum alone, without the support of the full complement of pastoral "arts" that give them their bearing, experiential amplification, and spiritual utility—the combination of attributes that produces what Mary Carruthers calls the *ductus* of meditative guidance and "invention" (*The Craft of Thought*, 11–82, 116–17). Without such "support" (her term for what the meditative as well as pastoral arts ideally provide to spiritual pursuit), pithy sayings are merely a kind of cognitive noise, convening their audience under the aspect of a common worldliness and offering a specious simulacrum of sagacious "content" without transferrable substance or trajectory. Shapin's observations on the "competent" uses of proverbs as situation-bound, dependent on assessment of their appropriate conditions for use, are also germane, both to William's sense of the proper uses of this rhetorical gambit and to Langland's several scenes staging encounters between two seemingly incongruent but submerged discursive premises—often as contrary pressures applied in dialogue to a familiar adage.

William's sense of the right use of such dicta emphasizes the aspects of pastoral care that this "art" shares with other "professional" expert practices, all of which depend for their success on situational specificity and experience over time, whether those of physicians, guides to penitents or pilgrims, or the custodians of Truth's treasury. As legal and medical professionals well understood (and as "feed a cold, starve a fever" illustrates), the maxims and aphorisms in which their "arts" were digested and transmitted are neither universal philosophical propositions nor succinct "folk" wisdom but extremely condensed forms of craft-knowledge, sometimes opaque and tautological to those most in need of it.[16]

The second felicity in William's deployment of the adage is thus a formal one, manifested in his use of it to illustrate the apt argumentative use of analogy and similitude. His double vehicle for his point adduces two similar applied "arts," those of the physician and those of the travel guide: as expert practices these cannot proceed through prescription or universal *doxa* alone but can be exercised to good effect only in temporal extension, and in consideration of the experiential particularities of the case, by those well-practiced in the art.[17] "Arts" or "crafts" denote in Langland's usage such expert practices as these, not systematic "sciences" or bodies of settled knowledge: a lament for the modern decline of the crafts of both "lered" and "lewed," from weather lore through agronomy to "gramer þe ground of al," forms part of Anima / Liberum-Arbitrium's comprehensive account of charity in action (C.17.69–111; cf. B.15.354–86, and further below). Though scornful of spotty or misapplied learning, Langland, like William, values efficacy in these "arts" over learned virtuosity in mastering them for their own sake. The site and medium for the success of the pastoral arts is not the schoolroom but the shared temporal and phenomenal world; they define a "common place" in which the truths of the faith may be offered to imaginatively compelling embodiment in particular circumstances and thereby further reinforce the bonds of shared experiential knowledge that sustains the mutual charity mandated by gospel injunction and example.

This is the aspect of pastoral as distinct from specifically doctrinal discourse elided by the Priest's response to the "teachable moment" presented by Truth's missive and Piers's mediation. For the Priest, the pastoral mandate to "kenne it þee on Englissh" is primarily an institutional imperative, demanding above all a regulatory rather than instructive response. In its combination of doctrinal orthodoxy and pastoral insufficiency, this reassertion of the categorical prerogative of the ordained resembles that of Arundel's Constitutions: his "construing" offers a renewed enunciation of credal rectitude whose only concession to the condition of its users is its memorably compact form. Yet the competent pastoral practitioner must offer more than the stark binary determination of the condition of a conscience as "diseased" or "healthy," pardoned or unpardoned, or of the soul's journey on "right" or "wrong" paths. Overlooked in his reactive response to the challenge of the moment is the more ample opportunity it affords to Piers (and ultimately, after several forays in this and other didactic registers in the course of Vision 3, to the poetic persona): to exemplify in action, and in the figurative design and rhetoric of the poem from this point onward, the "orthopraxis" capable of sustaining the folk in their extended course of communal and individual healing. This is the task into which the projected pilgrimage is "translated" at the end of Vision 2, with Piers and the dreamer as its mutually reflecting embodiments; in neither of these avatars is the prerogative of the priest, or the "truth" of his credal dictum, the main point at issue.

Flawed preparation of the pastoral clergy for the demands of their practice, and the defective performance that follows from it, may be the most persistent topical preoccupation (some would say distraction) of the third vision—especially in its B version, where the almost obsessive resurfacing of this topic amid a broader expository trajectory is often called "digressive" by commentators—but there is strong evidence that the revising poet took pains to assimilate his concern with pastoral efficacy into the larger argumentative program of Vision 3. The preponderance of C's alterations in this portion of the poem address not the theology of the dreamer's suppositions in dialogue but the placement, figurative vehicles, and rhetorical posture most useful for addressing the effects of the *ignorancia sacerdotium*, as well as defects of individual will, that bear on the primary objective and focus of the "inward journey" traced in this vision: the imaginative habituation of the Christian subject to those uses of figuration that support his return to the creator, and therefore those capabilities in the pastoral clergy that ought properly to inform their intervention in a "spiritual public health crisis."[18] As Ymaginatif explains the uses of imaginative figuration as grounded in "clergie" in the final dialogue of Vision 3, these are not confined to the prefigurative method of reading scripture that Auerbach defined as *figura* but includes all forms of metaphoric embodiment, on whatever scale, from formal similitude through implicit analogy through "parabolic" instantiation and expository *picturae*. As a "likening logic" (C.14.190; B.12.269) Ymaginatif's art offers a rhetoric of probability rather than proof—and is fundamental to the arts of "pastours and poetes" alike.

As a life in charity and love of God is the gospel imperative enjoined by Jesus on "all of either sex" (as the Fourth Lateran Council designated the imagined human universe to which his redemptive mission was addressed), and cultivating it among God's folk the ultimate objective of the many late-medieval manuals designed for "handling sin," so every Christian is called to reimagine the world and its uses to this end, as a "kynde" form of devout "sowle-hele," as well as a form of Christian mutual aid that differs in rhetorical character and ecclesiastical authority from the inculcation of correct doctrine. While the latter office is reserved to ordained ministers of God ("and noon othyr"), mutual guidance and edification is "a gostly almesdede, to whych euery man es bounde that hath cunnynge" and involves broad and heterogeneous deployment of several kinds of edifying "craft."[19] From Galatians 6:2, "Bear one another's burdens [and thus you fulfill the law of Christ]," the poet extrapolates the gospel imperative to share with others not only "oure catel" but "oure konnyng," in a B-version passage (B.11.212–32) introducing the second of the three points of the "poverty sermon" that amplifies the "lesson" of Trajan in what initially seems a counterintuitive direction.[20] The C version cancels this passage, relocating its citation of Galatians 6:2 into the long similitude that develops the latter half of the C version's newly introduced "patient poverty" excursus (C.12.172–C.13.99) as a schematic contrast between two hypothetical embodiments of what a later age would call "wayfaring Christians," a Merchant and a Messenger, and the spiritual impediments they encounter in travel to the same destination. This important C addition, dividing B.11 into two passus, is significantly inserted between B's two immediately adjacent citations (as B.11.286a and 287) of the Introit psalm for the entrance of the priest at Mass (Ps. 42:1, *Judica me deus*, and 42:6, *Spera in deo*, the first and last verses of the portion of the psalm to be recited at this moment: *Brev.* 2:481).[21] One effect of C's transplantation of Galatians 6:2 is to dissociate more decisively than does B the gospel injunction to perfection (Matt.19:21)—including its admonition to "poverty" as the renunciation of worldly attachments—from the apostolic mandates specific to the pastoral clergy.[22]

The varied uses the poet "makes" of his vast and varied treasury of pastoral figuration "to kepe with a comune" appear on several scales of magnitude—from brief schematic *divisiones* of a term or topic, through the surprising replacement of one (largely implicit) figurative vehicle by another that offers a more compelling way to engage a familiar credal truth, to large-scale hypotheses that embody pastoral dicta governing a large expository trajectory—yet are never stated overtly. Because the poet's extended narrative framework gives much wider scope to the latter than do the usual pastoral expository genres and occasions for expounding those shorter "citations" whose imprint in the poem is well-documented, I conclude a selective overview of Langland's figurative armature by identifying one large-scale figure that indicates the *ductus* of the entirety of Vision 3, yet is so skillfully woven into the narrative and dialogic structure that it has remained largely invisible: It is what for the "fit audience" of the poem goes without saying.

THE ARTS AND CRAFTS OF "PASTORS AND POETES"

Vision 3 unfolds as an *ars legendi* for the desirous soul, and it is hardly incidental to the direction of this extended dialogic sequence that an encounter with a pair of friars serves as its waking catalyst (C.10.7–60; B.8.6–61; A.9.6–52), providing a vestibule or entry porch to the array of figurative modes that support the narrative course of Vision 3. In their initial appearance in this sequence, the friars are not portrayed as venal purveyors of "cheap grace" (as the dreamer later complains: C.12.4–10a; B.11.53–8), still less as legitimate objects of his proudly schoolish distaste for their guidance (C.10.20–29; B.8.20–25; A.9.16–21), but as contemporary master-professionals of the arts of argumentative as well as affective figuration, especially to the lay devout, as forms of "construing" necessarily grounded in common experience and "common knowledge." Similarly, the intensive use of proverbs, sententiae, maxims, and other notionally "popular" forms of compact figurative language in the midsection of the poem calls attention to the paradoxical character of these tropes in pastoral use: though propositionally and epistemically "weak" (and hence vulnerable to the dreamer's denigration of the friars' use of them on "philosophical" grounds), they are heuristically robust in focusing on tacit common experience as the proper scene and means in which the care of souls (quite literally) *takes place*.

Langland stages this paradox of pastoralia in the denouement of the second vision, splitting between Piers and the Priest the situated truth it brings to the fore. As Piers embodies the limits of idealized pragmatic craft-knowledge of the field to remedy the vices of its folk and sustain their will to self-renewal, the Priest's "kenning" discloses his peremptory premise that what does suffice for pastoral guidance of such folk is the kind of English "construing" that reduces Latin content and bearing to axiomatic formulations that the "lewed" can "wel reporte and holde"—much as Arundel's Constitutions, in Watson's characterization of their effect ("Censorship and Cultural Change," 828), specify a de facto maximum rather than minimum knowledge of the faith necessary to every Christian. The dramatic standoff embodies the dual imperatives of pastoral care: in the Priest's "construing," memorable (if here largely unsuccessful) translations of catechetical truths into usable vernacular recognitions; in Piers's response, the seeming impossibility of sustaining a "version of contemplative living" compatible with continued performance of daily work (the phrase is that of Watson, "Pastoral Theology and Spiritual Perfectionism," 83, 94–97). This conundrum is posed in varying forms in the ensuing narrative: first in the musings that end the A version of Vision 3 and are engaged further in the BC continuation of that vision and then on several later occasions in the episodic sequence of the long versions.[23] This recurrent confrontation presents schematically what may be considered a "type-scene" of the long versions, in which the incipient division between word and deed is depicted not as a topic for satiric anatomy, as in the first two visions, but as the perennial condition that must be negotiated by the skillful use of the arts of "pastours and poetes." Explored dialectically by the poem itself, this experiential "truth" is pointedly not coextensive with that embodied by either of Truth's designated emissaries at this juncture, which is why the dreamer must ponder further the enigma offered by the denouement of the second vision.

The impasse with which the Dowel dictum ends the second vision proves to be a recurrent device in the poem for anatomizing the interacting registers of pastoral counsel in argumentatively pivotal episodes; as Hanna has observed, "Langland chooses never to present [the discourse] of parochial instruction thoroughly dissociated from other social languages." Extending Burrow's seminal analysis of the second vision, he and other recent analysts have shown that Langland typically achieves his distinctive effects by doubling the figuration that encompasses the key dialogic point at issue.[24] Watson has termed the segment of the poem between the Pardon denouement and the meeting of Hawkyn and Patience in B.13–14 the "testing of the Piers hypothesis." Enacting in a sequence of dialogic encounters an argumentative reprise of the standoff between the Priest and Piers that ended Vision 2, the encounter of Patience and Hawkyn (which ends Vision 4 in B), Watson claims, places "Patience's extremism and Hawkyn's shoddy cloak . . . under equal critical scrutiny." In this portion of the poem *patientes vincunt* is an often reiterated "proverbial" axiom, as "patient poverty" is an important definitional focus of this dialogic sequence, where the term does not (as the poetic persona anticipates) define a preferred vocation or manner of life, but that spiritually receptive state of "studious anticipation" (Gehl, 160; see n. 12 above) in which figurative representation can best impress on the soul its proper nature and object.

The ideational concerns identified by Watson in this portion of the poem have several distinctive idiomatic and stylistic markers, and it is these formal correlatives of its argument that most concern me here. Foremost among them is the clustering of the kind of sententious dictum usually labeled "proverbial" by most annotators since Skeat: though sometimes discussed as if it typified the poet's style of citation generally, it is a strong tropism only in the dialogues of the central third of the poem. After Patience's encounter with Hawkyn Activa Vita—another major concentration of what Watson (101) calls "slogans" in the exercise of pastoral guidance—the encapsulated dicta in the following encounters, which rehearse the Incarnation and Redemption as the defining acts around which human history coheres anew, tend to be apostolic and prophetic verses proper to the liturgical celebration of these events, while the Latin inclusions of the final two passus reprise the citational techniques of earlier visions, thus pointedly revisiting the slippery grounds beneath all human efforts to wield resonant commonplace to one's own benefit. The central third of the narrative thus anatomizes the forms and uses of sententious idiom itself as well the special case of it that initiates the sequence: the unreflective notion that, for lack of the requisite repertory in its hearers, "vernacular" pastoral discourse cannot move much beyond such saws.

The project of the poet's third vision and its coda is to delineate the "competent" use of such pastoral resources as those William "translates" from the schools and to enlist them in effective self-scrutiny. The method of this sequence is serial trial, refinement, and replacement of the figurative premises of "ordinary language" for thinking about the extraordinary truths of the Redemption.[25] That not all proverbs are explicitly figurative presented no obstacle to their medieval exposition as subsets of *parabolae*, implicit brief analogies, similitudes, comparisons; as Shapin notes (732), the proverbial and the metaphoric are, for purposes of argument, in equally bad odor with philosophers, and for the same reasons. Defined by exegetes as a constructed likeness for an expository or argumentative purpose, the parable as similitude in memorably brief form shared some of the discursive properties of *proverbiae* as "figures of thought."[26] They were fully continuous in pastoral use with such historical exempla as those gathered in Valerius Maximus's *Facta et dicta memorabilia*, used according to the principles of Cicero and Quintilian in demonstration and argument, as these had informed William's distribution of them (as proverbs, parables, similitudes, and examples) across his suite of resources for pastoral edification. Alanus de Insulis's *Parabolae* (comparisons), a compendium of analogies for use in preaching, orders its six sections according to the increasing amplitude of its illustrations, from one to six couplets; Langland's use of several of these—not simply as adventitious citations (Peace's celebratory "note" of "poesie" at the end of the Easter passus is the best known of these) but as unmarked frameworks for his own narrative development—shows his familiarity with the "artistic" principles as well as the referential treasury such works offered to poetic practice.

In addition to the concentration of capsule *sententiae* in this central segment of the poem, two further unremarked semantic patterns in its long versions support my claim that Langland's "poetics" are advertently displayed as such in Vision 3, and their right uses carefully expounded. "Poetes" in Langland's usage are those sages of antiquity, whether classical or scriptural, whose wisdom adumbrates and supports the moral theology of the New Law and the terms of salvation offered by the Incarnation and the institution of the church. The term is used in the poem only in Vision 3 (and with increased frequency in the C version)—with one indicative exception: the extended lament of Anima / Liberum-Arbitrium in the fourth vision (C.17.74–124; cf. B.15.347–86) for the modern decline of all human expert crafts that involve perspicacity in guidance of others, from astrology to agronomy, culminating in "gramer þe ground of al" (C 108; B 372), the craft of "constru[ing] kyndely þat poetes made" as well as composition; in B it also includes the (multilingual) epistolary art (B.15.376), impoverished unless it includes facility in French as well as Latin and English. In short, it is literate "craft" as expert practice, not "knowledge" as systematized *scientia*, that receives its most searching examination in the middle of the poem, as the prerequisite to its own principled continuation as a craft advertently akin to that of the pastor.

Another indicative Langlandian usage concentrated in this part of the poem is the word "skile" for the expository tropes that are a distinctive and defining (though not exclusive) feature of Scripture's discourse; see, for example, B.11.1 (C.11.160) and C.13.130, at the beginning and end of her long appearance in Vision 3, in her only speaking role in the poem. Frequently rendering the Latin *rationes*, "skiles" are reasons in argument or explanations in demonstration, particularly those based on a figurative analogy or hypothesis (cf. Chaucer, *Hous of Fame* 726–8; and see MED s.v. "skil," n., 4.a, b; 5.a,b,c; 7, and "skillen," v.(1), 5.b). "Skile" also denotes ability or expertise at these expository activities, which include both verbal *distinctiones* and felicitous explanatory analogies (as at C.18.84, where the three degrees of the fruit of the Tree of Charity are called "a good skile"); it may also denote a difficult interpretive figure or crux (as at B.12.216) that great clerks cannot easily "assoile" (resolve). In a pattern that glosses her name, Scripture in the poem personifies the written (which in the poet's usage is never limited to holy writ and its expositors) as matter for the provision of "clergie," a capability that in the poet's lexicon is most accurately rendered by "godly literacy" and denotes powers more capacious than those that govern the performative or commentative activities of the ordained. Scripture is the immediate catalyst for the events that extend Vision 3 into the long versions, initiating and volubly dominating its latter half. In her reappearance in Vision 4, however, where at Conscience's behest she silently serves "sondry metes manye" to the banquet guests, she does not speak, her "skiles" now fully subsumed in the staged actions of the occasion and its narrative consequences.

The banquet that begins Vision 4 serves as a coda to Vision 3, presenting ostensive definitions of the poet's understanding of both Scripture and Clergie as the chief informants of pastoral art. While Conscience is its primary host, it is Clergie's promised presence there that in B excites the dreamer eagerly to accept an invitation to dine among the high-literate (B.13.22–24); in C, however, it is Reason whose advertised presence piques the dreamer's interest (C.15.26–7, though he is not a guest but a chief officer of the household, "styward of halle"), and Conscience's role as host is more strongly seconded by Clergie, who in this version has apparently been promoted to virtual cohost of the event (C.15.25). The change may be understood as a figurative rectification of the seemingly indecorous conclusion of the B version's banquet scene, where Conscience, accompanied by Patience, somewhat abruptly departs his own assembled party of dinner guests to seek "parfitnesse," leaving the hall effectively in Clergie's charge. Clergie, however, declines to bid formal farewell to the departing Conscience (B.13.203–14), instead soberly warning, in a prolepsis of the final two passus, that "thou shalt se þe tyme" in future when "þou art wery forwalked" and will wish for Clergie's supportive presence. C cancels these monitory parting words of Clergie, replacing them with a fuller and more gracious farewell by Conscience; this version also underscores the figurative premise that supports this outcome by inserting earlier in the scene a sudden brief speech by the formerly unacknowledged Piers (C.15.137–49; see Kane-Donaldson's note, p. 156, on the lection "ȝent," and cf. B.13.130–35a), beginning with the dictum *patientes vincunt*. In C, Piers is thereby made a prosopopoeia of this saying (in a fashion similar to the sudden appearance and disappearance of Trajan as personified corroboration of Scripture's dictum on divine mercy); in B (though, as Skeat noted, it has no exact counterpart in scripture) this dictum, along with similar watchwords (B.13.127: Matt. 22:37 and Ps. 15:1) is strongly identified with Piers by the wiser members of the company, who therefore suspend further attempts to solve the riddle of Dowel "til Piers come and preue þis in dede" (B.13.133). Piers's sudden manifestation and equally sudden vanishing, marveled at by all, thus stages in C not only an anticipation of Piers's fuller subsequent identification as a figure or avatar of Christ but also a reprise of his confrontation with the Priest at the end of Vision 2. Like the earlier encounter, this one embodies in counterposed parties the paradox of pastoral figuration that recurs throughout the poem, in which memorably riddling words are confronted by equally resonant and enigmatic deeds (illustrated in the contraposition of Scripture's words and the first-person voicing of Trajan's exemplarity, as well as in the encounter of Patience and Hawkyn). Yet in the poem these are embodied in scenarios that initially produce interpretive dissonance rather than mutual confirmation among these dramatized varieties of figuration.

The banquet is staged as a festive occasion at a learned institution such as an episcopal court (B calls it the "court of Conscience"), and though never explicitly so designated, Clergie is apparently imagined as its chancellor, as William de Montibus was at Lincoln: the chapter's second in command with chief responsibility for maintaining its collective learned capabilities in good working order. Clergie's B-version warning to the departing Conscience is thus tantamount to William's setting of the "do well" dictum as an admonition on the right use of such adages and figures in support of "godly literacy"; similarly, Piers's close identification by the company with the "slogan" later offered by Patience to Hawkyn as spiritual bread marks the larger bearing of his brief appearance at the banquet: to make explicit the imperative of penitential humility that is prerequisite to doing well, and with it the penitential *ductus* of the entire dialogic sequence of Vision 3. Midway through it, the dreamer succeeds in framing his first genuinely productive and "true" figurative comprehension of the meaning of his, or any soul's, "election" (C.12.50–74a; B.11.115–139a): not, as he has imagined in the early stages of his quest to learn whether "y were chose or nat chose," as a once-and-for-all sorting of "predestinat" sheep from goats by a severely judging God at an ultimate disposition of souls, but rather as a perpetually renewed proffer of sustenance by a loving God to all whom he has "called" to "souke sauete" at his breast. The dreamer's substitution of the second figurative analogy for the first, as explanatory embodiment of the nature of the divine interest in human "doing" as occasion for *restauratio*, elicits from Scripture, for the first time in her long and often rebarbative engagement with the dreamer, hearty approval of his newly figured understanding, which she confirms with an adage of her own (Ps. 144:9), "His mercy is above all his works."

To the guests at this rarefied banquet of sense, the "skiles" of figuration are fundamental nourishment, summoned in the form of varying foodstuffs, ranging from plain to "delicat," to suit their recipients. These are drawn, without differentiation as to their authoritative standing, not only from holy writ or the fathers but also from the felicitous formulations of "poetes": for example, C.13.33–92, the excursus inserted in the C version into the already lengthy "poverty sermon" comparing the burdens of the traveling Merchant and Messenger, amplifies (through several medieval intermediaries, among them Alanus's *Parabolae*) an often quoted aphorism of Juvenal, "Cantabit uacuus coram latrone uiator" (*Sat.* 10.21–22), "the empty-handed traveler will sing in the presence of the thief." The Merchant–Messenger similitude handily illustrates how Scripture's "skiles" serve several expository purposes simultaneously, as both figures in it present moral and spiritual imperatives potentially in conflict: its exposition makes compelling arguments for both as exemplary, though the moral and spiritual metonyms they embody are differently weighted. For the larger *ductus* of this analogy in convening the desired "user-base" of the poem, it is noteworthy that both Merchant and Messenger are represented as having laudable moral and spiritual functions: the comparison does not propose a gradation of degrees of merit but embodies the variety of "conditions" that inflect the spiritual journey. The "assoiling" (resolution, conversion) of such figures, from apparent *enigmata* or *insolubilia* into forms that are intuitively supportive of deeper understanding, constitutes one of the poem's most frequent moves in a course of poetic "argument" that requires, as here, exploring alternative imaginings of the "same" aspect of the scheme of salvation.

Amplifying her account in *The Craft of Thought*, Mary Carruthers contrasts two main forms of Langland's usage: the plainer expository schema she terms *pictura*, and more rarefied and difficult tropes such as *enigma* or *obscuritas*. The former is "a cognitive trope address[ing] the need for clarity and organization . . . in receiving . . . or composing a work," while the latter is "a trope inviting meditation and speculation, . . . investigation and discovery"; the pleasure afforded by the latter is that of "a mind-game, not a school examination," and is meant to produce "wonder," conducing to an "emotional intention" (*motus animi*).[27] Yet while the distinction was well understood by rhetoricians, she concedes that in Langland's poem the difference between them is "far more obvious in theory than in practice." Where expository "clarity and organization" are called for in the poem, however, pictorial arrays (e.g., the "good skile" of the Tree of Charity) are invoked chiefly in its later stages. In its midsection, where the pastoral arts are most insistently under consideration, Langland heavily favors verbal over visual schemata, compact *dicta* offered for "unfolding": as Jill Mann has emphasized, "Langland's allegory is, to an unusual degree, rooted in ordinary language use."[28] In this portion of the poem, proverbial "saying" repeatedly inserts a moment of "embarrassment" as a characteristic pivot in the episodic development of the poem.[29] In Langland's hands, the embarrassment to philosopers posed by the proverbial, as Shapin has penetratingly analyzed its "heuristics," reveals, in one of the most unremarkable idioms of ordinary "natural"-language use, all the complexities of register and semantic instability that attend the poet's most arcane learned analogies. Yet is simultaneously declares an "epistemic advantage" (Shapin, 743) over these as an ever renewed effort to have the "last word": to render the question of valid knowledge an equally urgent question of its realms of utility and dispositive power for the soul in action. It thereby marks the point in the trajectory of the narrative where ordinary and extraordinary language declare their interdependence in the "arts" of both pastors and poets.

SHAPES TOO LARGE TO SEE

In her account of the intellectual foundations of imaginative figuration in the poem, Michelle Karnes ("Will's Imagination") revises prevailing views of the relations between "natural" and acquired knowledge (the domains of Kynde and Clergie) as these are usually parsed by critics, both in navigating the complex arguments of Vision 3 and in mapping the larger intellectual terrain within which later medieval literary and pastoral imaginative projects are understood. Noting the dominant critical tendency to "separate the lay from the clerical in the late-medieval period, cordoning devotional literature off from scholastic theology," and aligning these with different languages, she reflects in conclusion (56–57) on the "optimism" in the face of nature of the theologians of the twelfth century; among those she discusses are Langland's main intellectual forebears in the design of the "inward journey." She distinguishes their lucid representational practices from the greater density of Langland's late-medieval figurative depictions, not only of generative "nature" but also of the phenomenal social world and the material cosmos. Karnes thereby identifies the terms in which one may understand the intricate figurative tropisms of Langland's late-medieval "period style" (as Robertson has identified it, though without defining its distinguishing rhetorical rather than iconographic features) in relation to the philosophical allegiances that underwrite it. "The intellectual difficulty of experience in *Piers*, as well as the poem's indebtedness to originally scholastic understandings of imagination, however, might encourage us to weaken those barriers. That nature no longer offers its secrets so freely in the late fourteenth century at least encourages us to recognize that reconciling the natural to the spiritual within one's own life took considerable intellectual effort" (57).

It is this overall "intellectual difficulty of experience" in the poem that leads me to ground the poet's methods and their rationale specifically in the pastoral arts, rather than in those features of the arts curriculum from which these were composed. William's canny placement of the Dowel dictum within a more capacious indication of the full scope of pastoral practice accurately identifies its character as an art of *predication*, in the grammatical as well as rhetorical sense of the term: hypothetical positings of those states of affairs in human existence that elicit experimental reflection, through which one may perceive what is normally unregistered in worldly action—those unregarded facts of ordinary life to which preachers in their perorations (*uton we hycgan*) have long redirected mindful attention. Unlike local objects of scholarly source-hunting and crux-busting, the largest-scale pastoral figures in the poem offer themselves to discovery only slowly and tentatively, as they are also less amenable to the kinds of demonstration that normally govern critical explication of "quotations" as well as local tropes. Their rewards to a user of the poem are similarly realized only gradually but are for that reason more deeply productive, because their fundamental premise is only fitfully visible, hidden in plain sight: to recognize them is simultaneously to acknowledge the role of habituated "knowledge" in the reading and reflecting mind rather than as a formal motif in a "text."

I conclude with one example of such a deeply assimilated pastoral figure, which seems to me the key organizing trope in the intellectual and figurative design of Vision 3 as a whole, supporting the entire experiential *ductus* of the "inward journey." Its deep but simple premise is that the true "natural" state of humankind since the Flood is that of a man perpetually on the verge of drowning. The proper remedy for this condition, however, is not more learning but better "craft," an imperative memorably expressed in one of the most often repeated dicta of the penitential tradition: "penance is the second plank in shipwreck." This pastoral "saying" does not appear anywhere in the verbal surface of the poem, though it is strongly indicated by the two analogical hypotheses offered to the dreamer by his first and last informants of Vision 3. Its submerged similitude richly deserves (and will receive elsewhere) fuller philological exploration in its own right, as a "saying" with a complex literary and rhetorical history—almost all of which Langland mobilizes to significant effect over the course of Visions 3 and 4. Here I identify it only in the briefest summary sketch, to show the affinities of Langland's procedures to the crafts of figuration recommended by William de Montibus.

Few readers have noted the neat chiastic pairing of the two didactic analogies that bracket Vision 3 as variants of the same figurative premise. The two friars who in its waking preface respond to the persona's query for directions to Dowel ignore his truculent reception of their first effort (which he apparently discounts as mere *parti pris* mendicant apologetics), and by way of a second attempt they propose a "forbisne" in the form of a figurative hypothesis (C.10.30–55; cf. B.8.26–56; A.9.22–47). They invite him to consider the prospects of survival for a man in a small boat amid heavy seas and to compare the chances of one who loses his balance but rights himself and manages to remain within the craft with those of one who falls out of the boat entirely. In the last dialogue of Vision 3, Ymaginatif proposes a similar hypothetical exercise (C.14.104–13; B.12.160–73) in summation of his argument about the uses of edifying figuration as engaging both natural and acquired skill ("kynde" and "clergie"): he invites the dreamer to compare the chances of survival for two men cast directly into open water, one of whom knows how to swim, while the other lacks that skill. Despite the omission of the boat as vehicle in the second example, the pragmatically obvious answer to both leading questions evokes the well-known figure of the "ship of faith," depicted in later medieval iconography as the Navicella, outside of which there is no rescue from the flood—a figure that in turn recalls Christ's summoning of Peter to walk toward him on the water (Matt.14:22–33), and the apostle's initial faltering in his miraculous progress as his faith wavers. Giotto's monumental use of this motif as an image (now largely destroyed) for the west portal of old St. Peter's in Rome may have increased its influence in this period as an entry figure, but it is in any case a demonstratively apt choice for the introductory position in a large-scale program of figuration that expounds the mediating role of the church as the body of the faithful in restoring humankind to its creator.[30] This redoubled figure is rich with further scriptural associations, as is the contrast between the friars' vestibular use of it to signify the sacramental supports of the church, and Ymaginatif's later suggestion that the pursuit of "perfection" mobilizes a broader and more freelance form of "clergie," the skill of figurative reflection that supports the soul's efforts to return to its creator amid the buffeting currents of the world. Both hypotheses entail acknowledgment that the swimmer's powers of action, impaired by the categorically sinful character of postdiluvian humankind, are ultimately insufficient to effect his rescue from drowning in a flood of this magnitude. Yet this condition is not cause for despair: patient poverty thereby becomes the paradoxical embodiment of the circumstances in which that saving "plank" is presented to humankind.

As an image for the sustaining power of faith, both are based on 1 Timothy 1:19 ("circa fidem naufragaverunt": "By rejecting conscience, certain persons have suffered shipwreck in the faith"). The pastoral commonplace extrapolated from it, however, is so pervasive in the penitential literature of the period that it scarcely acknowledges a single source, and is never quoted in the poem in Latin or English. In its most frequently cited form, "Penitentia est secunda tabula post naufragium," it is usually attributed to Jerome (*Epistola* 130.9) by the many ecclesiastics who cite it in works on penance. Among these is William de Montibus, who quotes it as the opening dictum of the section "De penitentia" of his treatise *De septem sacramentis* (Goering, ed. 2.13, p 492); its wide currency in later-medieval penitential literature was secured by its citation in Raymond of Pennaforte's influential *summa*.[31] Anterior to both Raymond's and William's citation, it appears, as Canon 72 of Dist. 1, in the assemblage of dicta on the necessity of penance that forms the largely self-contained *Tractatus de penitencia* incorporated into the *Decretum* of Gratian.[32]

The adage also has a sturdy lineage in the epistolary literature on the moral and spiritual interiority of the devout ascribed to Jerome in the middle ages. Jerome cites the dictum in a letter to the newly vowed virgin Demetrias, written some thirty years after his more famous letter on the same topic to the virgin Eustochium (which includes his report of God's accusation of him as Ciceronian rather than Christian: *Ep.* 22.30). These two epistles for women religious (neither now considered the genuine work of Jerome; see note) are among the most often cited of Jerome's pastoral counsels. The "shipwreck" figure in the later epistle revisits metaphorically his rehearsal earlier in the letter (*Ep.* 130.7) of the flight from the sack of Rome by Demetrias's grandmother Proba, who sold her estates and with her small family set forth for Africa in a boat, in a vain attempt to escape the conquerors' cruelties that in turn echoes the sea-escapes of a host of antique heroes. But as a figure for imperilment in one's faith, shipwreck makes its earlier patristic appearance in Tertullian, *De poenitentia: ut naufragus alicuius tabulae fidem.*[33] In Seneca, the figure is one in a series contrasting public honors as "unduly coveted" benefits, which always elicit grateful acknowledgment, with several "less showy" that are seldom recognized as such, either by their recipients or others. The former is illustrated by the conferral of an estate, the latter by a plank offered to the grasp of one shipwrecked. Among other undervalued benefits enumerated by Seneca are those done by "him who gives useful advice . . . him who holds you back when you would rush into crime . . . him who strikes the sword from the hands of the suicide . . . him who by his power of consolation brings back to the duties of life one who was plunged in grief, and eager to follow those whom he had lost"—as well as the deeds of one who sits at the bedside of the sick man and who, "when health and recovery depend upon seizing the right moment, administers food in due season, stimulates the failing veins with wine, or calls in the physician to the dying man. Who can estimate the value of such services as these?" It cannot have escaped the notice of the early church fathers, still less their high-medieval literate heirs in the *summae confessorum*, that this *rota* of "less showy" benefits closely parallels the Works of Mercy.

The argumentative bearing of Tertullian's treatise also informs the representation of penance as the *second* plank, the first being baptism. He is at pains to distinguish the perpetually restorative spiritual efficacy of penance from the view of it implicit in the early Christian practice of publicly performed penance as, like baptism, an unrepeatable act. Early in his quest for Dowel in Vision 3, the dreamer grounds his hope for salvation in baptism as the sacrament that permanently secures one's "chosen" condition and is a necessary (though not sufficient) condition for salvation; reiterating this claim in a gratuitous further display of his doctrinal mastery, he adds a homegrown analogy to explain that it is also unrepeatable (C.12.59a–67; B.11.124a–136). The second restorative sacrament, however—as he has just affirmed, to Scripture's hearty approval—is perpetually available to quench the thirst of all whom Christ calls to his breast; it is this second route to "saufte" that is offered by contrition and penance. While both baptism and the eucharist are at various times likened to the salvific "waters" shed from Christ's side in sacrifice, the waters of the world that threaten to engulf the Christian are those in which the "plank" of contrition is a "second" means of avoiding drowning, succeeding the ark in which Noah and his family escaped the first such deluge of worldliness, as Wit explicates this event earlier in Vision 3. The figurative superimposition of the two sacraments, of water and blood, each enacting an interior transformation in the soul, is pervasive in later medieval figuration; the complex iconography of the Adoration of the Mystic Lamb in the Ghent altarpiece of 1432 is but one instance of many.

The excursus of Vision 3 on the powers of pastoral figuration, given a full rationale by Ymaginatif in its conclusion, is the precondition for Piers's return to the poem, to personify "crafts" more fundamental than those entailed in the governance of the earthly church. Paradoxically, it is in the course of the "inward journey," from which Piers is largely absent as referent or actant, that his broader figural significance as metonym for the proper spiritual praxis of all the faithful—as Peter saved from drowning to become the founder of the true church—receives its intellectual justification. When in consequence of this short course in figurative pedagogy the dreamer (or, more important, the reader of the poem) shows sufficient improvement to be capable of benefit from the rich fare to be had at the "clergial" table set at the beginning of Vision 4, Piers can return once more to the episodic process of the poem. His gnomic wisdom proves more compelling than the inkhorn riddles of the Doctour of Divinity as guest of honor, and draws the dreamer, and with him the reader, to resume the quest to penetrate through ever deeper readings the enduring imaginative centrality of the elusive Piers.

The crisis over the "dowel" dictum thus specifies the poem's "fit audience" not as the imagined subjects of the post–Lateran IV "Pecham syllabus," Christian *mediocres* needing elementary catechetical instruction to "know" the necessary and sufficient conditions for their salvation, but simply as Piers's heirs, late-medieval devout successors to the intended readers of Egerton 613, to whom the "dowel" aphorism proposes the same turn of spiritual attention that it induces in Piers, from solicitude for the world's work to the interior labor of "sowle-hele." As William warns against the (merely) memorable as sufficient grounding for spiritual *paideia*, so Langland systematically stages in Vision 3 the point he elaborates in endless variation: that vernacular poetic discourse on matters of faith and morals involves a principled appropriation of "clergial" arts, to restore the treasury of ecclesiastical commentative thought to its primal capacity for pleasing surprise as sustenance for the commune.

PUBLISHED WORKS BY PENN R. SZITTYA

"Kicking the Habit: The Campaign against the Friars in a Fourteenth-Century Encyclopedia." In *Defenders and Critics of Franciscan Life: Essays in Honor of John V. Fleming,* edited by Michael F. Cusato and Guy Geltner. Leiden: Brill, 2009.

Review of *Dante and the Franciscans: Poverty and the Papacy in the "Commedia,"* by Nicholas R. Havely. *Modern Philology* 104, no. 2 (2006): 246–9.

"The Eternal Gospel." In *The Palgrave Literary Dictionary of Chaucer,* edited by Malcolm Andrew. New York: Palgrave Macmillan, 2006.

"William of St. Amour." In *The Palgrave Literary Dictionary of Chaucer,* edited by Malcolm Andrew. New York: Palgrave Macmillan, 2006.

Review of *Omne Bonum: A Fourteenth-Century Encyclopedia of Universal Knowledge: British Library MSS Royal 6 E VI–6 E VII,* by Lucy Freeman Sandler. *Speculum* 74, no. 2 (1999): 491–3.

"Dream Vision." In *The New Princeton Encyclopedia of Poetry and Poetics.* Rev. ed. Princeton: Princeton University Press, 1993.

"Domesday Bokes: The Apocalypse in Medieval English Literary Culture." In *The Apocalypse in the Middle Ages,* edited by Richard K. Emmerson and Bernard McGinn. Ithaca, N.Y.: Cornell University Press, 1992.

Review of *"Piers Plowman" and the New Anticlericalism,* by Wendy Scase. *Speculum* 67, no. 4 (1992): 1040–42.

The Antifraternal Tradition in Medieval Literature. Princeton, N.J.: Princeton University Press, 1986.

"The Trinity in Langland and Abelard." In *Magister Regis: Studies in Honor of Robert Earl Kaske,* edited by Arthur Groos. New York: Fordham University Press, 1986.

Review of *A Fourteenth-Century Scholar and Primate: Richard FitzRalph in Oxford, Avignon, and Armagh,* by Katherine Walsh. *Speculum* 58, no. 1 (1983): 249–51.

"Metafiction: The Double Narration in *Under Western Eyes.*" *ELH* 48, no. 4 (1981): 817–40. Reprinted in *Critical Essays on Joseph Conrad,* edited by Ted Billy. Boston: G. K. Hall, 1986. Reprinted in *Joseph Conrad, Critical Assessments of Writers in English,* edited by Keith Carabine. Bromley, England: Christopher Helm, 1992.

"'Sedens super flumina': A Fourteenth-Century Poem against the Friars," *Mediaeval Studies* 41 (1979): 30–43.

"The Antifraternal Tradition in Middle English Literature," *Speculum* 52, no. 2 (1977): 287–313.

Rejoinder to Carole K. Brown and Marion F. Egge, "The *Friar's Tale* and the *Wife of Bath's Tale*." *PMLA* 91, no. 2 (1976): 291–93.

"The Green Yeoman as Loathly Lady: The Friar's Parody of the *Wife of Bath's Tale*." *PMLA* 90, no. 3 (1975): 386–94.

"The Friar as False Apostle: Antifraternal Exegesis and the *Summoner's Tale*." *Studies in Philology* 71 (1974): 19–46.

"The Living Stone and the Patriarchs: Typological Imagery in *Andreas*, Lines 706–810." *Journal of English and Germanic Philology* 72 (1973): 167–74.

"Geomorgidd Larsmithes." *Old English Newsletter* 7 (1973): 1–2.

"The Angels and the Theme of *Fortitudo* in the *Chanson de Roland*." *Neuphilologische Mitteilungen* 72 (1971): 193–223.

See also *The Latin Works of John Wyclif.* http://tiny.cc/georgetown-szittya-wyclif.

PENN R. SZITTYA AS SCHOLAR AND TEACHER

Jo Ann Hoeppner Moran Cruz

Because of the wide range of Penn Szittya's scholarship, this volume offers here a brief survey of his critical works to supplement their bibliographical listing. Readers who are familiar with his writing or teaching in one area of literary studies might learn through this survey about his role in other areas. Penn Szittya has contributed magisterial publications on the medieval antifraternal tradition, pathbreaking scholarship on Chaucer, and articles on a range of Middle English and Anglo-Saxon literatures. His scholarly publications connect political theology; cultural history; ecclesiology; exegesis; social theory and historical theory; theories and practice of kingship; popular culture; the conjunction of learned and popular culture; and the literary, scriptural, and artistic world of references behind texts ranging from the Anglo-Saxon to the modern period. Although the audience for this body of work consists primarily of scholars of late-medieval literature, the interdisciplinarity of Penn's work should appeal more broadly to scholars across a range of disciplines. Penn's thematic foci stretch across Western medieval Europe, while his research plumbs sources in Anglo-Saxon, Latin, Old French, and Middle English. A masterful reader of texts, he joins this skill with a historicist sensibility as he contextualizes medieval literatures, placing them in both an English and a Continental context, adding a detailed knowledge of surviving manuscripts as well as the surrounding manuscript culture.

Penn's earliest scholarly contributions focused on some of the earliest vernacular texts. In his first article, published in 1971, Penn exhibits his trademark ability to approach texts from a thorough background in the extrinsic aspects of a text (as he puts it in this article), combined with an insightful intrinsic analysis of the text.[1] In this case his attention is on the Oxford manuscript of *La Chanson de Roland*. The article focuses on an unnoticed aspect of the epic: the literary and thematic roles of the archangels

Michael and Gabriel. By analyzing the parallel textual associations of Michael with Roland and of Gabriel with Charlemagne, as well as by presenting the scriptural and patristic qualities of each of these two figures, Penn argues for two heroic models. Michael and Roland represent martial courage, with all its attendant human vulnerabilities to pride and hastiness. Gabriel and Charlemagne represent a more deliberative, humble fortitude that is spiritually grounded. In the final analysis the poem poses a challenge to the kind of martial valor that privileges personal honor and produces the self-reliant and self-centered but still noble and heroic Roland. It posits, through Charlemagne and also Oliver, a different model of martial prudence, mediated by wisdom and concern for the larger community and spiritually sustained by Gabriel through Charlemagne. In the end, as Roland's soul is borne away by both angels, his death represents a synthesis of wisdom and valor that he did not exhibit while alive. This analysis, which brings the value of wisdom to our understanding of the hermeneutics of Frankish kingship, stands against a tradition of scholarship that sees Charlemagne as representative, above all else, of a martial, sacral, Christian kingship. It might also contribute to discussions of the role of wisdom in valorizing Angevin kingship.

In a 1973 article on the ninth- or tenth-century Anglo-Saxon poem *Andreas*, Penn brings a typological analysis to several fantastic elements in the poem, in the process suggesting that typological modes of analysis are particularly fruitful when applied to Old English hagiographical works.[2] In this case Penn convincingly suggests that scriptural passages from the Old Testament (3 Kings and 2 Paralipomenon) describing the iconography of Solomon's Temple are intended to signify the living stone of Christ, the corner foundation stone, and his church. By the stone's descent from the wall and its spoken word to the men in the Temple, the poem alludes to the transformation of the Old Law into the New Law of Christ's church, to Christ's miracles, and particularly to the redemption of souls, exemplified in the redemption of the souls of the patriarchs. This early article displays the depth of Penn's understanding of the role of scripture and the typological and mystical modes of thinking embedded in early English texts.

The next set of articles, published between 1974 and 1976, address Chaucer's *Canterbury Tales*, with foci on the *Summoner's Tale*, the *Wife of Bath's Tale*, and the *Friar's Tale*.[3] Penn argues that Chaucer's treatment of the notably indecorous *Summoner's Tale* is to be understood as simultaneously learned and obscene, making this tale a treat for the theologically inclined as well as for a popular audience. Penn's reading illustrates what a wealth of meaning can be gleaned through scriptural exegesis as he details a series of biblical and, in particular, Pentecostal parodic inversions of wind and fire as well as related liturgical and patristic meanings. The article exhibits Penn's deeply historicist sensibilities in his arguments associating the friars with Pentecost. This article begins to address the Middle English antifraternal literature that will preoccupy Penn's scholarship until and beyond the publication of his book *The Antifraternal Tradition in Medieval Literature* in 1986. Penn's most immediate goal in this article is to connect the *Summoner's Tale* with the ways in which antifraternalism was argued and to suggest that Chaucer's allusive and ironic focus, which inverted analogies between Christ's apostles and the Summoner's friar, provides a means for understanding the unity of the tale. In doing so he draws from the range of Pentecostal typologies in Isidore of Seville, Augustine, and Bede and from treatments of the liturgy by John Beleth, William Durandus, and others. Penn argues that Thomas's "gift," the friar's speechlessness, the first fruits of Pentecost, and references to Moses and Elijah "all reinforce allusively the Pentecostal pattern within the tale and prepare for the joke to come."[4] Penn's argument not only rests on the biblical, liturgical, and patristic allusions in the tale but also gains force from the historical association of the friars with Pentecost—the date of their General Chapters—and the self-identification of the friars with the apostolic preaching mission. The extent to which the Summoner's friar quotes Christ's own words, particularly Christ's speech to his disciples in Matthew 23 in defense of the friars' apostolic claims, while failing to measure up to them in his own life, becomes the measure of his hypocrisy, greed, and pridefulness.

The comic self-inflated friar of Chaucer's text, whose actions are far removed from the original vision of St. Francis, mirrors many of the criticisms launched against the friars in the thirteenth and fourteenth centuries in the writings of William of St. Amour (who saw the friars as pseudo-apostles), in the *Roman de la Rose's* Fals-semblant, in "Pierce the Ploughman's Crede," and in Jack Upland. The article concludes by citing those biblical and apostolic allusions in Chaucer that echo the antifraternal literary tradition—for example, the false modesty surrounding the friar's use of the term *magister* (which is equated with Christ's forbidding the title *rabbi* to his disciplines) and the critique of shepherds of the church "penetrantes domos" (2 Tim. 3:6), thereby trespassing in the spiritual realm of the parish clergy and perhaps also morally within the household.

The next Chaucerian article, "The Green Yeoman as Loathly Lady: The Friar's Parody of the Wife of Bath's Tale," roused some debate in the *Proceedings of the Modern Language Association*. Penn's article, which ties together the three tales of the Wife of Bath, the Friar, and the Summoner, focuses on the hostility between Friar and Summoner and also between the Wife of Bath and the Friar, examining the extent to which *The Friar's Tale* echoes and undermines *The Wife of Bath's Tale* as well as the Wife herself. The Friar is looking both backward and forward. He is, at one level, obviously attacking the Summoner while, at a structural and linguistic level, he is attacking (parodying) the Wife of Bath's idealized conception of women, romance, and shape-shifting magic. The Summoner becomes the inverse of the Wife of Bath's knight, plighting troth to a demon rather than the Loathly Lady, and with far worse consequences. Further evidence for unity within these tales, Penn suggests, lies in the ongoing discourse surrounding "maistrie"—certainly in marriage, for the Wife of Bath, but with regard to authority in general, in all three tales. Thus, the Christian paradox that "masters shall be servants and servants shall be masters," played out in *The Wife of Bath's Tale*, is subverted by both the Friar and the Summoner.[5]

In a response, Carole K. Brown and Marion Egge argue that Penn's article did not uncover the contrasting moral lectures embedded in *The Wife of Bath's Tale* and *The Friar's Tale*. Leaving aside Penn's argument for the unity of the three tales, they concentrate on the contrasting moral response of the Friar to the Wife of Bath. Penn's response to their comment asks merely that their comments take his arguments at face value. More important, however, is that, in typical Szittyian methodological manner, he requests that they do what he does so well, which is to take into better account the context in which the moral interpretation rests. To consider the kind of complications that arise by contextualizing is exactly the strength of Penn's entire body of work.

In 1977, Penn published "The Antifraternal Tradition in Middle English Literature" in *Speculum*. This article, which was to form the nucleus of his subsequent 1986 book, addresses the attacks on the friars by William of St. Amour as part of the controversies between the secular clergy and the fraternal orders at the University of Paris in the 1250s and 1260s. Penn traces the impact of these attacks on the English literary tradition in the fourteenth and early fifteenth centuries. In so doing, he attends to the symbolic, highlighting the exegetical nature of the polemics and the theological use of biblical typologies characteristic of William of St. Amour's antifraternal writings. The article looks at several strands of antifraternal discourse found in William of St. Amour's writings that were then taken up in the conventions of English antifraternal writings. William of St. Amour saw the friars in terms of salvation history, responding to the radical Joachimite notions expressed by Gerard da Borgo San Donnino that the new orders of friars had arisen to combat Antichrist and that their presence inaugurated a new age, a new gospel, an eternal gospel, and a new law that would supplant the gospel of Christ. William responds by inverting the role of the friars, making them the precursors of Antichrist. He attacks them by means of biblical analogues. The friars, according to William of St. Amour, are prefigured in the friar-like Pharisees who called themselves *magistri* (cf. Matt. 23 and John 1:38), Christ having warned his disciples against them,[6] and in the pseudo-apostles of St. Paul's time (2 Cor. 11:13; 2 Tim. 3:6; 2 Thess. 3:6–12)[7]—a particularly effective charge, given the apostolic model of life followed by St. Francis and the *antichristi* predicted for the last days (2 Tim. 3:1-6).[8]

This article then looks at the variety of English poets and writers who took up these arguments. They include Chaucer, Langland, Gower, Thomas Wilton, Richard Kilwington, Richard FitzRalph, Wyclif, and the anonymous authors of a variety of texts. The English tradition is invoked briefly at various points; but the main thrust of the article is to "redefine the nature of antifraternalism" in terms of conventional literary, symbolic, and exegetical influences. The refrains of the antifraternal discourse, Penn is at pains to point out, have more to do with literary continuities than with the actual abuses of friars. Fleshing out the English antifraternal discourses will form the bulk of Penn's book.

In 1979, in an article on a fourteenth-century poem ("Sedens super Flumina") against the friars, Penn provided an annotated edition of the work.[9] Penn addresses the date and authorship of this vitriolic Latin poem. Concluding that it is of disputed authorship (and not by Peter Pateshull, as John Bale thought), Penn suggests that its origins can be located ca. 1357–1360, at a time of controversy between Richard FitzRalph, archbishop of Armagh, and the friars; it is paired with a poem in praise of the friars.

A subsequent published piece, from 1981, provocatively departs from the medieval world to make a foray into modernist studies.[10] Penn's analysis of Joseph Conrad's *Under Western Eyes* has been characterized as a key re-evaluation of the novel and has been reprinted twice.[11] In this Russian political novel, Conrad disguises his own imaginative effort with a protagonist who also disguises himself. These "two kinds of concentric fictions" are complicated by the fact that the protagonist, Razumov, is himself a writer. The fictional duplication of the novel produces duplicative images, events, places, and people. Penn explores the relationship between Conrad the author, the language teacher who reads Razumov's diary, and Razumov the diary writer.[12] Whether this narrative technique lends authenticity to Razumov's story or only complicates it depends on the stance of the English-language teacher. The latter's frequent declarations of incomprehension suggest both the gulf between Western and Eastern thinking and the incompetence and perhaps inauthenticity ("interpretive failures") of the narrator. These elements heighten the reader's sense of the novel's psychological and aesthetic dimensions, but they also place the reader in an interpretive quandary. How can the reader tell what is fictional falsehood and what is fictionally "true"? The relationship between fiction and reality becomes fraught, metafictionally confused, tied up, Penn suggests, not only with the contrived identity of Razumov but also with the "double identity" of Conrad himself as reflected in his two narrators.

In 1986, Penn published "The Trinity in Langland and Abelard," an intriguing article that explores the Trinitarian language in William Langland's *Piers Plowman*, passus 9, 16, and 17 of the B-text. This language derived from the twelfth-century Victorine tradition that influenced Langland but perhaps is even more remarkably similar to the images and metaphors used by Abelard. In particular, the article points to Abelard's figure of a lute player whose playing corresponds to the power of God and whose hand, as instrumental agent, is a similitude of the son's wisdom. Meanwhile, the sounding strings, produced by the combination of art and hand, correspond to the effects of the Holy Spirit.[13] Penn ends the article with a challenge to Langland scholars to investigate the path whereby Abelardian Trinitarian ideas may have reached England, through either manuscripts of Abelard's own works or those of his disciples, to influence Langland's Trinitarian overlay in the B-text.

That same year Penn published his magisterial work *The Antifraternal Tradition in Medieval Literature*,[14] a study that argues that the attacks on the friars derived less from any historical reality on the ground than from a symbolic, eschatological, and biblical tradition focused on salvation history, a tradition that William of St. Amour initiated. William's thirteenth-century Parisian debates influenced in turn a variety of English literary treatments of the friars by the second half of the fourteenth century. This book opened up the history of this literary tradition, which had, for the most part, been overlooked by historians and scholars of medieval literature. Penn begins and ends his study with William Langland. In between he traces the history of antifraternal literature from Paris to England, contextualizing it not in terms of the historical orders of friars or any failings they may have had but rather in terms of the arguments against the friars. The movement of the friars into the universities brought up questions about where the friars fit in terms of biblical prophecy and prefiguration, particularly pressing questions since the friars themselves claimed apostolic authority. Beginning with William of St. Amour, whose antifraternal writings in the 1250s and 1260s shaped much of the subsequent discourse, Penn traces the scriptural sources for William's sense of an immanent end based on biblical exegesis and prophecy, grounded in salvation history. Based, as William was, in an exegesis of scriptural texts and its glosses, the friars became, for William, prefigured in the Pharisees and the pseudo-apostles as signs of the coming of Antichrist. The Pharisees, hypocrites of their time, according to scripture, prefigured the hypocritical friars of William's time. Further, William argued, the friars had no claim to apostolic authority; nor were they sent by Christ to preach.

Nearly a century later, William of St. Amour's writings and influence surfaced in England. While there is only one record of a William of St. Amour manuscript in England before 1350, by the second half of the fourteenth century his ideas had been taken up by a number of English writers, including Chaucer and Langland. In tracing surviving manuscripts and book lists from 1350 to 1450, Penn documents an impressive range of antifraternal writings, from encyclopedic compilations to parish manuals to monastic treatises and Wycliffite texts.[15] In the slow transmission from Paris to England, however, the apocalyptic strain so prevalent in William of St. Amour was to give way to a greater concern with ecclesiological arguments against the friars. Penn then analyzes the antifraternal writings of

Richard FitzRalph, archbishop of Armagh. Like William of St. Amour, he uses biblical exegesis, but with a primary focus on the hierarchy of the church, where the friars are seen as interlopers. Like the Levites, FitzRalph suggests, the friars were outside the common law of the Church. Subsequent chapters follow the antifraternal discourse in Wycliffe's writings and those of his followers. While many of Wycliffe's arguments are idiosyncratic, much of his writing follows the William of St. Amour tradition. As the literary traditions reflecting the antifraternal theme shift into the English poetic tradition, the same biblical texts brought to bear on antifraternalism by William of St. Amour continue to be touchstones. While many of the poems connect the friars with eschatological expectations and the coming of Antichrist, generally the eschatology fades, or the expectations become vague, while the ecclesiology remains central. Poetically, the hypocrisy of the friars is a major focus, as is the concern with vagrancy and begging. The chapter on Chaucer, focusing as it does on the comedic present, goes back once more to *The Summoner's Tale.* The book then concludes with a revealing analysis of *Piers Plowman*, and especially of the last passus, that is directed to the centrality of antifraternalism in salvation history (with the friars as agents of Antichrist); in the moral contours of Langland's concern with word and work, moral restitution and accounting; and in the gathering omens of an approaching End. With this book, Penn has laid out a roadmap for all scholars who care to track the intellectual pilgrimage of an exegetical, theological, eschatological, and ecclesiological set of arguments against the friars. It should be difficult for any scholars of late-medieval literature and history to ignore this tradition and not to be on the alert for it in the texts they examine. It is the wide contextual lens, grounded in biblical exegesis, that gives this study its staying power and makes it the pathbreaking work that it is.

After the publication of his book on antifraternal literature, Penn published two additional articles. His 1992 article "Domesday Bokes: The Apocalypse in Medieval English Literary Culture" investigates the term *Domesday Boke* as it is associated with the 1086 census of manors, lands, and persons in newly conquered England.[16] While exploring the cultural meaning of the association of written text with christocentric kingship and analyzing the analogical and symbolic meanings attached to the Domesday Book, Penn presents an overview of a history of apocalyptic texts circulating in England. In the process he also sketches an outline for a much needed fuller literary history of the Apocalypse in England. Penn lays the groundwork for such a history by delineating the most active time periods for the circulation of apocalyptic texts. He then analyzes the apocalyptic hermeneutics behind a number of them, including *Pearl* as well as texts from the Arthurian romance tradition. Tracing the location of surviving manuscripts, he aligns Latinate and vernacular traditions as well as learned and popular expectations. In 2009 he published an article entitled "Kicking the Habit: The Campaign against the Friars in a Fourteenth-Century Encyclopedia."[17] Taking a title that he briefly considered using for his book, Penn explores a manuscript that had earlier intrigued him. *Omne bonum*, written in the 1360s and early 1370s by James le Palmer, a clerk in the exchequer, is a unique example of a secularly conceived encyclopedia, privately funded. It is composed alphabetically, with an elaborate program of illumination, written in James's own hand and on vast proportions (unfinished, the manuscript runs to nearly 1,100 folios).[18] Penn's article, after contextualizing and describing the manuscript, examines one alphabetical entry entitled "Fratres mendicantes." One of the longer entries in the encyclopedia, it was most likely originally a separate pamphlet that was later incorporated into the encyclopedia, and it is notably antifraternal in its sentiments. James incorporates material from William of Pagula's *Summa summarum*, the Franciscan Rule, canon-law glosses, and the antifraternal writings of William of St. Amour, Jean d'Anneux, Richard FitzRalph, and Thomas de Wilton. It is, in a sense, a brief historical compendium of writings against the friars, done in the context of a fascination with canon law, among the bureaucratic business of the exchequer, and, Penn argues, in an atmosphere that valued productive labor. The text ends with the rubric of an excerpt from Thomas de Wilton's *Questio on able-bodied begging* (c. 1327): "xxxvii How the blessed Bernard spoke against the mendicant friars running around the country and frequenting the courts of magnates and, idle, not laboring with their hands."[19]

Penn was also a master teacher, much beloved by his students; his courses ranged from the Vikings to Dante, including a variety of courses on Chaucer and the foundational course, The Age of Dante, for the Medieval Studies program at Georgetown University. With no teaching assistants to assist him with the demands of his writing-intensive approach, Penn directly shaped the intellectual development of hundreds of students. His *circumlectio* (reading around) research projects were pages of reading notes, written in whatever way a student chose to take notes, with introductory comments on each reading, interspersed thoughts on the readings in progress, and highlights of the reading project at the end. The students were asked to do the kind of insightful reading that is required in writing a paper, but they did not have to write the paper. Undistilled, these notes could range up to fifty or sixty pages per student. Each *circumlectio* was read in detail by Penn, who would comment on the reading experience of the student, suggest other ways to think about the material, offer further bibliographical suggestions, argue with the excerpted texts or with the student's take on them, or praise the student's perspicacity. It was a poorer student who did not take advantage of the opportunity to have this "conversation" with Penn, but the time it took to respond was demanding and a measure of Penn's commitment to the educational experience of his students, many of whom have gone on to do graduate study in programs at Oxford, Yale, Toronto, Cornell, Notre Dame, Fordham, York, Exeter, UCLA, Leuven, the CEU in Budapest, Georgetown, and elsewhere. In today's contested terrain of higher education, when many critics are questioning whether university faculty focus too much on research and not enough on teaching, Penn's ability to work with students at every level, his wry humor, and his deep well of kindness, combined with academic rigor and depth of scholarship, made him a much admired teacher and colleague.

This volume is a labor of love from colleagues and former students to a colleague and mentor who, happily in retirement, continues to pursue scholarly projects. His influence not only as a major critical voice in his field, but also as a teacher-scholar, deserves this thoughtful recognition from those who miss and value him.

THE DESIRE TO WRITE THINGS DOWN: A POETIC PALIMPSEST ON CERTAIN REMARKS BY PENN SZITTYA

Mark McMorris

PREFACE TO TEXT

The genre of the profile has strict requirements: verisimilitude, a correspondence between internal character and exterior setting. Like a photographer, the writer must situate his subject against a purposeful background. This setting is meant to mark invisible dispositions, but obliquely, like signs that promise—only promise—the revelations of allegory. I think Penn would dislike any plan to write a profile of his virtues, because in his view the things he worked on are more consequential, and more fascinating, than the man who did the work. Any gesture honoring Penn has to enfold these things. Although canny in his judgments, persistent in his aims, inclined toward boldness in his decisions, he did not care whether a result was ascribed to his labor. More than most people I worked with, Penn was willing to let others stand in the light he had engineered. Not a profile, then, but a hybrid sprung from Penn's words and postured as a setting, a studio that solicits an oblique analogy between a minor medieval civil servant and any modern poet, between vellum and immortality, between a palimpsest and poetics, and a writer's way of making a profile that looks nothing like the original to which it is indebted—this is the proposal. Dante leaves Vergil behind. The profile sustains a region that blends memory and hypothesis.

TEXT

Penn Szittya knows Italian, English, French, and Latin. Probably many other tongues. He likes to use all of his languages in his correspondence. Sometimes I sent him an email late at night. Sometimes Penn would reply that same night with other languages mixed in.

Penn Szittya sent the only email I can remember receiving that urged the horses of the night to run slowly, which I took to mean he kept Ovidian vigil: "lente currite, noctis equi!" (run slowly, horses of the night). But he may have meant the more sinister plea from Faustus:

> O lente, lente currite, noctis equi!
> The stars move still; time runs; the clock will strike;
> The devil will come, and Faustus must be damn'd.
>   (Marlowe, *Doctor Faustus*, B text 5.2.141–43)

Thus he admonished me to go to sleep, lest the sunlight find me bowed over the keyboard like a distracted creature, searching for an alibi. The devil will arrive promptly in any event.

Penn Szittya kept a rotating Lannan Foundation Chair inside his office, which he occupied as head of department, for a long time. The chair was a symbol and a joke—treating literally the name of an academic honor. The chair was black. The chair was not for sitting. This chair was also endowed.

Penn Szittya likes people and literature, liked to manage a large unruly department, likes to listen to Bach, likes to photograph birds and to send the photos to his friends, likes to do hard labor in beautifying his house, likes to meet and dine with writers, likes to celebrate diversity, because I suppose it reminded him of the medieval capacity to think fluidly about boundaries.

Penn Szittya never had so much fun with furniture as he did that year.

Penn Szittya is the sort of man who meets with all comers and listens to their tales. Not long ago he met Sheikha Mozah bint Nasser al-Missned, the wife of the emir of Qatar. It was in the middle of a lake, or in the middle of the Persian Gulf. They discussed cultural topics (and education's role), how to make a place belong to its time, how to make the time equal to ambitious plans. Penn later dined with her on top of a skyscraper overlooking the streets of Doha and the sea. Sheikha Mozah bint Nasser al-Missned was keen to modernize Qatar, and Penn Szittya was keen to listen and to assist.

An art involved with social and political life is of a kind to solicit the interest of Penn Szittya. This is because poetry shares hand and mind with other practices of everyday life, weaving and shearing, tales told at a tavern to spur the hours along, ploughing and mowing—*Works and Days, Georgics, Piers Ploughman*—as the season requires.

Penn Szittya is the only medievalist in the United States to have met Nigerian novelist Helon Habila at a French restaurant. This is a fact worth pondering, for what it says about transnational modernity.

It is Penn Szittya's habit to trust in the mind of other people. He assumes that anyone would like to read Ovid at night, or Marlowe, instead of Yours truly, that anyone might know the conclusion to *Inferno*, or want to know it, to know the best of Cavalcanti, or be able to see that "Vigilate!" means not "Keep the night watch on the battlements of the town" but "Go to sleep!"

Penn Szittya is from all places. Once he said he was of Hungarian ancestry, another time another, and so on. When pressed, he was inclined to say Yes, or to say No with elegance. On the matter of the name, he seemed proud of a secret history, one that Borges might write involving a library and a disorderly encyclopedia, discovered in a garden with illusory magnolias.

Penn Szittya liked the idea of "poetics and social practice" because, I suppose, it captured the making of culture by lots of people, some of whom couldn't necessarily write or read a book: Charlemagne, king of the Franks, for example, whom Gibbon treats with frank disrespect.

Penn Szittya once recited the last line of Dante's *Inferno* in the hearing of Dinaw Mengestu. When choosing a title for his novel, Mengestu remembered both the voice and the English translation: *The Beautiful Things That Heaven Bears*.

Penn Szittya could have been CEO of General Electric or ambassador to the Russians during the Cold War. One of his favorite words was *synergy*, but why, for God's sake?

I meant to ask Penn Szittya whether Charlemagne ever did learn to write proper Latin, this being the sort of question bound to annoy a medievalist. On the other hand, I admit, Hegel is not bothered by Charlemagne's illiteracy.

In time, as Penn Szittya knows, politics engulfs every motive.

German was the tongue least used of the major European tongues in the lattices of Penn Szittya's correspondence with me. Nor did I ever hear from him a word of Portuguese, though, of course, Penn knows all languages, since he is from everywhere.

Not professionally concerned with the writers of the twenty-first century, nonetheless he felt, as I recall, their practical import to the social world, which enfolds everyone: synergy.

Or Penn Szittya could have been a psychotherapist, or he could have run a large urban hospital, where all complain about their beds, as in Baudelaire, or in another life he could have been an ornithologist, a historian of the baroque, a Freedom Rider—though he probably was a Freedom Rider—a skilled football player on the Hungarian national team.

————

Penn Szittya once lectured on the medieval artist book for the Lannan Center for Poetics and Social Practice. (This was an event organized by my friend Ward Tietz.) A giant screen showed images of Dante Gabriel Rossetti's diagrams for the *Commedia*, a square with three interior circles, or segments of the Plan—*Inferno, Purgatorio, Paradiso*—and each circle opened onto the next, so that Dante might complete the sequence, from Dark Wood to the Face of Light.

Penn Szittya's lecture went next to his major theme: the palimpsest. In medieval England, a minor official of the state got hold of more than one thousand sheets of quality vellum and dedicated his lifetime to writing on these sheets. The clerk filled them with writing, but there was an extended "preface": fourteen folios of tinted drawings based on stories from the Bible. As we can see, the minor civil servant was both a supervisor of illuminators and an amateur scholastic. Wordy past all toleration, he knew how to keep silent too: the visual preface has no language.

I dwell on this detail for a reason. The medieval guys were fanatical writers—I don't say they were poets. But they loved to write things down. The minor civil servant withholds writing to begin with. He relies on pictures to show his meaning, deferring the alphabet until later. The interchange of script and image corresponds to a tendency in modernist and contemporary poetry: the unmanageable *signans*. As social practice, writing tends to want to elude the dictates of taxonomy. This, in addition to its visual dimension, is what Penn Szittya knew in choosing his topic. The book has the outlandish savor of an inexplicable desire—a sustained gesture toward the closed text, a gesture that in the end produces a text that is generically unmoored and open to further indefinite inscription: The scribe left many pages blank. "I thought that if I could put it all down, that would be one way," John Ashbery says. "And next the thought came to me that to leave all out would be another, and truer, way."

Penn Szittya clicked through his slides, offering comment. The earliest folios depict biblical tales (usually four panels to a page), the fifteenth folio shows the *arma Christi* (hammer, tongs, rooster, crown of thorns, sponge for the vinegar, ladder, nails, and so forth), but the sixteenth folio depicts the face of God like a Golden Sun, looking down benevolently and radiantly on the earth (see appendix 1, below). Penn Szittya called this sequential layering a palimpsest—strictly, a "conceptual" palimpsest—a surface and an interior that holds the universe.

Following the initial matter (Bible stories, *arma Christi*, beatific vision), the reader encounters the thick of the book filled with writing. The scripted pages belong also to the palimpsest, Penn Szittya said. The title given to the whole by the minor civil servant is *Omne bonum*, All Good, and he means to say God's book, or God's face, or Christ's body, or the content of this here book, a sort of early encyclopedia.

The word *poetics* covers the idea of making. Penn Szittya said that in the medieval period, one word for a poet was *maker*. Since no one in the period knew Greek, it must be that the idea of the poet as maker evolved independently of the word *poiein*, as by happy chance. Or that the force of *poiein* lingered in literate places although the language it came from was unknown. Still yet, someone must have known Greek. (There's a book about this. There's a book about everything.)

The deed is the poem, the thought the poetics or principle of form, which one discovers and elaborates into a thesis about the making of poems. Which comes first? To literary critics—to Aristophanes of Byzantium— what matters is the stable order of taxonomy and priority. The modern scholar wants a clear and distinct perception of differences: a Cartesian geometry of verbal forms and practices.

Penn's thesis in the lecture was that *Omne bonum* is a kind of palimpsest— a conceptual palimpsest, as he said. He was using the word *palimpsest* in a metaphorical sense, to describe the relationship of all of the pages of *Omne bonum* to the page containing the golden semblance of God's face. My recollection of his thesis is that one perceives "beneath" the writing of all of the pages—as beneath the writing on the surface of a literal palimpsest—this visual page, the page with God's heliomorphic visage on display.

An explanatory detour: Some medieval manuscripts contain a riot of "babewyns" in the margins (see appendix 2). These anthropomorphic hybrids are not incidental to the scribe's purpose. Man is a pothead, a fish. The babewyns restate as image the central discourse of the Latin script and have to do with the mystery of God's creation (I think). For the world is a book of pages scattered by the hand of God. Gathered together again, the pictorial and lingual parts of a book, such as *Omne bonum*, introduce the reader to the face of God, or to the universe: All that is good is one.

(The Greek word *graphein* means alternatively "write" or "draw," two ideas in one gesture.)

Maybe it would be clearer if I could find a way to talk about *mappae mundi*, as Penn Szittya did. He showed an image of one of these documents in which the body of Christ apparently lies beneath the representation of the surface of the earth. Only the head, hands, and feet of God are visible. This is because these parts extend out from under into the margin surface of the map. All is God, Good.

Aside from helping to clarify the nature of the book as palimpsest, the *mappa mundi* is also indicative of a logic of space that Penn called attention to. The spatial positions of margin and center do not designate positions in a hierarchy of importance and authority. Since God dwells at the center of everything, the margins of the map, where God becomes visible, as the margins of an illuminated codex, where babewyns cavort, are not in fact marginal.

––––––

The images of the encyclopedia on the screen of the auditorium are pieces of a larger assembly organized by the alphabet rather than topically, as had been the case with other compendia of the epoch.

Meeting with one or another visual diagram—the beatific Sun face, or caskets opened at the Last Judgment—I imagine the scattering of leaves done by God at the creation to be the same task set for the book by the compiler, but in reverse. The minor official wants nothing to be lost of God's Idea. Ceaselessly plundering other books, harassing his sublime illuminators to rectify this detail or that, he gathers up the leaves of the universe and binds them each to each, like a wound.

To accomplish his task, the minor civil servant must multiply his time, or he must curtail his diligence to the king, in order to serve writing (drawing) to the full: *to graphein*. He has two secrets. During the day he serves the state; but at night, and in the intervals away from his office, he serves his own hunger, reading, annotating, compiling, and transcribing the totality of a cultural bequest. Not altogether transparent, he moonlights as a scholastic. The other secret is that the book he assembles from 115 sources is unique—there are no copies. Just as God made the universe once, and not a second time, *Omne bonum* exists in a single manifestation, in a single scriptorium. The clerk quells his graphorrhea by an *imitatio Dei* divulged only to himself. He writes a book with no thought of its replication and circulation.

Under such a circumstance, the scribe's labor is vulnerable to rumor and deceit, and false tales proliferate. Some declare that a copy of the book went to Jerusalem and dwells beneath the tomb of Solomon. Others hold that the clerk pioneered the logic of linguistic forms as the method of listing objects in metrical treatises. Who can decode these mysteries? I have my own version of the tale of the minor civil servant and his labor. The text goes astray. The landscape formed by inattention and faulty memory of the occasion on which Penn Szittya spoke replaces any desire for knowledge, and in my mind the *Omne bonum* flourishes in every entrepôt of the alphabet, the ruined city of the Phoenicians entrusted to the Ark of poetry.

In this city the scribe dwells with his sheep and toxic inks, formed from the blood of Saracens. Or in this city the scribe wears the smile of a heathen kneeling at the holy cradle. The sepulcher and the crèche are the same place in the city of the alphabet overrun by tropical plants. Or in this city the scribe follows the horses of the night in their slow-motion gallop, while the true scholastic, the real author of *Omne bonum*, begins to write down all good things that begin with the letter *E*. The constellations flicker like a candle blown out by a lover at the call of the beloved. Inside the city of candles, the body has no future, and the present no champion. The alphabet was and will be, outlasting the objects it calls by many names, in many tongues.

The tabulation of knowledge is not the goal of the author of the encyclopedia read by Penn Szittya in a London library. He glorifies God in his Book. His solitary vigil is the emblem of a poet's labor, not only because he writes by intertextual transposition, but because he writes a palimpsest, a medium of perpetual errantry and erasure. Lazarus replaces Jonah, the cave door replaces the whale's mouth. Indifferent to Rational taxonomy, the poet—the civil servant—is a collector of strange beasts, a junkyard man, a bricoleur (much more so than a *Philosophe*), and the document he assembles from heterogeneous sources is not the perfectible form of some other *Season in Hell*.

I like to imagine the insane compiler as a path the future did not choose to take, since I know very well what came to pass is that the grammarians of Alexandria and Byzantium returned to classify and to freeze the spontaneity of Greek verse, and the verse that learned from it.

In my tale, the author of the encyclopedia went into a separate future, where there was barely a grammar. But there was writing and drawing and terror, and there was a God of some sort to receive the palimpsest of the Good. The lintel space beneath which one enters a center for poetics and social practice might say the word *palimpsest*, looking toward the day of the rewriting of the tongues, the poetics of surfaces set end to end like the chain of stanzas in Villon. Inside the center for poetics sits the ruined statue of knowledge, holding Relation in one hand and Transit in the other. The sword that dangles above the statue has already fallen; the center glorifies making.

The encyclopedia man is there, in the future of the fallen sword. He believes in writing. He thinks that the land contains objects made by God but that it is not enough to be among these things. Some perish from sight; others dwell in remote Scythia, and exist as rumor. Others defy belief, and are relegated to the sphere of illusion. For these objects, then, the world provides no shelter. What protects them from vanishing—from their attenuated life as simulacra of God's mind—is the encyclopedia, because that which writing captures is the real. The world is a veil that writing uncovers to show the face of objects. He can do no more.

The plan of writing does not mirror the plan of the world. At first sight, writing produces anarchy, a lack of hierarchy. *Hostis, Hostarius, Hostia*: army, doorkeeper, host (for the Mass). Everything falls together like the sun collapsing into itself. *Incendarius*, a man sets fire to a house. *Dolor Dencium*, a man extracts a tooth using a gigantic pair of pliers. Here and there, pictures of devils with hairy bodies and horns, the wings of a bat. *Gutta Sciatica*: sciatic gout. These mysteries are contained in the face of God, or the sun, the palimpsest of all that is good.

When you think about it further, the encyclopedia man knows only two categories. The first category he calls God, the second category he calls perception, but he really means to say other books, or the Book. *Canis, Cignus, Draco, Griffes*: dog, swan, dragon, griffin (a hybrid animal). Blind in other ways, I think of a baffling nuance: quantum undecidability. The encyclopedia man cannot have known about this. If he thought that writing was the shadow of a cat both dead and alive, instead of being what it is, he would not have stolen the vellum—the thousand large folio sheets cut from the skin of three hundred sheep—to assemble the universe. He must believe that he writes that part of God's mind made legible to a Christian, which is to say, to a person, that he makes some part of the mind come into being.

––––––––

Common to all worlds is the manuscript, the vellum made from the skin of slaughtered sheep. Time is powerless over it. One irony of the world manuscript is that the writing borne by the vehicle of the page is the thing that dies. The page survives. Ephemerality invades the world and transience swallows it up. Somewhere in Avignon, a scribe copies the story of Noah for the millionth time. First he selects a codex from the jumble lying round about in disheveled piles. Those that do not burn well, he takes of their number and undoes the binding. A pumice stone rubs or scrapes the ink from the liberated pages. Presto! A clean surface for new content. The scribe labors to entrust Noah's story—for the millionth time—to the indestructible page. He feels that God has blessed his work. The diegesis holds him rapt. This is what we think. The artful letters that make it legible solicit his admiration and provide the mirror in which to glimpse the hand of the creator.

In this thought we are orthodox but mistaken. Of all men, the scribe knows that to carry out his task of love, he must destroy the love of another writer. The desire to write things down is cruel. Therefore, being filled with humility, he perceives the death of his own hand in the act of scraping the skin, in the act of setting out his inks, in the act of designing the beautiful rubrics, in the act of retelling for the millionth time that year the story of the flood. Another scribe will choose another tale perhaps and cover up the one he writes.

In the relentless downfall of writing repeated without terminus, only the vellum makes it to the future intact. The man in prison will use anything. He will write on toilet paper, on writing itself. The scribe has no technology to recover the treatise of Archimedes that he now covers over with the tale of the world's ending. In his mind, for he is one of those men modern before his time, Archimedes and Noah are equally the victims of writing, and equally the heroes of a pageant of futility. But the vellum, the secret pores of which he knows nothing, appears to him as the symbol of infinity: an *imperium sine fine*, the page that has neither end nor beginning. The vehicle that bears writing as a body bears the child, as heaven bears beautiful things, is the true content of the history of texts.

A murmur—Penn Szittya telling me that he once lived on an Apache reservation. These whispers move in and out of silence. Sometimes, hearing them, I believe that I have found the key to the origin of Cubism. The Cubist surface is an assembly of whispered beginnings. The past looks like that eventually: a flock of whispers temporarily illuminated by declining sunlight. Put forward as a hypothesis of *l'inconnu*, the Cubist surface, like anyone's past, participates in its mystery. It was never about the multiplicity of perspectives as an overthrow of the hegemony of the vanishing point. An object has been dismantled, but it is the face of God. Again and again the canvas repeats the palimpsest of the encyclopedia. A whisper of replaceable origins, each letter of the alphabet like the previous letter, a simultaneity of layers, text and ghostly subtext (Archimedes), the mask and the face, laid end to end.

One detail of the making of the encyclopedia that I remember four years later is that a thousand folio sheets of vellum requires the slaughter of 300 sheep. It takes a man quite a few hours to kill 300 sheep with fourteenth-century technology. I don't have all the facts, but I imagine that the sheep shed their proverbial docility and reacted badly to the attack. After the first dozen or so had been garroted, or stabbed, or piked, or beaten with an iron bar, or drowned, or what have you, the other 288 sheep probably began to run away. The desire to write things down forces an immediate decision: Is it worth it? To hunt down terrified sheep and put them to the axe. But that is all behind us now. The sheep have gone to the sheep-god in sheep-heaven, and the minor civil servant sits down and arranges his pens and inks, and beside his stool there rises up a tower of vellum folio pages, freshly cut. He picks up a pen and begins to write down the universe, or God's face, beginning with the initial object named by the letter *A*, the *ovum* and *fons*, the molecule from which the sequence draws its life. Nothing can be done except by way of the beginning, he says. Penn Szittya points to a paragraph on Albania—and I remember understanding that the civil servant had fallen into an abyss, a bottomless obsession that could always be fed, since the number of names is infinite. A few years later, some heretics tried to avoid this problem by asserting that God limits himself. But these men were mercifully slaughtered.

————

The fate of writing is that of unseen traces, lying on top of the page, underneath the previous eddy, beside the edifice dwells another language, below the surface a surface—this palimpsest of desire signals the gift of writing, a text written down to be written over, because the manuscript partakes of illusion.

————

Penn Szittya belongs inside the space of transit, what with his languages refusing to stay in one place, what with him being a scholar of a time with no national borders.

Penn Szittya stands beneath an image of a medieval encyclopedia, a sphere containing the sum of all random knowledge beaming like the sun, a palimpsest, Penn says, in which nothing is lost, no detail of earthly life too small to enclose by writing.

Penn Szittya is speaking Italian like a Florentine. I am certain that he is from the city of Dante and Michel Angelo. Talking with me and Dinaw Mengestu, he quotes from *Inferno*:

> Lo duca e io per quel cammino ascoso
> intrammo a ritornar nel chiaro mondo;
> e sanza cura aver d'alcun riposo,
>
> salimmo sù, el primo e io secondo,
> tanto ch'i' vidi de le cose belle
> che porta 'l ciel, per un pertugio tondo.
>
> E quindi uscimmo a riveder le stelle.

(34.133–39)

APPENDIX 1: THE HOLY FACE

Vision of Benedict and Paul. © The British Library Board. BL MS Royal E. VI, f.16.

APPENDIX 2: BABEWYNS

These images of babewyns were shown by Penn Szittya in his lecture on *Omne bonum.*

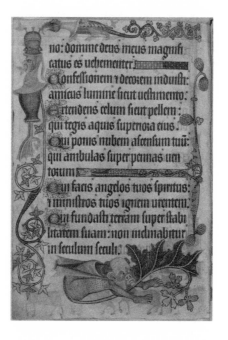

Luttrell Psalter, Psalm 103. Babewyns in the left and lower margins. © The British Library Board. BL MS Add. 42130, f.182v.

NOTES

INTRODUCTION / SEETA CHAGANTI

1. http://tiny.cc/lannan-about; Adrienne Rich, "Why I Refused the National Medal for the Arts," *Los Angeles Times*, 3 August 1997 (http://tiny.cc/MED-poetical [18 July 2011]).

2. http://tiny.cc/lannan-about.

3. See, for example, Michelle Bolduc, *The Medieval Poetics of Contraries* (Gainesville: University Press of Florida, 2006); Mark C. Amodio, *Writing the Oral Tradition: Oral Poetics and Literate Culture in Medieval England* (South Bend, Ind.: University of Notre Dame Press, 2005); Katherine O'Brien O'Keeffe, *Visible Song: Transitional Literacy in Old English Verse* (New York: Cambridge University Press, 2006); Sarah Stanbury, *Seeing the* Gawain-*Poet: Description and the Act of Perception* (Philadelphia: University of Pennsylvania Press, 1991); Peggy McCracken, "The Poetics of Sacrifice: Allegory and Myth in the Grail Quest," *Yale French Studies* 95 (1999): 152–68; Robert J. Meyer-Lee, *Poets and Power from Chaucer to Wyatt* (New York: Cambridge University Press, 2007); Emily Steiner, *Documentary Culture and the Making of Medieval English Literature* (New York: Cambridge University Press, 2003); and Logan E. Whalen, *Marie de France and the Poetics of Memory* (Washington, D.C.: Catholic University of America Press, 2008).

4. On this conception of formalist poetic reading, see Seth Lerer, "The Endurance of Formalism in Middle English Studies," *Literature Compass* 1 (2003): 10–11.

5. Glending Olson, "Making and Poetry in the Age of Chaucer," *Comparative Literature* 31.3 (1979): 277. Here Olson suggests that Deschamps' use of the name *Philomela* to designate the nightingale provides "a means of rendering one's work more 'poetical.'"

6. Deborah M. Sinnreich-Levy, "Deschamps' *L'Art de dictier*: Just What Kind of Poetics Is It?" in *The Rhetorical Poetics of the Middle Ages: Reconstructive Polyphony: Essays in Honor of Robert O. Payne*, ed. John M. Hill and Deborah M. Sinnreich-Levy (London: Associated University Presses, 2000), 36: "Deschamps espouses an expressive poetics that rises from whatever urges the poet must express or whatever subjects he must explain."

7. *Middle English Dictionary*, s.v. "poetical," http://tiny.cc/MED-poetical.

8. John Lydgate, *The Fall of Princes*, ed. H. Bergen, Early English Text Society, e.s. 123 (London: Oxford University Press, 1924; repr., 1967), 9.3325. Elsewhere in the poem as well, *processe* designates a narrative account (1.127, 3.2143, 9.716).

9. *Middle English Dictionary*, s.v. "profunde."

10. Related to this point are discussions of the quality of the literary itself as medieval audiences perceived it. A. S. G. Edwards and Derek Pearsall, for instance, maintain that the distinction between the literary and the nonliterary "was well understood in the Middle Ages"; see "The Manuscripts of the Major English Poetic Texts," in *Book Production and Publishing in Britain, 1375–1475*, ed. Jeremy Griffiths and Derek Pearsall (Cambridge: Cambridge University Press, 1989), 271, n. 1. Responding to this assessment, Seth Lerer argues that we must be mindful of both modern and medieval anthologizing and collecting practices in order accurately to perceive medieval literary culture's own "self-conscious articulation of its modes of making and its media of transmission." Lerer, "Medieval English Literature and the Idea of the Anthology," *PMLA* 118, no. 5 (2003): 1253.

11. Olson, "Making and Poetry," esp. 273–75. See also O. B. Hardison Jr., "Rhetoric, Poetics, and the Theory of Praise" (1962), repr. in *Landmark Essays on Rhetoric and Literature*, ed. Craig Kallendorf (Mahwah, NJ: Hermagoras Press, 1999), 79–99.

12. Judson Boyce Allen, *The Ethical Poetic of the Later Middle Ages: A Decorum of Convenient Distinction* (Buffalo: University of Toronto Press, 1982), 13, 289.

13. Paul Zumthor, *Toward a Medieval Poetics*, trans. Philip Bennett (Minneapolis: University of Minnesota Press, 1992), 13, 18.

14. Rita Copeland and Ineke Sluiter, eds., *Medieval Grammar and Rhetoric: Language Arts and Literary Theory*, AD 300–1475 (New York: Oxford University Press, 2009), 33, 40.

15. Roman Jakobson, "What Is Poetry?" in *Language in Literature*, ed. Krystyna Pomorska and Stephen Rudy (Cambridge, Mass.: Harvard University Press, 1987), 377–78.

16. Jakobson, "What Is Poetry?" 378.

17. Michel de Certeau, *The Practice of Everyday Life*, trans. Steven F. Rendall (Berkeley: University of California Press, 1984), xi. Within the context of his own reading of practices, de Certeau arrives at a related formulation about poetry and the world. Songs, he notes, "exist *alongside* the analysis of facts, as the equivalent of what a political ideology introduces *into* that analysis" (17).

18. Jakobson, "What Is Poetry?" 378.

19. John Oliver Hand and Martha Wolff, *Early Netherlandish Painting: The National Gallery of Art*, The Collections of the National Gallery of Art: Systemic Catalogue (New York: Cambridge University Press, 1986), 76.

20. Extensive conservation treatment after 1993 revealed that much of the Annunciation's "subtlety" was preserved in its transfer from panel support to canvas. See E. Melanie Gifford, "Van Eyck's Washington Annunciation: Technical Evidence for Iconographic Development," *Art Bulletin* 81, no. 1 (1999): 115, n. 1. This is the case despite the fact that the nineteenth-century technique of transfer to canvas has long been considered problematic and even "dangerous." Ulrich Schiessl, "History of Structural

Panel Painting Conservation in Austria, Germany, and Switzerland," in *The Structural Conservation of Panel Paintings: Proceedings of a Symposium at the J. Paul Getty Museum, 24–28 April 1995,* ed. Kathleen Dardes and Andrea Rothe (Los Angeles: Getty Conservation Institute, 1998), 220.

VISUAL TRANSLATION IN FIFTEENTH-CENTURY ENGLISH MANUSCRIPTS / RICHARD K. EMMERSON

1. For linguistic translation and the literary canon, see especially *The Oxford History of Literary Translation in English,* vol. 1, *To 1550,* ed. Roger Ellis (Oxford: Oxford University Press, 2008); and *The Idea of the Vernacular: An Anthology of Middle English Literary Theory, 1280–1520,* ed. Jocelyn Wogan-Browne, Nicholas Watson, Andrew Taylor, and Ruth Evans (University Park: Pennsylvania State University Press, 1999).

2. David Freedberg, *The Power of Images: Studies in the History and Theory of Response* (Chicago: University of Chicago Press, 1989), 206.

3. For Chaucer's "transformative adaptation," see Barry Windeatt, "Geoffrey Chaucer," *Oxford History of Literary Translation,* ed. Ellis, 137–48, esp. 145–46.

4. Alex Potts, "Sign," in *Critical Terms for Art History,* ed. Robert S. Nelson and Richard Shiff, 2nd ed. (Chicago: University of Chicago Press, 2003), 20–34 (at 21).

5. Roger Chartier, *The Order of Books: Readers, Authors, and Libraries in Europe between the Fourteenth and Eighteenth Centuries,* trans. Lydia G. Cochrane (Stanford: Stanford University Press, 1994), 3.

6. See Tim William Machan, "Manuscript Culture," in *Oxford History of Literary Translation,* ed. Ellis, 29–44 (at 43).

7. See Kathleen L. Scott, "Design, Decoration, and Illustration," in *Book Production and Publishing in Britain, 1375–1475,* ed. Jeremy Griffiths and Derek Pearsall (Cambridge: Cambridge University Press, 1989), 31–64; and Hélène Toubert, "La mise en page de l'illustration," in *Mise en page et mise en texte du livre manuscrit,* ed. Henri-Jean Martin and Jean Vezin (Paris: Éditions du Cercle de la Librairie-Promodis, 1990), 353–420.

8. Stephen G. Nichols, "Introduction: Philology in a Manuscript Culture," *Speculum* 65 (1990): 1–10 (at 8).

9. Ardis Butterfield, "*Mise-en-page* in the *Troilus* Manuscripts: Chaucer and French Manuscript Culture," *Huntington Library Quarterly* 58 (1996): 49–80 (at 49).

10. Richard K. Emmerson, "Middle English Literature and Illustrated Manuscripts: New Approaches to the Disciplinary and the Interdisciplinary," *JEGP* 105 (Jan. 2006): 118–36 (at 136), drawing on W. J. T. Mitchell, "The Pictorial Turn," in *Picture Theory: Essays on Verbal and Visual Representation* (Chicago: University of Chicago Press, 1994), 11–33.

11. Roger Ellis, "The Translator," in *Oxford History of Literary Translation,* ed. Ellis, 108.

12. Thelma S. Fenster and Jocelyn Wogan-Browne, trans., *The History of Saint Edward the King* (Tempe: Arizona Center for Medieval and Renaissance Studies, 2008), 28. For the role of the miniatures, see also Deirdre Ann Carter, "History and Hagiography in Mathew Paris's Illustrated Life of Edward the Confessor" (master's thesis, Florida State University, 2009).

13. See especially Mary Carruthers, *The Craft of Thought: Meditation, Rhetoric, and the Making of Images, 400–1200* (New York: Cambridge University Press, 1998).

14. See Lawrence G. Duggan, "Was Art Really the 'Book of the Illiterate'?" *Word and Image* 5 (1989): 227–51.

15. Jeffrey F. Hamburger, "Rewriting History: The Visual and the Vernacular in Late Medieval History Bibles," *Zeitschrift für deutsche Philologie* 124 (2005): 260–308 (at 270).

16. A. S. G. Edwards and Derek Pearsall, "The Manuscripts of the Major English Poetic Texts," in *Book Production and Publishing in Britain,* ed. Griffiths and Pearsall, 257–78.

17. The two volumes are in the multivolume work *A Survey of Manuscripts Illuminated in the British Isles*, ed. Jonathan J. G. Alexander: Lucy Freeman Sandler, *Gothic Manuscripts 1285–1385,* 2 vols. (London: Harvey Miller, 1986); and Kathleen L. Scott, *Later Gothic Manuscripts 1390–1490,* 2 vols. (London: Harvey Miller, 1996). Scott's catalog will be cited as "Scott cat." by entry number, or by volume and page number, or by illustration number.

18. British Library, Royal 20.D.IV; see Sandler, *Gothic Manuscripts,* cat. 136. For early manuscripts linking images to Middle English texts, see Richard K. Emmerson, "Visualizing the Vernacular: Middle English in Early Fourteenth-Century Bilingual and Trilingual Manuscript Illustrations," in *Studies in Manuscript Illumination: A Tribute to Lucy Freeman Sandler,* ed. Carol Krinsky and Kathryn A. Smith (London: Harvey Miller, 2008), 187–204.

19. Scott examined more than nine hundred fifteenth-century illustrated manuscripts. More-comprehensive lists will be included in a new series edited by Scott, *An Index of Images in English Manuscripts: From the Time of Chaucer to Henry VIII, c. 1380–c. 1509.*

20. See, for example, J. J. G. Alexander, "Foreign Illuminators and Illuminated Manuscripts," in *The Cambridge History of the Book in Britain,* vol. 3, *1400–1557,* ed. Lotte Hellinga and J. B. Trapp (Cambridge: Cambridge University Press, 1999), 47–64. As Julian M. Luxford notes, late-medieval English book illustration is "an opportunity-rich but neglected field." See Luxford, review of *Tradition and Innovation in Later Medieval English Manuscripts*, by Kathleen L. Scott, *Speculum* 86 (2011): 804.

21. For comparison with English royal patronage, see J. J. G. Alexander, "Painting and Manuscript Illumination for Royal Patrons in the Later Middle Ages," in *English Court Culture in the Later Middle Ages,* ed. V. J. Scattergood and J. W. Sherborne

(London: Duckworth, 1983), 141–62. For French manuscripts see Claire Richter Sherman, *Imaging Aristotle: Verbal and Visual Representation in Fourteenth-Century France* (Berkeley: University of California Press, 1995); and *Imagining the Past in France: History in Manuscript Painting, 1250–1500*, ed. Elizabeth Morrison and Anne D. Hedeman (Los Angeles: Getty Publications, 2010), with excellent bibliography.

22. National Library of Scotland, Adv. 19.2.1 (London, ca. 1330). Unfortunately, most of its images are lost. See *The Auchinleck Manuscript*, introduction by Derek Pearsall and I. C. Cunningham (London: Scolar, 1977).

23. See Scott cat. 1; Otto Pächt and J. J. G. Alexander, *Illuminated Manuscripts in the Bodleian Library Oxford*, vol. 3 (Oxford: Clarendon, 1973), no. 676; *The Vernon Manuscript: A Facsimile of Bodleian Library, Oxford, MS. Eng. Poet. A.1.*, ed. Ian Doyle (Cambridge: D. S. Brewer, 1987); and Maide Hilmo, *Medieval Images, Icons, and Illustrated English Literary Texts: From the Ruthwell Cross to the Ellesmere Chaucer* (Aldershot: Ashgate, 2004), 125–36. One native Middle English text, the *Prick of Conscience*, is illustrated by a historiated initial (fol. 265r).

24. See Scott cat. 13, vol. 1, illus. 61–62; Pächt and Alexander, *Illuminated Manuscripts in the Bodleian*, vol. 3, no. 793; and Frank Grady, "Contextualizing *Alexander and Dindimus*," *Yearbook of Langland Studies* 18 (2004): 81–106. First copied in Flanders around 1340, the manuscript was brought to England around 1375 and probably owned by Thomas of Woodstock. The Middle English text was added 1400–10.

25. See Scott cat. 12; and A. S. G. Edwards, "The Manuscript: British Library MS Cotton Nero A.x.," in *Companion to the "Gawain"-Poet*, ed. Derek S. Brewer and Jonathan Gibson (Cambridge: D. S. Brewer, 1997), 197–220, which reproduces the images and makes a strong case for their later addition.

26. Paul F. Reichardt, "'Several Illuminations, Coarsely Executed': The Illustrations of the *Pearl* Manuscript," *Studies in Iconography* 18 (1997): 119–42. Scott defends "several positive aspects of the drawings" (Scott cat., vol. 2, p. 67).

27. John M. Bowers, *The Politics of "Pearl": Court Poetry in the Age of Richard II* (Cambridge: D. S. Brewer, 2001), 191. In Hilmo's view, the plain style of the images responds to Lollard iconophobia; see *Medieval Images*, 145–47.

28. Edwards, "Manuscript," in *Companion to the Gawain Poet*, 219.

29. See Jennifer Lee, "The Illuminating Critic: The Illuminator of Cotton Nero A.x.," *Studies in Iconography* 3 (1977): 17–46. I agree with Hilmo that the images both unify the manuscript and shape its reception; however, her ingenious argument that they depict a spiritual quest culminating in Gawain's return to Arthur's court—allegorized as the heavenly Jerusalem (*Medieval Images*, 159)—is unpersuasive.

30. San Marino, Huntington Library, EL 26 C 9 (ca. 1405). See Scott cat. 42; and Derek Pearsall, "The Ellesmere Chaucer and Contemporary English Literary Manuscripts," in *The Ellesmere Chaucer: Essays in Interpretation*, ed. Martin Stevens and Daniel Woodward (San Marino, Calif.: Huntington Library, 1995), 263–80.

31. Representative is Martin Stevens, "The Ellesmere Miniatures as Illustrations of Chaucer's *Canterbury Tales*," *Studies in Iconography* 7–8 (1981–82): 113–34. See also Derek Pearsall, "Beyond Fidelity: The Illustration of Late Medieval English Literary Texts," in *Tributes to Kathleen L. Scott: English Medieval Manuscripts: Readers, Makers, and Illuminators,* ed. Marlene Villalobos Hennessy (London: Harvey Miller, 2009), 197–220, esp. 199–202; and Hilmo, *Medieval Images,* 168–95.

32. For later depictions see Betsy Bowden, "Visual Portraits of the Canterbury Pilgrims: 1484(?)–1809," in *The Ellesmere Chaucer,* ed. Stevens and Woodward, 171–204.

33. Richard K. Emmerson, "Text and Image in the Portraits of the Ellesmere Taletellers," in *The Ellesmere Chaucer,* ed. Stevens and Woodward, 143–70. Hilmo curiously implies that the choice was between depicting the pilgrims or "portraying potentially idolatrous images in illustration of the tales" (*Medieval Images,* 160).

34. V. A. Kolve, *Chaucer and the Imagery of Narrative: The First Five Canterbury Tales* (Stanford, Calif.: Stanford University Press, 1984).

35. Ibid., 2.

36. Ibid., 8.

37. Ibid., 67.

38. Jonathan J. G. Alexander, "Art History, Literary History, and the Study of Medieval Illuminated Manuscripts," *Studies in Iconography* 18 (1997): 51–66 (at 54).

39. V. A. Kolve, *Telling Images: Chaucer and the Imagery of Narrative* (Stanford, Calif.: Stanford University Press, 2009).

40. Richard K. Emmerson, review of *Telling Images,* by V. A. Kolve, *Studies in the Age of Chaucer* 32 (2010): 441–45 (at 443).

41. See Derek Pearsall, "The Manuscripts and Illustrations of Gower's Works," in *A Companion to Gower,* ed. Siân Echard (Cambridge: D. S. Brewer, 2004), 73–97.

42. See Joel Fredell, "Reading the Dream Miniature in the *Confessio Amantis,*" *Medievalia et Humanistica* n.s. 22 (1995): 61–94; and Thomas J. Garbáty, "A Description of the Confession Miniatures for Gower's *Confessio Amantis* with Special Reference to the Illustrator's Role as Reader and Critic," *Mediaevalia* 19 (1996): 319–43. Two manuscripts also include portraits of Gower; see Jeremy Griffiths, "*Confessio Amantis*: The Poem and Its Pictures," in *Gower's "Confessio Amantis": Responses and Reassessments,* ed. Alastair J. Minnis (Cambridge: D. S. Brewer, 1983), 163–78.

43. See Peter C. Braeger, "The Illustrations in New College MS. 266 for Gower's Conversion Tales," in *Gower: Recent Readings,* ed. Robert F. Yeager (Kalamazoo, Mich.: Medieval Institute Publications, 1989), 275–310. For Morgan M.126, see Scott cat. 120, vol. 1, illus. 442–44; Patricia Eberle, "Miniatures as Evidence of Reading in a Manuscript of the *Confessio Amantis* (Pierpont Morgan MS M.126)," in *Gower: Recent Readings,* ed. Yeager, 311–64; and Martha Driver, "Printing the *Confessio Amantis*: Caxton's Edition in Context," in *Re-visioning Gower: New Essays,* ed. R. F. Yeager (Asheville, N.C.: Pegasus Press, 1998), 269–303.

44. Richard K. Emmerson, "Reading Gower in a Manuscript Culture: Latin and English in Illustrated Manuscripts of the *Confessio Amantis*," *Studies in the Age of Chaucer* 21 (1999): 143–86.

45. In addition to *Troy Book* and *Fall of Princes*, Lydgate's *Lives of Saints Edmund and Fremund*, *Siege of Thebes*, and *Pilgrimage of the Life of Man* were illustrated; see Scott cat. 78, 89, 111, 112.

46. Although concerned with French and German literature, an excellent study of this function is by Ursula Peters, *Das Ich im Bild: Die Figur des Autors in volkssprachingen Bilderhandschriften des 13. bis 16. Jahrhunderts,* Pictura et Poesis 22 (Cologne: Böhlau Verlag, 2008), esp. "Illustrationsmodus und 'Autorfunktion,' " 23–37.

47. See Lesley Lawton, "The Illustration of Late Medieval Secular Texts, with Special Reference to Lydgate's *Troy Book*," in *Manuscripts and Readers in Fifteenth-Century England: The Literary Implications of Manuscript Study*, ed. Derek Pearsall (Cambridge: D. S. Brewer, 1983), 41–69.

48. For example, Manchester, Rylands University Library, MS Eng. 1 (late 1440s) includes sixty-four marginal paintings in addition to miniatures delineating the poem's structure; see Scott cat. 93.

49. Scott cat. 110, vol. 1, illus. 412–15 (1450s). The poem is also richly illustrated in Huntington Library, HM 268 (1440–50); see Scott cat. 79A, vol. 1, color pl. 11, illus. 305–09.

50. Anne D. Hedeman, *Translating the Past: Laurent de Premierfait and Boccaccio's "De Casibus"* (Los Angeles: Getty Publications, 2008).

51. See Scott cat. 119; Victoria Kirkham, "Decoration and Iconography of Lydgate's *Fall of Princes (De casibus virorum illustrium)* at the Philadelphia Rosenbach," *Studi sul Boccaccio* 25 (1997): 297–310; and James R. Tanis, ed., *Leaves of Gold: Manuscript Illumination from Philadelphia Collections* (Philadelphia: Philadelphia Museum of Art, 2001), 208–10, no. 72. These images tend to undermine Lydgate's theory of translation as discussed by Nicholas Watson, "Theories of Translation," in *Oxford History of Literary Translation*, ed. Ellis, 73–91, esp. 84.

52. See Pächt and Alexander, vol. 3, no. 886; and Kathleen Scott, "The Illustrations of *Piers Plowman* in Bodleian Library MS Douce 104," *Yearbook of Langland Studies* 4 (1990): 2–86. The uniqueness of its images is quite evident when it is compared to two near-contemporary illustrated manuscripts of John Mandeville's *Travels*, both in the British Library: Royal 17.C.xxxviii and Harley 3954. See Scott cat. 70A and 70B.

53. See Richard K. Emmerson, "Beyond the Apocalypse: The Human Antichrist in Late Medieval Illustrated Manuscripts," in *Waiting in Fearful Hope: Approaching a New Millennium*, ed. Christopher Kleinhenz and Fannie LeMoine (Madison: University of Wisconsin Press, 1999), 86–114, esp. 96–99, fig. 5.6. On the mnemonic features of the drawings, see Mary Carruthers, *The Book of Memory: A Study of Memory in Medieval Culture* (Cambridge: Cambridge University Press, 1990), 228–29. For their

linking of textual passages, see Phillipa Hardman, "The Mobile Page: 'Special Effects' in Some Late Medieval Manuscripts," in *Tributes to Kathleen L. Scott*, ed. Hennessy, 101–13.

54. Denise L. Despres and Kathryn Kerby-Fulton, *Iconography and the Professional Reader: The Politics of Book Production in the Douce "Piers Plowman"* (Minneapolis: University of Minnesota Press, 1999).

55. Ralph Hanna III, *"Piers Plowman* and the Radically Chic," *Yearbook of Langland Studies* 13 (1999): 179–92 (at 179).

56. Of course, effective reception history requires recognizing "the competence or intelligence or receptivity of the receiver," as Pearsall notes ("Beyond Fidelity," 198). Two successful examples are by Kathryn A. Smith, *Art, Identity and Devotion in Fourteenth-Century England: Three Women and their Books of Hours* (London: British Library, 2003); and by Marilynn Desmond and Pamela Sheingorn, *Myth, Montage, and Visuality in Late Medieval Manuscript Culture: Christine de Pizan's Epistre Othéa* (Ann Arbor: University of Michigan Press, 2003).

57. Kathryn Kerby-Fulton with Denise Despres, "Fabricating Failure: The Professional Reader as Textual Terrorist," *Yearbook of Langland Studies* 13 (1999): 193–206 (at 205).

58. For the *Troilus* frontispiece, see Scott cat. 58; *Gothic: Art for England, 1400–1547*, ed. Richard Marks and Paul Williamson (London: V&A Publications, 2003), no. 171; and Derek Pearsall, "The *Troilus* Frontispiece and Chaucer's Audience," *Yearbook of English Studies* 7 (1977): 68–74. For Cambridge University Library, MS Gg.4.27 (ca. 1420), see Scott cat. 43; Geoffrey Chaucer, *Poetical Works: A Facsimile of Cambridge University Library Gg.4.27*, ed. M. B. Parkes and Richard Beadle, 3 vols. (Cambridge: D. S. Brewer, 1979–80); and Kolve, *Chaucer and the Imagery of Narrative*, 264–67.

59. Pearsall, "Beyond Fidelity," 202.

60. Barbara Nolan, *The Gothic Visionary Perspective* (Princeton: Princeton University Press, 1977), xiii.

61. Freedberg, *Power of Images*.

62. Hilary Maddocks, "Seeing Is Believing: Reading the Deadly Sins in Deguileville's Pilgrimage of the Lyfe of the Manhode in the State Library of Victoria," in *Imagination, Books, and Community in Medieval Europe*, ed. Gregory Kratzmann (South Yarra, Australia: Macmillan Art Publishers, 2010), 205–11 (at 208).

63. See Jessica Brantley, *Reading in the Wilderness: Private Devotion and Public Performance in Late Medieval England* (Chicago: University of Chicago Press, 2007).

64. Pearsall, "Beyond Fidelity," 197.

65. On ways in which medieval translators understood their work, see Watson, "Theories of Translation," in *Oxford History of Literary Translation*, ed. Ellis, 73–91; and J. D. Burnley, "Late Medieval English Translation: Types and Reflections," in *The*

Medieval Translator: The Theory and Practice of Translation in the Middle Ages, ed. Roger Ellis (Woodbridge, Suffolk: D. S. Brewer, 1989), 37–53.

66. Helen Phillips, "Nation, Region, Class, and Gender," *Oxford History of Literary Translation,* ed. Ellis, 45–69 (at 61). Phillips does not comment on illustrated manuscripts of Scrope's translation. For these see Scott cat. 94 and 105; and Marilynn Desmond, "Reading and Visuality in Stephen Scrope's *Translatio* of Christine de Pizan's *Othéa,*" in *Thresholds of Medieval Visual Culture: Liminal Spaces,* ed. Elina Gertsman and Jill Stevenson (Woodbridge, Suffolk: Boydell and Brewer, 2012).

67. British Library, Cotton Tiberius A.vii, Scott cat. 89; see Michael Camille, "The Iconoclast's Desire: Deguileville's Idolatry in France and England," in *Images, Idolatry, and Iconoclasm in Late Medieval England: Textuality and the Visual Image,* ed. Jeremy Dimmick, James Simpson, and Nicolette Zeeman (Oxford: Oxford University Press, 2002), 151–71, esp. 161–68.

68. David Summers, "Representation," in *Critical Terms for Art History,* 2nd ed., ed. Nelson and Shiff, 14.

69. Rudolf Arnheim, *Visual Thinking* (Berkeley: University of California Press, 1969), 246. As Michael Baxandall notes in *Patterns of Intention: On the Historical Explanation of Pictures* (New Haven, Conn: Yale University Press, 1985), a verbal description of a picture "is a representation of thinking about a picture more than a representation of a picture" (5).

70. The fundamental distinction between visual art as based in space and literary art as based in time was classically argued by Lessing in *Laocoon: An Essay upon the Limits of Painting and Poetry,* trans. Ellen Frothingham (1766; New York: Farrar, Straus, and Giroux, 1965). On the problematic correspondence of visual and verbal, see also Mitchell, *Picture Theory,* 151–81; and James Elkins, *On Pictures and the Words That Fail Them* (Cambridge: Cambridge University Press, 1998).

71. See Mary J. Carruthers, "*Ars oblivionalis, ars inveniendi*: The Cherub Figure and the Arts of Memory," *Gesta* 48 (2009): 99–117.

72. Norman Bryson, *Word and Image: French Painting of the Ancien Regime* (Cambridge: Cambridge University Press, 1981), 6.

73. On the distinction between content and subject see Meyer Schapiro, "On Perfection, Coherence, and Unity of Form and Content" (1966), in *Theory and Philosophy of Art: Style, Artist, and Society* (New York: George Braziller, 1994), 33–49, esp. 41–43.

74. This necessity characterizes not only literary critical but also art-historical scholarship. As Donald Preziosi notes in *Rethinking Art History: Meditations on a Coy Science* (New Haven: Yale University Press, 1989), "the discipline has maintained its focus upon the 'what' of signification to the near exclusion of the 'how'" (49).

75. Michael Camille, *Mirror in Parchment: The Luttrell Psalter and the Making of Medieval England* (Chicago: University of Chicago Press, 1998), 46. For the manuscript

as mirror of medieval life, see Michelle P. Brown, *The World of the Luttrell Psalter* (London: British Library, 2006).

76. As Potts comments, "There is a long tradition of cultural common sense that considers the visual image to be somehow more natural, offering up a replica of reality rather than a conventionally coded representation of it as in language" ("Sign," 24).

77. Ernst Robert Curtius, *European Literature and the Latin Middle Ages,* trans. Willard R. Trask (Princeton: Princeton University Press, 1963), 15; the original German edition was published in 1948.

78. On the conventionality of clothing in late-medieval images, see the introduction to *Illuminating Fashion: Dress in the Art of Medieval France and the Netherlands, 1325–1515,* by Anne H. van Buren and Roger S. Wieck (New York: Morgan Library and Museum, 2011), esp. "The Nature of the Images," 17–27.

79. W. J. T. Mitchell, *Iconology: Image, Text, Ideology* (Chicago: University of Chicago Press, 1987), 38. Jan-Dirk Müller makes a similar point, arguing that "visuality does not mean self-evidence." See "Writing–Speech–Image: The Competition of Signs," in *Visual Culture and the German Middle Ages,* ed. Kathryn Starkey and Horst Wenzel (New York: Palgrave Macmillan, 2005), 38.

80. On this problem see John V. Fleming, "Obscure Images by Illustrious Hands," in *Text and Image,* ed. David W. Burchmore, *Acta* 10 (1986 for 1983): 1.

81. Jeffrey F. Hamburger, "The Place of Theology in Medieval Art History: Problems, Positions, Possibilities," in *The Mind's Eye: Art and Theological Argument in the Middle Ages,* ed. Jeffrey F. Hamburger and Anne-Marie Bouché (Princeton: Princeton University Press, 2006), 11–31 (at 22).

82. Mary Clemente Davlin, *The Place of God in "Piers Plowman" and Medieval Art* (Aldershot: Ashgate, 2001).

83. Elizabeth Sears, "'Reading' Images," in *Reading Medieval Images: The Art Historian and the Object,* ed. Elizabeth Sears and Thelma K. Thomas (Ann Arbor: University of Michigan Press, 2002), 1–7 (at 2).

84. See especially Mitchell's *Picture Theory* and *Iconology.* For medieval issues, see Michael Camille, "Seeing and Reading: Some Visual Consequences of Medieval Literacy and Illiteracy," *Art History* 8 (1985): 26–49; Sandra Hindman, *Sealed in Parchment: Rereadings of Knighthood in the Illuminated Manuscripts of Chrétien de Troyes* (Chicago: University of Chicago Press, 1994); and Norbert H. Ott, "Word and Image as a Field of Research: Sound Methodologies or Just a Fashionable Trend? A Polemic from a European Perspective," in *Visual Culture and the German Middle Ages,* ed. Starkey and Wenzel, 15–32.

85. See Norman Bryson and Mieke Bal, "Semiotics and Art History," *Art Bulletin* 73 (1991): 174–208; and François Garnier, *Le langage de l'image au moyen âge: Signification et symbolique,* 2 vols. (Paris: Le Léopard d'Or, 1982, 1989). For important earlier

studies, see Meyer Schapiro, *Words and Pictures: On the Literal and Symbolic in the Illustration of a Text* (Paris: Mouton, 1973); and Schapiro's essays gathered in *Words, Script, and Pictures: Semiotics of Visual Language* (New York: Braziller, 1996).

86. Mieke Bal, *Reading Rembrandt: Beyond the Word–Image Opposition* (Cambridge: Cambridge University Press, 1991). For application to a medieval play manuscript, see Richard K. Emmerson, "Visualizing Performance: The Miniatures of Besançon MS 579 (*Jour du Jugement*)," *Exemplaria* 11 (1999): 245–72.

87. Paris, Bibliothèque nationale de France, fr. 12420; see Brigitte Buettner, *Boccaccio's "Des cleres et nobles femmes": Systems of Signification in an Illuminated Manuscript* (Seattle: University of Washington Press, 1996).

88. Anne D. Hedeman, "Presenting the Past: Visual Translation in Thirteenth- to Fifteenth-Century France," in *Imagining the Past in France*, ed. Morrison and Hedeman, 69–85 (at 78).

89. Mary C. Olson, *Fair and Varied Forms: Visual Textuality in Medieval Illuminated Manuscripts* (New York: Routledge, 2003), 180.

90. Nelson Goodman, *Languages of Art: An Approach to a Theory of Symbols* (Indianapolis: Hackett, 1976): "No amount of familiarity turns a paragraph into a picture; and no degree of novelty makes a picture a paragraph" (231).

91. Its first book is edited by Rosemarie Potz McGerr, *The Pilgrimage of the Soul: A Critical Edition of the Middle English Dream Vision* (New York: Garland, 1990). On authorship see xxvi–xxix.

92. Ibid., xlvii. See also Leslie Lawton, "Text and Image in Late Medieval English Vernacular Manuscripts," 4 vols. (Ph.D. diss., Univ. of York, 1982), 1:114–32. On its influence, see Rosemarie Potz McGerr, "Pageants, Scaffolds, and Judgment Scenes: The *Pilgrimage of the Soul* and the Iconography of Medieval Religious Drama," *Yearbook of Comparative and General Literature* 45–46 (1997–98): 3–35.

93. London, Lambeth Palace Library, MS 326 (ca. 1426); see Richard K. Emmerson, "Translating Images: The Decorated Page in French, English, and Latin Versions of Guillaume de Deguileville's *Trois Pèlerinages*," in *Poetry, Place, and Gender: Studies in Medieval Culture in Honor of Helen Damico*, ed. Catherine E. Karkov (Kalamazoo, Mich.: Medieval Institute Publications, 2009), 275–301, esp. 295–97. The popularity of Guillaume's three pilgrimage poems in the fifteenth century is suggested by the fact that a sequence of 202 marginal roundels based on the poems but unaccompanied by the poetic texts are painted in the margins of the Hours of Isabella Stuart (Cambridge, Fitzwilliam Museum, MS 62); see Richard K. Emmerson, "A 'Large Order of the Whole': Intertextuality and Interpictoriality in the *Hours of Isabella Stuart*," *Studies in Iconography* 28 (2007): 53–110.

94. Rosemarie Potz McGerr, "Editing the Self-Conscious Medieval Translator: Some Issues and Examples," *Text* 4 (1988): 147–61 (at 153). The compilers of the Carthusian

Miscellany (British Library, Add. 37049), which anthologizes some of the lyrics of the *Pilgrimage*, were probably attracted by the translation's orthodoxy; see Brantley, *Reading in the Wilderness*, 240–59. It is unfortunate that this important translation is not discussed in *The Oxford History of Literary Translation*.

95. See Lucy Freeman Sandler's entry in *The Splendor of the Word: Medieval and Renaissance Manuscripts at the New York Public Library*, ed. Jonathan J. G. Alexander, James H. Marrow, and Lucy Freeman Sandler (London: Harvey Miller, 2005), no. 94; and Scott cat. 74. For its provenance, see Victor Hugo Paltsits, "The Petworth Manuscript of 'Grace Dieu' or 'The Pilgrimage of the Soul,'" *Bulletin of The New York Public Library* 32 (1928): 715–20. The miniatures are available in color through the New York Public Library Digital Gallery (http://tiny.cc/nypl-digital-gallery), although the online images do not do justice to the bright colors and sheer brilliance of the original miniatures.

96. For descriptive terminology see Kathleen L. Scott, "Limning and Book-Producing Terms and Signs *in situ* in Late-Medieval English Manuscripts: A First Listing," in *New Science Out of Old Books: Studies in Manuscripts and Early Printed Books in Honour of A. I. Doyle,* ed. Richard Beadle and A. J. Piper (Aldershot: Scolar Press, 1995), 142–88.

97. Armando Petrucci, "Reading in the Middle Ages," in *Writers and Readers in Medieval Italy: Studies in the History of Written Culture,* ed. and trans. Charles M. Radding (New Haven: Yale University Press, 1995), 132–44 (at 138).

98. McGerr shows that the "archetypal program" included at least thirty and perhaps thirty-seven scenes; see *Pilgrimage of the Soul,* xlv–l. Sandler (*Splendor of the Word,* 404) lists only twenty-five miniatures for Spencer 19, failing to note the last (fol. 111r).

99. The presence of this figure has not been noticed by earlier scholarship.

100. See Scott cat. 1:217; Sandler, *Splendor of the Word,* 404; and the image details provided by the New York Public Library Digital Gallery.

101. Death with its dart is a medieval commonplace best known from *Everyman.* Two illustrated *Soul* manuscripts depict Death in their introductory images (see McGerr, *Pilgrimage of the Soul,* 127).

102. Scott cat. 1:217. Sandler is more accurate: "The pilgrim's soul led 'to judgment' by his guardian angel, a devil alongside" (*Splendor of the Word,* 404).

103. Pearsall, "Beyond Fidelity," 203. To make his point, Pearsall contrasts images in Chaucer manuscripts to Sir William Russell Flint's early-twentieth-century watercolors (203–5). The comparison is inapt, however, because Flint paints narrative scenes from the *Canterbury Tales.*

BARN OF UNITY OR THE DEVIL'S CHURCH? SALVATION
AND ECCLESIOLOGY IN LANGLAND AND THE WYCLIFFITES /
J. PATRICK HORNBECK II

I am grateful for assistance in the writing of this essay to Penn Szittya and Julia Lamm, who both reviewed a very early draft (in the form of my 2003 undergraduate honors thesis), and to Helen Cooper and the other members of the Cambridge University Medieval Reading Group, where I presented a version of this argument.

1. Avery Dulles, *Models of the Church* (Garden City, N.Y.: Image Books, 1974; expanded ed., New York: Image Books, 2002).

2. Dulles, 2002, 98–102.

3. See, for instance, Pamela Gradon, "Langland and the Ideology of Dissent," *Proceedings of the British Academy* 66 (1980): 179–205; Christina von Nolcken, "Piers Plowman, the Wycliffites, and Pierce the Plowman's Creed," *Yearbook of Langland Studies* 2 (1988): 71–102; and David Lawton, "Lollardy and the *Piers Plowman* Tradition," *Modern Language Review* 76 (1981): 780–93, where he famously argued that "the Lollards had Langlandian sympathies" (793).

4. John Bale, *Illustrium Maioris Brittaniae Scriptorum . . . Summarium* (Ipswich: Overton, 1548), 474–75; *Scriptorium Illustrium Maioris Brytannie Catalogus* (1557–59; repr., Farnsworth: Gregg International, 1971), 450–56.

5. On the appropriation of Langland's poem for polemical purposes under the Tudors, see Seymour Baker House, "Literature, Drama, and Politics," in *The Reign of Henry VIII: Politics, Policy, and Piety*, ed. Diarmaid MacCulloch (New York: St. Martin's Press, 1995), 181–201.

6. In addition to the works cited at n. 3 above, see Anne Middleton, "The Audience and Public of *Piers Plowman*," in *Middle English Alliterative Poetry and Its Literary Background*, ed. David Lawton (Cambridge: D. S. Brewer, 1982), 101–23.

7. This has been the trajectory of much recent work on Wyclif and Lollardy: In addition to my book *What Is a Lollard? Dissent and Belief in Late Medieval England* (Oxford: Oxford University Press, 2010), see, among many others, Ian Christopher Levy, "Grace and Freedom in the Soteriology of John Wyclif," *Traditio* 60 (2005): 279–337; "John Wyclif and the Primitive Papacy," *Viator* 38 (2007): 159–89; Jill C. Havens, "Shading the Grey Area: Determining Heresy in Middle English Texts," in *Text and Controversy from Wyclif to Bale: Essays in Honour of Anne Hudson*, ed. Helen Barr and Ann M. Hutchinson (Turnhout: Brepols, 2005), 337–52; and Jeremy Catto, "Fellows and Helpers: The Religious Identity of the Followers of Wyclif," in *The Medieval Church: Universities, Heresy, and the Religious Life: Essays in Honour of Gordon Leff*, Studies in Church History, Subsidia 11 (Woodbridge: Boydell, 1999), 141–61.

8. This and the following paragraph are borrowed from a longer discussion of the history of the doctrine of salvation in my *What Is a Lollard?* 27–31. For further detail,

see Alister McGrath, *Iustitia Dei: A History of the Christian Doctrine of Justification*, 3rd ed. (Cambridge: Cambridge University Press, 2005).

9. As will be evident even from the titles of some of the works, cited here, on Langland's theology, the term *semi-Pelagian* has gained broad currency in scholarship on *Piers Plowman*; it is worth pointing out, however, that the term was originally coined in the context of technical fifth- and sixth-century disputes over Augustine's teachings about predestination. Even in that milieu, as Rebecca Harden Weaver has argued, it is something of a misnomer. See *Divine Grace and Human Agency: A Study of the Semi-Pelagian Controversy* (Macon, Ga.: Mercer University Press, 1996).

10. William Langland, *The Vision of Piers Plowman: A Critical Edition of the B-Text*, ed. A. V. C. Schmidt (London: J. M. Dent, 2001), Prol.14, 16. Unless otherwise noted, all subsequent quotations from the poem will be from Schmidt's edition of the B-text and will appear in parentheses in the main text.

11. David Aers, *Salvation and Sin: Augustine, Langland, and Fourteenth-Century Theology* (Notre Dame, Ind.: University of Notre Dame Press, 2009), esp. chap. 4.

12. Denise Baker, "From Plowing to Penitence: *Piers Plowman* and Fourteenth-Century Theology," *Speculum* 55 (1980): 715–25; for this reading, see also John Lawlor, "*Piers Plowman*: The Pardon Reconsidered," *Modern Language Review* 45 (1950): 449–58; and Rosemary Woolf, "The Tearing of the Pardon," in *Piers Plowman: Critical Approaches*, ed. S. S. Hussey (London: Methuen, 1969), 50–75.

13. Robert Adams, "Piers's Pardon and Langland's Semi-Pelagianism," *Traditio* 39 (1983): 367–418; in agreement with Adams are Nevill Coghill, "The Pardon of Piers Plowman," *Proceedings of the British Academy* 30 (1944): 303–57; Robert Frank, *Piers Plowman and the Scheme of Salvation* (New Haven: Yale University Press, 1957); and Mary Carruthers, "*Piers Plowman*: The Tearing of the Pardon," *Philological Quarterly* 49 (1970): 8–18.

14. Emily Steiner, *Documentary Culture and the Making of Medieval English Literature* (Cambridge: Cambridge University Press, 2003), 135, 127.

15. Steiner, *Documentary Culture*, 140–41.

16. Baker, "From Plowing to Penitence," 722.

17. William Langland, *Piers Plowman by William Langland: An Edition of the C-Text*, ed. Derek Pearsall (Berkeley: University of California Press, 1979), 9.290.

18. 109.300–4.

19. The section with which Langland introduces the pardon scene in all extant versions of the poem, including the Z-text, seems to imply that the pardon guarantees the salvation of all people. Here, the verb *impugnede* means "to dispute the authority or validity of"; the priest is not impugning so much the pardon itself as Piers's faulty interpretation of the pardon. See *Middle English Dictionary*, s.v. "impugnen," http://tiny.cc/med-impugnen.

20. On the C text's overall emphasis on free will, see Britton J. Harwood, "The Character 'Liberum Arbitrium' in the C-Text of *Piers Plowman*," *Philological Quarterly* 52 (1973): 680–95.

21. See Richard Firth Green, "John Ball's Letters," in *Chaucer's England: Literature in Historical Context*, ed. Barbara Hanawalt (Minneapolis: University of Minnesota Press, 1992), 176–200.

22. See Matt. 18:23–35.

23. Szittya's discussion of this scene appears in the introduction to his classic study *The Antifraternal Tradition in Medieval Literature* (Princeton: Princeton University Press, 1986).

24. On this point, see David Aers, *Sanctifying Signs: Making Christian Tradition in Late Medieval England* (Notre Dame, Ind.: University of Notre Dame Press, 2004), chap. 2.

25. Janet Coleman, *Piers Plowman and the Moderni* (Rome: Edizioni di storia e letteratura, 1981), 36–41.

26. On Holcot, an excellent study is still Heiko Oberman, "*Facientibus quod in se est Deus non denegat gratiam*: Robert Holcot, O.P., and the Beginnings of Luther's Theology," *Harvard Theological Review* 55 (1962): 317–42.

27. James Simpson, *1350–1547: Reform and Cultural Revolution*, vol. 2 of *The Oxford English Literary History*, ed. Jonathan Bate (Oxford: Oxford University Press, 2002), 361.

28. Norman P. Tanner, ed., *Decrees of the Ecumenical Councils*, 2 vols. (Washington, D.C.: Georgetown University Press, 1990), 1.426. This argument draws on the longer discussion in *What Is a Lollard?* of Wyclif's soteriology and its place in modern studies of his thought (see n. 7 above), 31–35.

29. John Stacey, "John Wyclif as Theologian," *Expository Times* 101 (1990): 134–41 at 138.

30. For Wyclif's definition of the true church as the congregation of the predestined, see, among others, J. Loserth, ed., *De ecclesia* (London: Trübner, 1886), 2–3, 7, 37, 58; R. L. Poole, ed., *De civili dominio*, 4 vols. (London: Trübner, 1885), 1.288, 358; and J. Loserth, ed., *Opera minora* (London: C. K. Paul, 1913), 176.

31. For the best account of Wyclif's *dominium* theology, see Stephen E. Lahey, *Philosophy and Politics in the Thought of John Wyclif* (Cambridge: Cambridge University Press, 2003).

32. This gem of a comment comes from Louis Brewer Hall, *The Perilous Vision of John Wyclif* (Chicago: Nelson-Hall, 1983), 228.

33. Unfortunately, many literary critics who have written about the influence that Wyclif and Wycliffite ideas had on writers like Langland have all too readily accepted the conventional account of Wyclif's so-called predestinarianism. For example, see,

in an otherwise masterful study of *Piers Plowman*, James Simpson, *Piers Plowman: An Introduction*, 2nd ed. (Exeter: University of Exeter Press, 2007), 201.

34. Levy, "Grace and Freedom" (see n. 7 above); see similar accounts by Stephen E. Lahey, *John Wyclif* (Oxford: Oxford University Press, 2009); Anthony Kenny, *Wyclif* (Oxford: Oxford University Press, 1985); and Hornbeck, *What Is a Lollard?* chap. 2.

35. John Wyclif, *On Universals*, trans. Anthony Kenny (Oxford: Clarendon Press, 1985), XIV/98–100.

36. Levy, "Grace and Freedom," 313.

37. Levy, "Grace and Freedom," 330.

38. John Wyclif, *Trialogus*, ed. G. Lechler (Oxford: Clarendon Press, 1869), 296; *De officio regis*, ed. A. W. Pollard and C. Sayle (London: Trübner, 1887), 147.

39. Poole, ed., *De civili dominio* (see n. 26 above), 1.38, 282–84.

40. The appropriate terminology for late-medieval dissenters has recently been the subject of much controversy: Should they be called "Lollards," "lollards," "Wycliffites," or something else? There is not room in this essay to engage these questions at the level they deserve, so for convenience, since I am for the most part discussing the works of Wyclif and his immediate successors, I have chosen to use "Wycliffite(s)" throughout.

41. Lilian M. Swinburn, ed., *The Lanterne of Li3t*, Early English Text Society, o.s. 151 (London: Kegan Paul, Trench, Trübner, 1917), 23, lines 3–4.

42. *Lanterne*, 136, lines 13–17.

43. For further discussion, see *What Is a Lollard?* (see n. 7 above), 49–50.

44. Anne Hudson and Pamela Gradon, eds., *English Wycliffite Sermons*, 5 vols. (Oxford: Clarendon Press, 1983–96), 2.55.53–58; 3.229.47–48; 2.100.82–84; these texts are cited by volume, sermon, and line numbers.

45. In *What Is a Lollard?* chap. 2.

46. Norman P. Tanner, ed., *Heresy Trials in the Diocese of Norwich, 1428–1431* (London: Royal Historical Society, 1977), 61, 73, 49.

47. On the procedures followed in English heresy trials, see Anne Hudson, "The Examination of Lollards," in *Lollards and Their Books* (London: Hambledon Press, 1985), 124–40; for skeptical views on the stereotyping effects of late-medieval inquisitorial records, see, among others, R. N. Swanson, *Church and Society in Late Medieval England* (Oxford: Blackwell, 1993); and Shannon McSheffrey and Norman P. Tanner, eds., *Lollards of Coventry, 1486–1522* Camden Fifth Series 23, (Cambridge: Cambridge University Press, 2003). In *What Is a Lollard?* I have set out the case for the rehabilitation of some inquisitorial records (xi–xviii).

48. Similar remarks, stressing the invisible aspect of the church, appear in the trials of Thomas Bikenore of Salisbury diocese (1443) and John Crud and John Baile of Ely diocese (1457), among others. Chippenham, Wiltshire and Swindon History Centre

D1/2/10, fols. 52v–54v; Cambridge, Cambridge University Library, Ely Diocesan Records MS G/1/5, fol. 130b.

49. *Lanterne*, 44, lines 6–14.

CHRISTIAN POETICS AND ORTHODOX PRACTICE: MEANING AND IMPLICATION IN SIX CAROLS BY JAMES RYMAN, O.F.M. / JOHN C. HIRSH

The research for, and some of the writing of, this study took place in 2009 when I was the George S. Yip Visiting Fellow at Magdalene College, Cambridge. I am most grateful to Duncan Robinson, the Master, to Professor Helen Cooper, and to all of the fellowship for the warm welcome and the generous support I received there. I am further grateful to the Syndics of Cambridge University Library both for continuing access to its collections and for permission to republish, from CUL MS Ee.1.12, certain of Ryman's carols.

1. Penn Szittya has developed a reading of dissent throughout *The Antifraternal Tradition in Medieval Literature* (Princeton: Princeton University Press, 1986), particularly in his treatment of William of St. Amour (62–122) and Richard FitzRalph (123–51). The topic is still in the process of definition, with definitions of *orthodox* and *official* and of *subversive* and *dissenting* much contested. See, among many places, Rita Copeland, ed., *Criticism and Dissent in the Middle Ages* (Cambridge: Cambridge University Press, 1996), in particular the chapters by James Simpson (215–43) and Steven Justice (289–43). See further Simpson, *1350–1547: Reform and Cultural Revolution*, vol. 2 of *The Oxford English Literary History*, ed. Jonathan Bate (Oxford: Oxford University Press, 2002), passim.

2. There is an early biographical study by A. G. Little, "James Ryman—A Forgotten English Poet," *Archaelogia Cantiana* 54 (1942): 1–4; and one specifically on his carols, by David L. Jeffrey, "James Ryman and the Fifteenth-Century Carol," in *Fifteenth-Century Studies: Recent Essays*, ed. R. F. Yeager (Hamden, Conn.: Archon Books, 1984): 303–20. Ryman recently has been the subject of a thoughtful study by Karl Reichl, "James Ryman's Lyrics and the Ryman Manuscript: A Reappraisal," in *Bookmarks from the Past: Studies in Early English Language and Literature in Honour of Helmut Gneuss*, ed. Lucia Kornel and Ursula Lenker (Frankfurt am Main: Peter Lang, 2003), 195–227. Reichl has some further remarks on this much neglected author in "The Middle English Carol," in *A Companion to the Middle English Lyric*, ed. Thomas G. Duncan (Cambridge: D.S. Brewer, 2005), 150–70; as does Bernard O'Donoghue, "'Cuius Contrarium': Middle English Popular Lyrics," in *A Companion to the Middle English Lyric* (210–26), where he points out that E. K. Chambers and F. Sidgwick's anthology *Early English Lyrics: Amorous, Divine, Moral, and Trivial* (London: A. H. Bullen, 1907; repr., New York: October House, 1966) represented Ryman's carols as the product of

"a pious and unimaginative ecclesiastic" (Chambers and Sidgwick, 202; cited by O'Donoghue, 211). Pious and also orthodox James Ryman certainly seems to have been, but, *pace* Chambers, Sidgwick, et al., that circumstance hardly makes him either unimaginative or unlearned.

3. On Wyclif's theology of the Eucharist, see Anne Hudson, *The Premature Reformation: Wycliffite Texts and Lollard History* (Oxford: Clarendon Press, 1988), 281–90. Ryman's allusions to the sacraments are largely uninflected and as a rule simply reflect the contemporary devout understanding, though, as we shall see, he is at pains to articulate certain less common Christian teachings concerning both the Trinity and Christ's human and divine natures.

4. Richard L. Greene, ed., *The Early English Carols*, 2nd ed. (Oxford: Clarendon Press, 1977), cliv–clv. "Ryman's body of verse, dull as much of it is, provides valuable testimony as to the methods which he and doubtless other carol-writers followed in producing songs of this type" (clv). But Greene also allows that Ryman was at least productive, writing about a quarter of all extant English carols earlier than 1550. It should be remembered too that many of Ryman's lyrics were inscribed to be sung, and that circumstance informed their composition, a point Reichl effectively posed at 220–21. And for some students of music at least, Ryman's lyrics have retained their appeal. Christopher Rathbone has adapted Ryman's lyrics in his opus 72, *Nunc Natus Est Altissimus* (South Hutton, York: Banks Music, 1999). It is very much to be hoped, of course, that as this most graceful and prolific poet becomes better known, such compositions as Rathbone's will increase in number, and that students of music will help students of literature better to appreciate and understand these simple but rich compositions. A new edition of Ryman's work would of course speed the process.

5. See Nicholas Love, *Mirror of the blessed lyf of Jesu Cristie*, ed. Michael Sergeant (Exeter: University of Exeter Press, 2005); and Margaret Aston, and *Thomas Arundel: A Study of Church Life in the Reign of Richard II* (Oxford: Clarendon Press, 1967) for two studies showing the power both of enforcement and persuasion that ecclesiastical authority enjoyed, and what forms they could take. Ryman chose a different way.

6. The manuscript and the colophon are discussed by Reichl, "Reappraisal," 195–98; the bracketed readings in the colophon recorded above have been erased in the manuscript. Reichl's "Reappraisal" also contains, among other things, an interesting and considered section, "Ryman and the Critics" (213–14), which enlarges, if judiciously, the critical appreciation of Ryman's work. Two recent studies further emphasize the importance of manuscript study in developing a new understanding of medieval English carols: Kathleen Palti, "An Unpublished Fifteenth-Century Carol Collection: Oxford. Lincoln College MS Lat. 141," *MAE* 77 (2008): 260–78; and Seeta Chaganti, "Choreographing *Mouvance*: The Case of the English Carol," *Philological Quarterly* 87, nos. 1–2 (2008): 77–103, which discusses, among other things, the element of dance in carols. Douglas Gray has examined their association with lyrics in "Fifteenth-Century

Lyrics and Carols," in *Nation, Court, and Culture: New Essays on Fifteenth-Century Poetry*, ed. Helen Cooney (Dublin: Four Courts Press, 2001), 168–83.

7. Greene, 341; see contra Reichl, "Reappraisal," 197–98 and 205–6.

8. Julia Boffey and A. S. G. Edwards, eds. *A New Index of Middle English Verse* (London: British Library, 2005).

9. Greene, ed., *The Early English Carols*. Earlier, the lyrics were edited by J. Zupitza, "Die Gedichte des Franziskaners Jakob Ryman," *Archiv für das Studium der Neueren Sprachen und Litteraturen* 89 (1892): 167–338. The edition is without critical commentary. *The Cambridge University Library Catalogue of Manuscripts* (Cambridge: Cambridge University Press, 1857; repr., Hiedesheim: Georg Olms Verlag, 1980) shares Greene's low judgment of Ryman's work, which it may have influenced: "These hymns, which are little more than translations from the Latin service books, relate chiefly to the Virgin" (2.12).

10. Both of these teachings were developed by the fifth century. The hypostatic union was defined in the Council of Chalcedon, on which see *The Acts of the Council of Chalcedon*, 3 vols., trans. Richard Price and Michael Gaddis (Liverpool: Liverpool University Press, 2005: repr. with corrections, 2007), especially "The Christological Crisis" (1.17–37) and "The Theology of Chalcedon" (1.56–85). The bibliography for any discussion of the role of the Trinity in medieval culture is of course enormous, but for its position in fifteenth-century painting see François Bœspflug, *La Trinité dans l'art d'Occident (1400–1600): Sept chefs-d'oeuvre de la peinture*, 2nd edition (Strasbourg: Presses universitaires de Strasbourg, 2006); see 17–29 for a general introduction to the topic. In fifteenth-century England, allusions to the Trinity were everywhere apparent, whether in manuscript illumination, theological discourse, or private devotion. I have written about some such references in the Paston Letters in *The Revelations of Margery Kempe: Paramystical Practices in Late Medieval England* (Leiden and New York: E. J. Brill, 1989), 12–15. The references to the Trinity in Margaret Paston's correspondence in particular anticipate Ryman's allusions and indicate the breadth of knowledge that the poet could reasonably expect from a devout and literate layperson.

11. Richard Cross, *The Metaphysics of the Incarnation: Thomas Aquinas to Duns Scotus* (Oxford: Clarendon Press, 2002), 121. I am indebted as well to Cross's *Duns Scotus* (New York: Oxford University Press, 1999), esp. 113–26, and to his "Scotus's Parisian Teaching on Divine Simplicity," in *Duns Scot à Paris, 1302–2002*, ed. Olivier Boulnois et al. (Turnhout: Brepols, 2004), 519–62.

12. Cross, *Duns Scotus*, 114, 116. For a further refinement of Scotus's teaching on the Trinity, see Richard Cross, "Duns Scotus on Divine Substance and the Trinity," *Medieval Philosophy and Theology* 11 (2003): 181–201, where he discusses the sense in which we can speak, in Scotus, of "the three divine persons as one *substance* and one *God* . . . and what, according to Scotus, are the theological consequences of accepting his claim that the divine nature is an immanent universal" (183).

13. See further Cross, "The Substance–Accident Model: (3) Duns Scotus," chap. 5 of *Metaphysics of the Incarnation*, 121–36. I have drawn on this perceptive chapter through-out. In chap. 3, Cross also treats from Bonaventure to William of Ware (77–88). In chap. 4, Cross treats the substance–accident model in Giles of Rome and his opponents (89–120).

14. On the related point concerning Christ's uniqueness, which I cannot develop here, see Cross, "Some Points of Christological Consensus," chap. 4 of *Metaphysics of the Incarnation*, 147–55; in particular within this chapter see "The Incarnation and the Divine Essence," 147–51, and "The Incarnation of Just One Divine Person," 151–52. For a briefer treatment of the topic see too Cross's *Duns Scotus*, 114–17.

15. Marc Ozilou and Gilles Berceville, "Théologie médiévale: Entre logique et mystique. La théologie universitaire," in *Histoire de la théologie*, ed. Jean-Yves Lacoste (Paris: Éditions du Seuil, 2009), 264. For treatments of the devout and practical implications of Scotus's thought, see Olivier Boulnois, *Duns Scot: La rigueur de la charité* (Paris: Les Éditions du Cerf, 1998), 131–42.

16. I have not the space here to develop Scotus's treatment of divine freedom and love, but see in particular Steven Dumont, "Henry of Ghent and Duns Scotus," in *Medieval Philosophy*, ed. John Marenbon (London and New York: Routledge, 1998; repr., 2004), 291–328, and Alan B. Wolter, O.F.M., and *Duns Scotus on the Will and Morality*, ed. and trans. William A. Frank (Washington, D.C.: Catholic University of America Press, 1997), 3–16, 57–60.

17. Reichl, "Reappraisal," 221; Jeffrey, 315.

ENABLED AND DISABLED "MYNDES" IN *THE PRICK*
OF *CONSCIENCE* / MOIRA FITZGIBBONS

1. Except where otherwise indicated, all citations from *The Prick of Conscience* are taken from *The Pricke of Conscience: A Northumbrian Poem*, ed. Richard Morris (Berlin: A. Asher, 1863). A new edition of the text will be very welcome when it arrives. In-text citations of the poem refer to line numbers.

2. For important discussions of vernacular theology, see Nicholas Watson, "Censorship and Cultural Change in Late-Medieval England," *Speculum* 70 (1995): 822–64; *The Idea of the Vernacular: An Anthology of Middle English Literary Theory, 1280–1520*, ed. Jocelyn Wogan-Browne, Nicholas Watson, Andrew Taylor, and Ruth Evans (University Park: Pennsylvania State University Press, 1999); *English Language Notes* 44, no. 1 (2006): 75–137; and Vincent Gillespie, "Vernacular Theology," in *Middle English*, ed. Paul Strohm (Oxford: Oxford University Press, 2007), 401–20.

3. A useful overview of different facets of knowledge and rationality in *Piers Plowman* is provided in Randolph Quirk's "Langland's Use of *Kind Wit* and *Inwit*," *Journal of English and Germanic Philology* 52 (1953): 182–88. Watson ("Censorship," 853) points out that Nicholas Love explicitly rejects the authority of "kyndely reson" in *The Mirror*

of the Blessed Life of Jesus Christ. As Kantik Ghosh has noted, however, Love continues to make use of the term "resonable" and its variations as part of his polemical strategy. See Ghosh, *The Wycliffite Heresy: Authority and the Interpretation of Texts* (Cambridge: Cambridge University Press, 2002), 161–65. Later in the fifteenth century, of course, the "doom of resoun" constitutes a key component of the ideas of Reginald Pecock: See Stephen Lahey, "Reginald Pecock on the Authority of Reason, Scripture, and Tradition," *Journal of Ecclesiastical History* 56 (2005): 235–60.

4. See *A Descriptive Guide to the Manuscripts of the "Prick of Conscience,"* eds. Robert E. Lewis and Angus McIntosh (Oxford: Medium Ævum Monographs, 1982), as well as A. I. Doyle, "Ushaw College, Durham, MS 50," in *The English Medieval Book: Studies in Memory of Jeremy Griffiths*, ed. A. S. G. Edwards, Vincent Gillespie, and Ralph Hanna (London: British Library, 2000), 43–49; A. S. G. Edwards and Theresa O'Byrne, "A New Manuscript Fragment of the *Prick of Conscience,*" *Medium Ævum* 76 (2007): 305–7; and *A New Index of Middle English Verse*, ed. Julia Boffey and A. S. G. Edwards (London: British Library, 2005), esp. 227–28.

5. I will use "madness" throughout this chapter (as opposed to phrases like "mental illness") since it most closely approximates the Middle English word "wode." For a discussion of the utility of the term "madness," see Aleksandra Pfau, "Protecting or Restraining? Madness as a Disability in Late Medieval France," in *Disability in the Middle Ages: Reconsiderations and Reverberations*, ed. Joshua R. Eyler (Surrey: Ashgate, 2010), 94–95. See also *Middle English Dictionary*, s.v. "wode."

6. For an exploration of ways this question was posed and addressed within another medieval context, see Margaret Trenchard-Smith, "Insanity, Exculpation, and Disempowerment in Byzantine Law," in *Madness in Medieval Law and Custom*, ed. Wendy J. Turner (Boston: Brill, 2010), 39–56. Mary Carruthers points out the centrality of memory to conceptualizations of human identity: "A person without a memory, if such a thing could be, would be a person without moral character and, in a basic sense, without humanity" (*The Book of Memory: A Study of Memory in Medieval Culture*, 2nd ed. [Cambridge: Cambridge University Press, 2008], 14).

7. Lewis and McIntosh, *Descriptive Guide*, 14, 11.

8. See J. A. Burrow, *Medieval Writers and Their Work: Middle English Literature, 1100–1500*, second edition (Oxford: Oxford University Press, 2008), 21; Burrow states that "there is no reason to quarrel" with the absence of *The Prick of Conscience* from the literary canon.

9. See Watson, "Censorship," 832, 835, as well as his essay "The Politics of Middle English Writing" in *Idea* (esp. 338).

10. Nicole Rice, *Lay Piety and Religious Discipline in Middle English Literature* (Cambridge: Cambridge University Press, 2008), 14.

11. Howell Chickering, "Rhetorical *Stimulus* in the *Prick of Conscience,*" in *Medieval Paradigms: Essays in Honor of Jeremy DuQuesnay Adams*, ed. Stephanie Hayes-Healy

(New York: Palgrave, 2005), 194–97. I am very grateful to Dr. Chickering for providing me with a copy of this chapter.

12. Cf. Robert Mannyng, *Handlyng Synne*, ed. Idelle Sullens (Binghamton: Center for Medieval and Early Renaissance Studies, 1983), and *Speculum Vitae*, ed. Ralph Hanna, Early English Text Society, o.s. 331 and 332 (Oxford: Oxford University Press, 2008). *Jacob's Well* is not available in a complete edition. *Jacob's Well: An English Treatise on the Cleansing of Man's Conscience*, ed. Arthur Brandeis, Early English Text Society, o.s., 115 (London: Kegan Paul, Trench, Trübner, 1900), contains the collection's first fifty sermons. The remaining forty-five were edited by Clinton Atchley in "The 'Wose' of *Jacob's Well*: Text and Context" (Ph.D. diss., University of Washington, 1998).

13. Chickering, "*Stimulus*," 219, 193.

14. Ibid., 202.

15. Ibid., 212.

16. The poet is not devoid of misogyny—he describes the womb as a "foul thyng" (524–25), for example—but he expends little energy in this direction. Although he conjures up the common image of a "faire woman" who is inwardly "wlatsom" (579–83), for example, his denunciation of people obsessed with clothing focuses at length on the vain habits of "yhong men" (1525).

17. *Middle English Dictionary*, s.v. "wit," "minde," and "skil." Other terms and phrases used to indicate mental activity within the text include "insight" (e.g., 253) and "thynk in hert" and variants (e.g., 407, 6562, 6585, 6801).

18. For analysis of the relationship between animal and human reason within *Piers Plowman* and other late medieval texts, see Quirk, 182–85.

19. The active engagement with the present, past, and future depicted here recalls Carruthers's characterization of memory as "an agent, a power, not just a receptacle" (*Book of Memory*, 68).

20. "Þarfor ilk man þat of dede has mynde/Dredes gretely þe dede here thurgh kynde" (1776–77); "For whiles [the sinful] lyf þai have na mynde/ Of God, bot forgettes hym, als ay unkynde" (2050–1).

21. "For swa hardy es na man, ne swa balde / In þis werld, nouther yhung ne alde, / If he myght right consayve in mynde, / How grysely a devel es in his kynde" (6855–58).

22. Chickering, "*Stimulus*," 205.

23. For example, see the initial appearances of Consience, Kynde Wytt, and Resoun on 48, 51, and 102 of *Piers Plowman: A New Annotated Edition of the C-text*, ed. Derek Pearsall (Exeter: University of Exeter Press, 2008).

24. For explorations of the way these questions emerge within *Piers Plowman*, see Quirk; Carruthers, "The Character of Conscience in *Piers Plowman*," *Studies in Philology* 67 (1970): 13–30; Andrew Galloway, "*Piers Plowman* and the Schools," *The Yearbook of Langland Studies* 6 (1992): 89–107; and Galloway, "The Making of a Social Ethic

in Late-Medieval England: From *Gratitudo* to "Kyndenesse," *Journal of the History of Ideas* 55 (1994): 365–83.

25. Galloway, "Social Ethic," 374.

26. When he does remark on social distinctions, it is generally so that he can emphasize their irrelevance in the face of death and judgment: "Dede wil na frendshepe do ne favour, / Ne reverence til kyng ne til emperour, / Ne til pape, ne til bisshope, ne na prelate, / Ne til other man of heghe estate," and so on (1884–87).

27. Although I will focus on the interplay between oral and written forms of communication here, it is important to remember the poem's role in the combined appeal that the "Prick of Conscience" stained-glass window at All Saints Church in York made to visual and textual literacies. The window presents the Fifteen Signs before Doomsday, along with lines from the poem itself. I am grateful to Dr. Shannon Gayk for sharing her research on this window and its resonance for our understanding of late-medieval literacy, especially her "Lyric Materialities: *The Pricke of Conscience* Window and Late-Medieval Lyricism" (paper, annual meeting, Modern Language Association, Philadelphia, December 2009).

28. Hanna, *Speculum Vitae*, lxxix. All in-text citations from the poem are by line number and are taken from Hanna's edition.

29. For a discussion of the *Speculum Vitae*'s authorship, see Hanna, lx–lxiii.

30. Other examples highlighting clerical knowledge include the following: "Ffor als þir clerkes fyndes writen and redes" (1682); "For þes clerkes þat gret clergy can / Calles man bathe Inner man and utter man" (5844–45); and "Ffor clerkes says þat knawes and sese" (7595).

31. Other passages that describe book learning in an inclusive way are "Bot ye sal understand and witte, / Als men may se in haly writte" (6252–53); "For þus we fynde wryten in boke" (6870); and "Als þe boke openly schewes us, / Whare we may fynd wryten þus" (7277–78).

32. A rough count reveals that in the first 2,000 lines of the poem, the *Conscience*-poet uses variants of the verb *seien* 80 times when referring to ideas expressed in writing. By contrast, the verb *speken* appears 4 times. Similarly, in the first 2,000 lines of *Speculum Vitae* the verb *seien* occurs 24 times when alluding to written ideas, as opposed to 3 occurrences of *speken*.

33. For a discussion of the relationship between *speak* and *say*, see the "signification" section of the *Oxford English Dictionary* s.v. "say (v.)," http://www.oed.com.

34. For a similar point about pedagogy, see Chickering, "*Stimulus*," 204, which suggests that the poet's repetitiveness may reflect "his desire to educate his audience."

35. The *Conscience*-poet makes a similar move when conceding that "Yhit som trowes, and swa may wel be" that parts of the actual Cross will appear at the Last Judgment (5291), although he sounds a bit skeptical about this possibility.

36. Geoffrey Chaucer, "The Nun's Priest's Tale," from *The Riverside Chaucer*, ed. Larry Benson (Boston, Houghton Mifflin, 1987), 259.

37. See also "Þus may I lyken, als I ymagyn" (9051), "I lyken here, after I ymagyn" (9116), and so forth.

38. See Mary Teresa Brady, "*The Pore Caitif*, Edited from MS Harley 2336 with Introduction and Notes" (Ph.D. diss., Fordham University, 1954), 174.

39. For a contrast to the willingness of the *Conscience*-poet to affirm the ability of his audience to imagine heaven on their own, see Michelle Karnes, "Nicholas Love and Medieval Meditations on Christ," *Speculum* 82 (2007): 397–99.

40. See Lewis and McIntosh, *Descriptive Guide*, 9, 40–41, 65–66, 74–75, 91–92, 97, and 118–19.

41. Cf. the discussion of the title from Morris's edition: "In þir seven er sere materes drawen / Of sere bukes, of whilk some er unknawen, / Namly til lewed men of England, / Þat can noght bot Inglise understand; / Þarfor þis tretice drawe I wald/ In Inglise tung þat may be cald/ Prik of Conscience als men may fele, / For if a man it rede and understand wele, / And þe materes þar-in til hert wil take, / It may his conscience tendre make, / And til right way of rewel bryng it bilyfe, / And his hert til drede and mekenes dryfe, / And til luf and yhernyng of heven blis, And to amende alle þat he has done mys" (9545–58).

42. Penelope Doob, *Nebuchadnezzar's Children: Conventions of Madness in Middle English Literature* (New Haven: Yale University Press, 1974), 10, 134–207.

43. Pearsall, *Piers Plowman C-text* , 175. He makes this suggestion in response to Langland's discussion of "lunatyk lollares" (9.107) who "walke, / With a good will, witteles, many wyde contreyes" (9.110–11). See below for an alternative interpretation of this passage. For a fuller exploration of the relationship between fervent religiosity and madness, see Jerome Kroll and Bernard Bachrach, *The Mystic Mind: The Psychology of Medieval Mystics and Ascetics* (New York: Routledge, 2005).

44. See, for example, pages 146 and 338 of M. C. Seymour et al., *On the Properties of Things: John Trevisa's Translation of Bartholomeus Anglicus De Proprietatibus Rerum* (Oxford: Clarendon Press, 1975).

45. See especially Wendy J. Turner, "Town and Country: A Comparison of the Treatment of the Mentally Disabled in Late Medieval English Common Law and Chartered Boroughs," in *Madness in Medieval Law and Custom*, ed. Turner, 17–38; and Aleksandra Pfau, "Crimes of Passion: Emotion and Madness in French Remission Letters," in *Madness in Medieval Law and Custom*, ed. Turner, 97–122. Other important discussions of the wide range of medieval representations of madness include Corinne Saunders's " 'The Thoghtful Maladie': Madness and Vision in Medieval Writing," in *Madness and Creativity in Literature and Culture* (New York: Palgrave, 2005), 67–87; Sylvia Huot's *Madness in Medieval French Literature* (Oxford: Oxford University Press, 2003); and Simon Kemp's *Medieval Psychology* (Santa Barbara: Greenwood Press, 1990). For analysis of

medieval attitudes toward disability in general, see Irina Metzler, *Disability in Medieval Europe* (New York: Routledge, 2006), as well as Eyler, ed., *Disability in the Middle Ages*.

46. See *A Book to a Mother: An Edition with Commentary*, ed. Adrian McCarthy (Salzburg: Institut für Anglistik und Amerikanstik, 1981), 17, 198.

47. McCarthy, *Book*, 126.

48. See Bridget of Sweden, *The "Liber Celestis" of St. Bridget of Sweden*, ed. Roger Ellis, Early English Text Society 291 (Oxford: Oxford University Press, 1987), 3.

49. *The Cloud of Unknowing and The Book of Privy Counselling*, ed. Phyllis Hodgson, Early English Text Society, o.s. 218 (Oxford: Oxford University Press, 1944), 84.

50. *The Book of Margery Kempe*, ed. Sanford Brown Meech and Hope Emily Allen, Early English Text Society, o.s. 212 (Oxford: Oxford University Press, 1940), 69–71, 54.

51. Ibid., 55.

52. Ibid., 17.

53. Pearsall regards these people as "feeble-minded" rather than mad; see *Piers Plowman C-text*, 175, and "'Lunatyk Lollares' in *Piers Plowman*," in *Religion in Poetry and Drama of the Late Middle Ages*, ed. Piero Boitani and Anna Torti (Cambridge: D. S. Brewer, 1990), 163–78. While this is clearly one possibility, I think Richard K. Emmerson's characterization of these "lollares" as "enigmatic figures" better reflects the ambiguities of the passage: See Emmerson, "'Or Yernen to Rede Redels?' *Piers Plowman* and Prophecy," *Yearbook of Langland Studies* 7 (1993): 64. Langland's frequent recourse to such phrases as "as hit were," "as hit semeth," and "to oure syhte" in passus 9.105–20 of the C-text seems to underscore the difficulty of verifying another person's mental condition.

54. Chickering, "*Stimulus*," 214.

55. Trevisa's translation of Bartholomew, for example, notes animals afflicted with "wodenes of humour," such as a "wood hound" (208). Literary writers of course made great use of this association, as in Chaucer's description of Palamon's fighting like a "wood leon" ("Knight's Tale," *Riverside*, 47).

56. See Doob, *Nebuchadnezzar's Children*, 54–94.

57. Seymour, *Properties*, 87.

58. Nicholas Love, *The Mirror of the Blessed Life of Jesus Christ*, ed. Michael G. Sargent (Exeter: University of Exeter Press, 2005), 71.

59. Seymour, *Properties*, 1082 and 1095.

60. The *Conscience*-poet's desire to paint with a broad brush may also account for the fact that he refrains from applying the term "wodenes" to God or Doomsday itself, as other writers regularly do: The writer of *Book to a Mother*, as mentioned above, alludes to Judgment Day as a "day of woodnes" (198) and asserts that God will display "wodnes" when damning the wicked (81).

61. See *John Mirk's 'Festial*,' ed. Susan Powell, Early English Text Society, o.s. 334 (Oxford: Oxford University Press, 2009), 1:30.

62. Mannyng, *Handlyng Synne*, ed. Sullens, 86.

63. Hanna, *Speculum Vitae*, 124.

64. See *Middle English Dictionary*, s.v. "clomsen."

65. See Mannyng, *Handlyng Synne*, ed. Sullens, 81, 113, as well as Powell, *Mirk's 'Festial,'* 177.

66. *Mirk's Festial*, ed. Theodor Erbe, Early English Text Society, e.s. 96 (Milwood: Kraus Reprint, 1974), 240, 249. I have cited this edition because this material is not included in volume 1 of Powell's edition.

67. *The Cloud of Unknowing* evokes a similar image when discussing contemplatives who allow their thoughts to go astray. Arguing that misguided contemplation is "woodnes & no wisdom," the *Cloud*'s author asserts that some people "trauayle þeire ymaginacion so vndiscreetly, at at þe laste þei turne here brayne in here hedes" (96). If this takes place, the victims "stare as þei were wode" and may well "go staryng wode to þe deuil" (97–98).

68. See Revelation 6:15–17.

69. Other writers shared the *Conscience*-poet's emphasis on the ability of madness to estrange people. For an account of Thomas Hoccleve's negotiation of the isolation involved in madness and its aftermath, see James Simpson, "Madness and Texts: Hoccleve's *Series*," in *Chaucer and Fifteenth-Century Poetry*, ed. Julia Boffey and Janet Cowen (London: King's College Medieval Studies, 1991), esp. 23–25.

70. See, for example, pages 91 and 151 of *Handlyng Synne*, ed. Sullens, which describe punishments suffered by sinners in front of individual witnesses (in the case of the first narrative) or the public at large (in the second).

71. McCarthy, *Book*, 116.

72. Bridget of Sweden, *Liber Celestis,* ed. Ellis, 72.

73. See Erbe, *Mirk's Festial*, 236–38.

74. For two slightly divergent accounts of the extent to which medieval people regarded mentally ill people as dangerous, see James R. King, "The Mysterious Case of the 'Mad' Rector of Bletchingdon: The Treatment of Mentally Ill Clergy in Late Thirteenth-Century England," in *Madness in Medieval Law and Custom*, ed. Turner, 57–80, and Pfau in *Madness in Medieval Law and Custom*, ed. Turner, esp. 106.

75. See Meech, *Margery Kempe*, 177–78. For a persuasive analysis of the crucial role this episode plays in Margery's construction of her own authority, see Stephen Harper, *Insanity, Individuals, and Society in Late-Medieval English Literature* (Lewiston, N.Y.: Edwin Mellen Press, 2003), 263–68.

76. These ideas are problematic in their own way; contemporary disability theorists have questioned both the use of disability as a metaphor for something else and the automatic assumption that cures are viable and necessary. See, for example, Lennard Davis's critique of disability metaphors within Joseph Conrad's *Heart of Darkness* in *Enforcing Normalcy: Disability, Deafness, and the Body* (New York: Verso, 1995), 44–45,

as well as Susan Sontag's seminal *Illness as Metaphor* (New York: Farrar, Straus and Giroux, 1978). For a discussion of assumptions regarding cures, see Lois Keith, *Take Up Thy Bed and Walk: Death, Disability, and Cure in Classic Fiction for Girls* (London: Women's Press, 2000).

77. Pearsall, *Piers Plowman C-text*, 9.125.

THE IDEA OF PUBLIC POETRY IN LYDGATEAN RELIGIOUS VERSE: AUTHORITY AND THE COMMON VOICE IN DEVOTIONAL LITERATURE / JOHN T. SEBASTIAN

1. Anne Middleton, "The Idea of Public Poetry in the Reign of Richard II," *Speculum* 53, no. 1 (1978): 94–114. I first encountered this article in a course on literature and dissent in late-medieval England taught at Georgetown University by this volume's honoree, Penn Szittya. It is a genuine honor to be able to dedicate this article to him and to thank him publicly for many years of inspiration and friendship. I would like to thank Seeta Chaganti for her careful reading of this essay and her many thoughtful suggestions for its improvement. I would like to thank as well the two anonymous readers for the Press.

2. Middleton, "Public Poetry," 95.

3. Scott-Morgan Straker, "Propaganda, Intentionality, and the Lancastrian Lydgate," in *John Lydgate: Poetry, Culture, and Lancastrian England,* ed. Larry Scanlon and James Simpson (Notre Dame, Ind.: University of Notre Dame Press, 2006), 121.

4. C. David Benson, "Civic Lydgate: The Poet and London," in *John Lydgate: Poetry, Culture, and Lancastrian England,* 148, 163–64.

5. Maura Nolan, *John Lydgate and the Making of Public Culture* (New York: Cambridge University Press, 2005), 4 (emphasis in original). For a response to Nolan's discussion of Lydgate's public values in *Serpent of Division*, see Andrew Galloway, "John Lydgate and the Origins of Vernacular Humanism," *Journal of English and Germanic Philology* 107, no. 4 (2008): 309–31.

6. Claire Sponsler, "Lydgate and London's Public Culture," in *Lydgate Matters: Poetry and Material Culture in the Fifteenth Century,* ed. Lisa H. Cooper and Andrea Denny-Brown (New York: Palgrave Macmillan, 2008), 27.

7. Middleton, "Public Poetry," 95–96.

8. Andrew Cole, *Literature and Heresy in the Age of Chaucer* (New York: Cambridge University Press, 2008), 19 (emphasis added).

9. The idea of images as books for the unlearned appears to have originated with Pope Gregory the Great at the end of the sixth century, for which see Celia Chazelle, "Pictures, Books, and the Illiterate: Pope Gregory I's Letters to Serenus of Marseilles," *Word and Image* 6 (1990): 138–53. Interestingly, both sides, orthodox and reformist, cited Pope Gregory as the authority for their positions. Wyclif and his followers maintained that since images were instructional tools, they needed to be free of the kinds of

aesthetic embellishment that might mislead the unlearned. See, e.g., Johannes Wyclif, *Tractatus de mandatis divinis accedit Tractatus de statu innocencie*, ed. Johann Loserth and F. D. Matthew (London: C. K. Paul, 1922), 155–56, and the anonymous vernacular treatise on images contained in British Library MS Addit. 24202 and edited by Anne Hudson in *Selections from English Wycliffite Writings*, Medieval Academy Reprints for Teaching 38 (Toronto: University of Toronto, 1997), 83–88. Defenders of the orthodox position, writing in both Latin and English, who cite Gregory's authority include the twelfth-century liturgist John Beleth, the fifteenth-century homilist John Mirk, and the anonymous author of the vernacular treatise known as *Dives and Pauper*.

10. For Louis Althusser, interpellation is an act of hailing or address in which the individual hailed is, through his or her response, constituted as a subject within an ideology. See Althusser, "Ideology and Ideological State Apparatuses (Notes towards an Investigation)," in *Lenin and Philosophy and Other Essays*, trans. Ben Brewster (London: New Left Books, 1971), 127–88. Lydgate's version of a moderate Christianity, represented as a more flexible and accommodating alternative to the extremes of either traditional orthodoxy or heterodox reform, is in an Althusserian sense no less ideological, and thus Lydgate's poetry constitutes his individual reader as a subject already complicit in the form of public devotion that he promotes through his verse.

11. Lydgate's turn to formal hybridity as a means of addressing complex public concerns in the secular realm is the subject of Maura Nolan's recent study. See Nolan, *Lydgate and the Making of Public Culture*, 3 and *passim*.

12. A good deal of Lydgate's shorter devotional verse was probably intended for circulation in inexpensive and disposable pamphlets, and so much of it remains undated. For an excellent recent discussion of Lydgatean ephemera, see Joel Fredell, "'Go litel quaier': Lydgate's Pamphlet Poetry," *Journal of the Early Book Society* 9 (2006): 51–73. There seems no reason, however, to doubt that *The Testament* is a product of Lydgate's later years following his retirement to Bury St. Edmunds, although we should be cautious in too quickly assigning Lydgate's religious writings to his Bury periods and his secular compositions to his days among the court in London or France. *The Testament* is also highly conventional on the one hand and freely experimental in terms of form and genre on the other, thereby rendering biographical statements about the poet on the basis of his poem subject to suspicion. *The Testament* is published in *The Minor Poems of John Lydgate*, pt. 1, ed. Henry Noble MacCracken, Early English Text Society e.s. 107 (London: Kegan Paul, Trench, Trübner, 1911; New York: Oxford University Press, 1911), 329–62. All subsequent references to the poem are to MacCracken's edition and appear parenthetically in the text. I have occasionally and silently emended Mac-Cracken's punctuation and capitalization in this and other poems.

13. Jennifer Bryan, *Looking Inward: Devotional Reading and the Private Self in Late Medieval England* (Philadelphia: University of Pennsylvania Press, 2008), 108, com-

ments that the "Pygmalion image echoes and inverts a simile from twenty lines earlier, in which Lydgate had compared himself to Lot's wife, frozen in the act of looking back (676)." It also points forward to the image of Jesus speaking from the crucifix, whose liveliness is attested in the repeated references to sacrificial blood.

14. One is reminded here of Long Will garbed in the habit of a hermit "unholy of werkes" in the opening lines of *Piers Plowman*.

15. Each of the five final stanzas concludes with some variation of the refrain "I gaf for the my blood in sacryfice" (865).

16. James Simpson, *1350–1547: Reform and Cultural Revolution*, vol. 2 of *The Oxford English Literary History*, ed. Jonathan Bate (Oxford; New York: Oxford University Press, 2002), 455 and 457, describes *The Testament* as a document "which is very self-conscious of its documentary status" but whose textual recollection of the past is ultimately undone by the focus on "the dramatic, present, *seen* experience of the 'popular' image" (emphasis in original). *The Testament* receives extended treatment in Shannon Gayk, *Image, Text, and Religious Reform in Fifteenth-Century England* (Cambridge: Cambridge University Press, 2010). The book was still forthcoming at the time of this writing, and I am grateful to Professor Gayk for sharing a prepublication version of her chapter on Lydgate, which makes an important contribution to the study of Lydgate's devotional verse, including *The Testament*.

17. Bryan, *Looking Inward*, 109.

18. Middleton, "Public Poetry," 95.

19. Ibid.

20. The text of the poem is published in *Minor Poems*, ed. MacCracken, 268–79.

21. Middleton, "Public Poetry," 99.

22. Scholars have begun to reassess Lydgatean aesthetics and poetics in order to gain some critical distance on the damning but persistent judgments of earlier generations of readers epitomized in the English antiquarian Joseph Ritson's withering condemnation of Lydgate's verse, "in which there are scarcely three lines together of pure and acurate [*sic*] metre," a claim rendered all the more rhetorically effective by appearing after a catalogue of the monk's compositions that extends to some twenty-two pages. See Joseph Ritson, *Bibliographia Poetica: A Catalogue of Engleish Poets of the Twelfth, Thirteenth, Fourteenth, Fifteenth, and Sixteenth Centurys, with a Short Account of Their Works* (London: C. Roworth, 1802), 88. For revisions to this assessment, see, e.g., Phillipa Hardman, "Lydgate's Uneasy Syntax," 12–35, and Larry Scanlon, "Lydgate's Poetics: Laureation and Domesticity in the *Temple of Glass*," 61–97, both in *John Lydgate: Poetry, Culture, and Lancastrian England*.

23. See, e.g., *An Holy Meditacyon*, *A Procession of Corpus Christi*, and *On the Image of Pity*, all edited in *Minor Poems*, ed. MacCracken.

24. The contest over control of lay piety in post-Wycliffite England has been well documented. Among recent contributions, see Simpson, *Reform and Cultural*

Revolution; Jeremy Dimmick, James Simpson, and Nicolette Zeeman, *Images, Idolatry, and Iconoclasm in Late Medieval England: Textuality and the Visual Image* (Oxford; New York: Oxford University Press, 2002); Kathleen Kamerick, *Popular Piety and Art in the Late Middle Ages: Image Worship and Idolatry in England, 1350–1500* (New York: Palgrave, 2002); Shannon Gayk, "Images of Pity: The Regulatory Aesthetics of John Lydgate's Religious Lyrics," *Studies in the Age of Chaucer* 28 (2006): 175–203; and *Image, Text, and Religious Reform*.

25. Cole, *Literature and Heresy*, 131. In the unquoted portion of this sentence, Cole goes further than I would in claiming that Lydgate is "plainly no anti-Wycliffite." Indeed Cole is at pains to paint Lydgate as a Wycliffite sympathizer throughout his chapter. While I disagree with Cole about Lydgate's allegiances, I nevertheless find the poet a less than staunch supporter of the mainstream and often severe ecclesiastical agenda represented by figures like Archbishop Arundel, whose policy of censorship has been so powerfully described in Nicholas Watson, "Censorship and Cultural Change in Late-Medieval England: Vernacular Theology, the Oxford Translation Debate, and Arundel's Constitutions of 1409," *Speculum* 70.4 (1995): 822–64.

26. In the prologue to book 1 of *Fall of Princes*, Lydgate praises that poem's patron, Humphrey, duke of Gloucester, for "hooli chirche meyntenyng in deed, / That in this land no Lollard dar abide" and as a secular political figure who "As verray support, vpholdere and eek guide / Sparith noon, but maketh hymsiluen strong / To punysshe all tho that do the chirche wrong" (1.402–3, 404–6). See Henry Bergen, ed., *Lydgate's Fall of Princes*, 4 vols., Early English Test Society e.s. 121–24 (London: Oxford University Press, 1924–27). Lydgate's description of Lollardy as a persistent and pressing concern for Lancastrian authority serves here simply as an otherwise nondescript occasion for celebrating Humphrey's prowess in the conventional terms of literary masculine heroism. Lydgate likewise styles his former benefactor and Humphrey's brother, Henry V, as "most myhti off puissaunce," and the person who

> Gaff me charge off entent most cleene,
> Thyng off old tyme to putte in remembraunce [i.e., *Troy Book*],
> The same Henry, for knyhtli suffisaunce,
> Worthi for manhod, rekynd kynges all,
> With nyne worthi for to haue a stall.
>
> To hooli chirch he was chieff defensour;
> In all such causes Cristses chosen knyht.
> To stroie Lollardis he sette al his labour. (1.5959–67)

Although Lydgate here names the Lollards, he does so in a way that is, in fact, less pointed than his oblique engagement with issues of concern to the Reformers in the poems discussed above.

27. Gayk, "Images of Pity," 177–78.

28. Middleton, "Public Poetry," 95.

NATURE'S *YERDE* AND WARD: AUTHORITY AND CHOICE IN CHAUCER'S *PARLIAMENT OF FOWLS* / NICK HAVELY

1. *Parliament of Fowls* (subsequently *PF*), lines 617–23. For the description of the formel on Nature's hand, see 372–78. The text cited is *Chaucer's Dream Poetry*, ed. H. Phillips and N. Havely (London: Longman, 1997), 219–80. All subsequent references to *PF* will be to this edition.

2. For the complete stanza on the formel's blush, see *PF* 442–48; see also *gentil plee* (485), *noyse* (491), and *veirdit* (525).

3. See *Teseida*, ed. Alberto Limentani, in *Tutte le opere di Giovanni Boccaccio*, vol. 2., ed. Vittore Branca (Milan: Mondadori, 1964), book 7, stanzas 81–82, and book 12, stanzas 39–42. For Emily in the *Knight's Tale*, see *The Riverside Chaucer*, ed. Larry D. Benson, 3rd ed. (Oxford; New York: Oxford University Press, 2008), *Canterbury Tales* (subsequently *CT*) I (A) 2300–11 (all subsequent references to *CT* and the *Troilus* will be to this edition). Alastair Minnis argues that "there was never any suggestion that the formel wished to be a lifelong follower of the chaste goddess [Diana]. She is therefore rather different from Emily in the *Knight's Tale*" (*Shorter Poems*, ed. Minnis, Oxford Guides to Chaucer [Oxford: Clarendon Press; New York: Oxford University Press, 1995], 303).

4. *Book of the Duchess*, in *Chaucer's Dream Poetry*, ed. Phillips and Havely, lines 1240–44, 1258, 1270.

5. Linda M. Paterson, *The World of the Troubadours: Medieval Occitan Society, c. 1100–c. 1300* (Cambridge: Cambridge University Press, 1993), 259.

6. See Minnis, *Shorter Poems*, 254, summarizing a range of critical views on the formel's "indecision"; and Kathryn L. Lynch, "The *Parliament of Fowls* and Late Medieval Voluntarism," *Chaucer Review* 25 (1990): 1–16 and 85–95, esp. 2–5, 6, 7, 86, 91–2.

7. Groundbreaking work on this aspect of literature and social practice has been done by Noël James Menuge, particularly in *Medieval English Wardship in Romance and Law* (Cambridge: Brewer, 2001); see esp. 6–9 for a review of previous scholarship on the subject. I am also much indebted to Dr. James Menuge herself for invaluable advice and references during work on an earlier draft of this essay.

8. *MED* s.v. "yerd" n. (2), sense 2 (a).

9. See Alanus, *De planctu naturae*, ed. N. M. Häring, in *Studi Medievali*, 3rd ser., 19, no. 2, 3rd ser. (1978): 810–13 (Prose 3); and *Le Roman de la Rose*, ed. F. Lecoy (Paris: Champion, 1965–70), l. 16752.

10. Nature assigns *legitimos malleos* to Venus in *De planctu* (Prose 5), ed. Häring, 845, l. 25; and there are a number of references to the use of *greffes*, *marteaus* etc. in Genius's sermon near the end of *RR*, e.g., ll. 19515, 19599, 19607. For *yerd/yard* in the sense of "penis," see *MED* s.v. "yerd" n. (2), sense 5, and *OED* "yard" sb 2, sense 11.

11. *De planctu* (Prose 8), ed. Häring, 871, l. 178 (*pastorali uirga excommunicationis eliminet*) and 872, l. 213 (*seuera excommunicationis uirga percutiat*). Genius is also endowed with a cleric's pastoral rod (*croce*, "crosier") by Amors in *RR* l. 19449.

12. See *Mediae Latinitatis Lexicon Minus*, ed. J. F. Niermeyer (Leiden: Brill, 1976), "virga," senses 2, 5, and 7. See also the *Lexicographical Notes of the British Medieval Latin Dictionary Committee*, http://tiny.cc/virga-medieval-latin, for "Virga and its derivatives," sense iv.

13. "Now were it worthi that ye were ybete" (*Troilus* 3.1169).

14. *Troilus* 3.135,139, 141, 143–44, 145–46.

15. See Charles Muscatine, *Chaucer and the French Tradition: A Study in Style and Meaning* (Berkeley: University of California Press, 1957), 161. On the reading of *Troilus* 3.1356–58, see Richard Firth Green, *A Crisis of Truth: Literature and Law in Ricardian England* (Philadelphia: University of Pennsylvania Press, 1999), 326.

16. D. W. Robertson, "The Concept of Courtly Love as an Impediment to the Understanding of Medieval Texts," in *The Meaning of Courtly Love*, ed. F. X. Newman (Albany: State University of New York Press, 1968), 1–18.

17. Robertson, "The Concept of Courtly Love," 15.

18. One further example of such playfulness in this scene at the beginning of Book 3 of the *Troilus* would be the hero's addressing his *lady right* as his *chief resort* (134)—a term that can mean generally "a source of assistance, of comfort, of solace etc., that to which one resorts for aid, for protection etc." but that is also recorded from the early fifteenth century in a legal sense and parliamentary usage: "the right of having final authority vested in one." It also comes to have the meaning of "final appeal" and even "superior authority." See *MED* s.v. "resort)e" n., sense 3(a) (citing *Troilus* 3.134) and sense 5.

19. See Peter Beidler, "Medieval Children Witness Their Mothers' Indiscretions: The Maid Child in Chaucer's *Shipman's Tale*," *Chaucer Review* 44, no. 2 (2009): 186–204. Beidler suggests (194) that *under the yerde* refers to the Wife's having "moral authority over" the *mayde child*, but he does not consider the phrase's legal and social significance. On the other hand, Skeat, in his commentary on the line in *Complete Works of Geoffrey Chaucer* (Oxford: Clarendon Press, 1894), 5:169, notes the parallel between *under the yerde* and *sub virga/sous la verge*.

20. *Riverside Chaucer*, 911B, citing S. L. Thrupp, *The Merchant Class of Medieval London* (Ann Arbor: University of Michigan Press, 1948), 151 and n. 150.

21. Barbara Hanawalt, *Growing Up in Medieval London: The Experience of Childhood in History* (New York and London: Oxford University Press, 1993), 179.

22. Ibid.: "Elite young women might go into a household for a period before marrying. A citizen's daughter, particularly an orphan, might have a period of service in another household, instead of entering into an apprenticeship."

23. See especially Elaine Clark, "City Orphans and Custody Laws in Medieval England," *American Journal of Legal History* 34 (1990): 168–87, table 2 (177); also 173, 174–76, 183, 186 (on the responsibilities of the city authorities and the guardians).

24. Thrupp, *The Merchant Class*, 196 and n. 9.

25. *Physician's Tale*, *CT* 6 (C), 72–92. See also Beidler, "The Maid Child in Chaucer's *Shipman's Tale*," 204.

26. On the levels of and sources for classification of birds in *PF*, see: J. A. W. Bennett, *The Parlement of Fowles* (Oxford: Clarendon Press, 1957), 149; D. S. Brewer, ed., *The Parlement of Foulys* (Edinburgh and London: Nelson, 1960), 114–15; P. A. Olson, "*The Parlement of Foules*: Aristotle's *Poetics* and the Foundations of Human Society," *SAC* 2 (1980): 53–69.

27. On Nature's kiss, see Kathryn L. Lynch, " 'Diana's "Bowe Ybroke': Impotence, Desire, and Virginity in Chaucer's *Parliament of Fowls*," in *Menacing Virgins: Representing Virginity in the Middle Ages*, ed. Kathleen Coyne Kelly and Marina Leslie (Newark: University of Delaware Press and Associated University Presses, 1999), 85; and Susan Schibanoff, *Chaucer's Queer Poetics: Rereading the Dream Trio* (Toronto: University of Toronto Press, 2006), 284–88.

28. Lisa J. Kiser notes how "the social construction of nature" is recognized in *PF* through the casting of Nature "in the image of a human, an aristocratic female, implicitly with royal standing"; see "Chaucer and the Politics of Nature," in *Beyond Nature Writing: Expanding the Boundaries of Ecocriticism*, ed. Karla Armbruster and Kathleen R. Wallace (Charlottesville: University Press of Virginia, 2001), 45.

29. Bennett, *The Parlement of Fowles*, 140–41 and 141, n. 1; Brewer, ed., *The Parlement of Foulys*, 119 (n. on lines 387, 390) where Brewer also notes that "by the end of the [fourteenth] century parliamentary practice seems to have clearly recognised the general and perpetual quality of the statute, in contrast with the more particular and less necessarily perpetual quality of the ordinance."

30. *PF* 491, 495, 496, 502, 526, 531–32. The Chancellor's role and the parliamentary uses of such terms are noted by Brewer, ed., *The Parlement of Foulys*, 37–8 and 119 (n. on lines 387, 390). Bennett (*The Parlement of Fowles*, 140 and n. 1) suggests that 531–32 recall the Commons' process of installing a Speaker. On the range of legal terms used, Bennett also notes that these "should not lead us to think that Chaucer has forgotten the parliamentary setting: they should rather remind us that parliament was still, in many of its functions, a court of law" (168–69).

31. Marion Turner, "The Carnivalesque," in *Chaucer: An Oxford Guide*, ed. Steve Ellis (Oxford: Oxford University Press, 2005), 392.

32. See David Aers, "*The Parliament of Fowls*: Authority, the Knower and the Known," *Chaucer Review* 16 (1981): 12, citing R. H. Hilton, *Peasants, Knights and Heretics* (Cambridge: Cambridge University Press, 1976), 8.

33. Bennett, *The Parlement of Fowles*, 174.

34. *Bracton on the Laws and Customs of England*, ed. George Edward Woodbine, trans. Samuel Edmund Thorne (Cambridge Mass.: Belknap Press and Selden Society), 2: 35–36.

35. See Benjamin Thorpe, *Ancient Laws and Institutes of England* (London: Public Records Commissioners, 1840), 236–7 (under *De Inculpacionibus*); also cited in Niermeyer, *Mediae Latinitatis Lexicon Minus*, s.v. "virga," sense 7. See also the term *sub virga et potestate* cited in relation to marriage by Robert C. Palmer, "Contexts of Marriage in Medieval England: Evidence from the King's Court circa 1300," *Speculum* 59 (1984): 50 and n. 26.

36. See: *Casus Placitorum and Reports of Cases in the King's Courts, 1272–1278*, ed. W. H. Dunham (London: Bernard Quaritch, 1952), 102 (1275); *Calendar of Wills Proved and Enrolled in the Court of Husting London, Part I: 1258–1358*, ed. Reginald R. Sharpe (London: John Francis, 1889), 105 (1292); and *Year Books of the Reign of King Edward I: Years XXXII–XXXIII*, ed. and trans. Alfred J. Horwood (London: Longman, Green, Longman, Roberts and Green, 1864), 183 (1304). *The Dictionnaire historique de la langue française*, ed. Alain Rey (Paris: Le Robert, 1992), gives the earliest reference for the term "être sous la verge de qqn" as 1226 (2232, col. 2).

37. For emphasis on the distinction between wardship of property held in burgage tenure and feudal wardship, see Clark, "City Orphans," 170.

38. S. F. C. Milsom, "The Origin of Prerogative Wardship," in *Law and Government in Medieval England and Normandy*, ed. George Garnett and John Hudson (Cambridge: Cambridge University Press, 1994), 223–44.

39. Scott L. Waugh, "Marriage, Class, and Royal Lordship in England under Henry III," *Viator* 16 (1985): 195.

40. Scott L. Waugh, *The Lordship of England: Royal Wardships and Marriages in English Society and Politics, 1217–1327* (Princeton: Princeton University Press, 1988), 204.

41. John Carmi Parsons, *Eleanor of Castile: Queen and Society in Thirteenth-Century England* (Basingstoke: Macmillan, 1994), 46, 90.

42. Chris Given-Wilson, *The English Nobility in the Later Middle Ages* (New York: Routledge, 1987), 152.

43. *Tractatus de legibus et consuetudinibus regni Anglie qui Glanvilla vocatur*, ed. and trans. G. D. G. Hall (Oxford: Clarendon Press, 1993), 85; see also 108; and Milsom, "The Origin of Prerogative Wardship," 239–40.

44. *Bracton on the Laws and Customs of England*, 2.256–57 and 255.

45. James Menuge, *Medieval English Wardship*, 83.

46. Sue Sheridan Walker, "Free Consent and Marriage of Feudal Wards in Medieval England," *Journal of Medieval History* 8 (1982): 129.

47. Gratian, *Decretum* C. 31 q.2 d.a.c.1, cited in Michael M. Sheehan, "Choice of Marriage Partner in the Middle Ages: Development and Mode of Application of a

Theory of Marriage," *Studies in Medieval and Renaissance History* 1, o.s. 11 (1978): 9, n. 15; reprinted in *Medieval Families: Perspectives on Marriage, Household, and Children*, ed. Carol Neel (Toronto: Medieval Academy of America, 2004), 157–91.

48. See: R. H. Helmholz, *Canon Law and the Law of England* (London: Hambledon, 1987), 151–52; John T. Noonan Jr., "Power to Choose," *Viator* 4 (1973): 427, 431; and (on the age of consent) James Menuge, *Medieval English Wardship*, 85n16, citing Gratian *Glossa ordinaria* ad 10.4.2.3 and the *Decretales Gregorii* 9.4.2.3.

49. *Bracton on the Laws and Customs of England*, 2: 257.

50. Walker, "Free Consent," 123, as against Noël James Menuge, "Female Wards and Marriage in Romance and Law: A Question of Consent," in *Young Medieval Women*, ed. Katherine J. Lewis, Noël James Menuge, and Kim M. Phillips (Stroud: Sutton, 1999), 167n6. A similar point is also made by James Menuge, *Medieval English Wardship*, 83n7.

51. *Statutes of the Realm, 1101–1713*, ed. Alexander Luders, Sir Thomas Edlyne Tomlins, John Raithby et al. (London: Record Commission, 1810–28), 1: 226.

52. *Statutes of the Realm*, 1.225, discussed by Waugh, *The Lordship of England*, 60.

53. Noonan, "Power to Choose," 431.

54. Gower's Valentine poem in the *Cinkante Balades*, cited by Brewer in his edition of *PF* (120), does not explicitly acknowledge this principle.

55. For Reason's approval of Nature's role in procreation and *amor naturel*, see *Roman de la Rose*, ed. Lecoy, lines 4379 and 5733–54. On Nature's "incompatible goals" here, see Elaine Tuttle Hansen, *Chaucer and the Fictions of Gender* (Berkeley: University of California Press, 1992), 119.

56. On *Havelok*, see Waugh, *The Lordship of England*, 194–95. More extensive discussion of this aspect of the romance, and comparison with a fourteenth-century legal case heard in the York consistory court, can be found in James Menuge, "Female Wards," esp. 155–60, and again in *Medieval English Wardship*, 87–94. For the legal definition and documentation of "force and fear" in these circumstances, see R. H. Helmholz, *Marriage Litigation in Medieval England* (Cambridge: Cambridge University Press, 1974), 90–94.

57. See Waugh, *The Lordship of England*, 214–15 and fig. 5.1.

58. Guardians at all social levels (including the king) were obliged not to impose on their wards marriages that would be "disparaging," i.e., inappropriate or unsuitable for social or certain other reasons. For the guidelines in urban wardship practice, see Clark, "City Orphans," 173; for the obligations of the king and other guardians of feudal wards (under Magna Carta, ch. 6, and subsequent statutes), see Nicholas Orme, *Medieval Children* (New Haven: Yale University Press, 2001), 326 and n. 103, and James Menuge, *Medieval English Wardship*, 3.

59. See especially Tuttle Hansen, *Chaucer and the Fictions of Gender*, 125–28, on the formel's "formidable voice" and her "power to disrupt the game"; and Lynch, "Diana's 'Bowe Ybroke,'" 87.

60. As Schibanoff points out in *Chaucer's Queer Poetics* (296), "the formel stipulates that her selection must be . . . completely free."

61. See Tuttle Hansen, *Chaucer and the Fictions of Gender*, 123, 139; and Minnis, *Chaucer's Shorter Poems*, 257, 303.

62. I am grateful to Seeta Chaganti, as editor of this volume, for the suggestion that "what the formel creates here through her phrasing is a kind of opposition to performative language, in Austinian terms—not only does her speech refuse to enact any change, but it also deliberately obfuscates its very relationship to action."

63. James Menuge, *Medieval English Wardship*, 83.

64. See note 50 above.

FABULOUS WOMEN, FABLES OF PATRONAGE: METHAM'S
AMORYUS AND CLEOPES AND BL MS ADDITIONAL 10304 /
KARA DOYLE

1. Seth Lerer, *Chaucer and His Readers: Imagining the Author in Late-Medieval England* (Princeton: Princeton University Press, 1993), 61.

2. A full bibliography on European medieval women as literary patrons and their potential influence on literary texts would be lengthy; three major works that have influenced my thinking here are Joan Ferrante, *To the Glory of Her Sex: Women's Roles in the Composition of Medieval Texts* (Bloomington: Indiana University Press, 1997), especially chapter 4; the essays in *The Cultural Patronage of Medieval Women*, ed. June Hall McCash (Athens: University of Georgia Press, 1996); and some of the essays in *Women and Literature in Britain, 1100–1500*, ed. Carol Meale (Cambridge: Cambridge University Press, 1993, 1996).

3. All citations of *Amoryus and Cleopes* are from Stephen Page, ed., *Amoryus and Cleopes* (Kalamazoo, Mich.: Medieval Institute Publications, 1999).

4. See Page, *Amoryus and Cleopes*, 12–14; also Page, "'Amoryus and Cleopes': Intertextuality and Innovation in a Chaucerian Poem." *Chaucer Review* 33 (1996): 201–8.

5. See also Roger Dalrymple, "*Amoryus and Cleopes*: John Metham's Metamorphosis of Chaucer and Ovid," in *The Matter of Identity in Medieval Romance*, ed. Phillipa Hardmann (Cambridge, U.K.: D. S. Brewer, 2002), 149–62, esp. 154–56.

6. See also Dalrymple, 160.

7. See Page, "Intertextuality," 208.

8. For the seminal argument about the fifteenth century's lack of appreciation for irony and ambiguity, see Paul Strohm, "Chaucer's Fifteenth-Century Audience and the Narrowing of the 'Chaucer Tradition,'" *Studies in the Age of Chaucer* 4 (1982): 3–32.

9. All citations of this translation are taken from the edition by Gustav Schleich, *Die mittelenglishe Umdichtung von Boccaccios De claris mulieribus nebst der latein-*

ischen Vorlage zum ersten Male vollständig herausgeben (Leipzig: Mayer and Müller, 1924). A leading numeral followed by a period indicates stanza number.

10. There are additional examples. In the same way, whereas Boccaccio does not hold back from condemning the brothels he credits Venus with inventing, the Middle English translator, in contrast, reserves judgment. At the end of the story of Manto, Boccaccio undermines her "goodness" by remarking that if she did indeed preserve her virginity as some sources say, it would be somewhat praiseworthy, except that she preserved it for the wrong God and committed many other heinous acts. This passage is likewise left entirely out of the Middle English translation. The translator also omits from the life of Artemisia Boccaccio's final remark that nature must have erred "in bestowing female sex on a body which God had endowed with a virile and lofty spirit." See Boccaccio, *Famous Women*, trans. Virginia Brown (Cambridge, Mass: Harvard University Press, 2003), 119.

11. Boccaccio, *Famous Women*, 9.

12. See Strohm, "Narrowing," passim.

13. See Sheila Delany, "Mothers to Think Back Through: Who Are They? The Ambiguous Example of Christine de Pizan," in *Medieval Texts and Contemporary Readers*, ed. Laurie A. Finke and Martin B. Shichtman (Ithaca: Cornell University Press, 1987), 177–97.

DOWEL, THE PROVERBIAL, AND THE VERNACULAR:
SOME VERSIONS OF PASTORALIA / ANNE MIDDLETON

1. The encounter occurs at C.9.281–93; B.7.107–18; A.8.89–100. All citations of *Piers Plowman* refer to the Athlone edition: *The A Version*, ed. George Kane (London: Athlone Press, 1960); *The B Version*, ed. George Kane and E. Talbot Donaldson (1975); *The C Version*, ed. George Russell and George Kane (1997).

2. The *locus classicus* for this term of art in studies of later medieval religious writings is Nicholas Watson, "Censorship and Cultural Change in Late-Medieval England: Vernacular Theology, the Oxford Translation Debate, and Arundel's Constitutions of 1409," *Speculum* 70 (1995): 822–64; Watson there notes (847) the "prescience" of the poem's representation of issues surrounding vernacular translation of religious texts and instruction. More directly pertinent here is his later essay, *"Piers Plowman*, Pastoral Theology, and Spiritual Perfectionism: Hawkyn's Cloak and Patience's *Pater Noster,"* YLS 21 (2007): 83–118, though my primary concern is the formal and rhetorical rather than ideational implications of the way these matters are represented in the poem. On the larger critical stakes of regarding Langland's poem as vernacular theology, see Katherine Zieman, "The Perils of *Canor*: Mystical Authority, Alliteration, and Extragrammatical Meaning in Rolle, the *Cloud*-Author, and Hilton," *YLS* 22 (2008): 131–63, esp. 131–36; also Michelle Karnes, "Will's Imagination in *Piers Plowman,"* JEGP 108 (2009): 27–58, esp. 35, and the section "Shapes Too Large To See," below.

3. Steven Shapin provides a thoughtful account of the ways in which "proverbial" utterance has historically been a key verbal metonymy for "false belief as a popular illness in need of learned therapy"; see his essay "Proverbial Economies," *Social Studies of Science* 31: 731–69. With a valuable typology of the form and "heuristics" of proverbial formulations in spoken exchange, and a survey of the main terms of critical discussion of proverbs by linguists and sociologists of language, he also provides an overview of the issues historically and philosophically at stake in long-standing debate, from Aristotle onward, on the "truth" of traditional "sayings"—as Barbara Herrnstein Smith has termed them (Shapin, 736–37), "speech without a speaker, self-sufficient verbal object(s) rather than . . . verbal act(s)." His discussion suggests ways in which late-medieval contestation over putatively "vernacular" theology restages broader and longer-standing debate over "natural-language" philosophizing generally; his account of the "heuristics of . . . expert practices" (as I suggest below, a prominent topic of concern in the midsection of the poem) is especially germane to the present essay.

4. On the gradational triad as a recommended expository device in sermon composition, as well as the structuring of a sermon around questions of "who, what, how," see, most recently, Sarah Wood, "*Ecce Rex: Piers Plowman* B.19.1–212 and its Contexts," *YLS* 21 (2007): 31–56, esp. 35–37; on the poet's term *skile* for this expository device among others in the pastoral arsenal, see further below. As a term of art, *Dowel* appears on only two occasions after Vision 3: in the Banquet scene (examined further below) that serves as coda to Vision 3 and preface to Vision 4, where the term is posed as the set topic for a riddling contest that elicits displays of definitional ingenuity among the learned; and in the penultimate vision, in which the three stages of the earthly career of the champion Christ are mapped by its three "degrees" (B.19 / C.21.15–182).

5. In *Proverbs, Sentences, and Proverbial Phrases, Mainly before 1500* (Cambridge, Mass.: Belknap; Harvard University Press, 1968), B. J. Whiting lists eight other medieval instances in English (D 278), only one of them antedating Langland's poem.

6. A letter writer to the *New York Times* (Consuelo Reyes, Feb. 20, 2007, D4) corroborates this traditional sense in the aphorisms of the physician Sir William Ostler, which in turn reflect the enduring role in medical education of the aphorisms of Hippocrates (on the use of maxims in medical and other "expert" practices, see Shapin, 757). Nor should "popular" oral tradition be invoked to explain the medieval passage of Hippocratic aphorisms to modern Europe: see Pearl Kibre, "*Hippocrates latinus*: Repertorium of Hippocratic Writings in the Latin Middle Ages," *Traditio* 38 (1982): 165–92; also R. W. Hunt, *The Schools and the Cloister: The Life and Writings of Alexander Nequam*, ed. M. Gibson (Oxford: Clarendon, 1984), 71 and notes.

7. *The Sermons of Thomas Brinton*, ed. Mary Aquinas Devlin. 2 vols., Camden Society 3rd ser. 55–56 (London: Offices of the Royal Historical Society, 1954), 2:318.

See further Andrew Galloway, *The Penn Commentary on Piers Plowman* (Philadelphia: University of Pennsylvania Press, 2006), 1:133–36 (on C.Pro.168–219; B. Pro.146–208). For *proverbialiter* the commonest near-synonym is *vulgariter*, which without further specification usually denotes a linguistic register rather than the language of performance, and is often applied to such pithy dicta in Latin records of preaching.

8. For the text of the letters, see Steven Justice, *Writing and Rebellion* (Berkeley: University of California Press, 1994), 13–14; on the rebels' use of the phrase see 114–24, esp. 119, n. 38; also Richard Firth Green, "John Ball's Letters: Literary History and Historical Literature," in *Chaucer's England*, ed. Barbara Hanawalt (Minneapolis: University of Minnesota Press, 1992), 176–200, esp. 185–86 and notes 61–65. Justice notes that the Piers of the rebel letters is pressed into ideological service in a role markedly different from the one initiated by this impasse: not as the penitent he becomes at this moment, but as manual worker bade to stay at home and continue to labor in solidarity to the ends there proposed: "if þe ende be weleþan is all welle."

9. Watson has noted ("Censorship and Cultural Change," 849) the absence of any surviving "clearly orthodox works after *Piers Plowman* in which a *rusticus* acts as a teacher." In "Pastoral Theology and Spiritual Perfectionism" (85–87), Watson discusses the 1510 pamphlet "How the Plowman learned his paternoster" as a later skirmish on what he terms the enduring "parochial battlefront" concerning the representation to the laity of "the more demanding theology that had lain behind the church's pastoral programme from the early thirteenth century."

10. Ralph Hanna, *London Literature, 1300–1380* (Cambridge: Cambridge University Press, 2005), 251–52. Betty Hill has described the manuscript—"British Library Egerton 613," *Notes and Queries* 223 (1978): 394–409, 492–501—and devotes the second part of her article to the text that contains the phrase (item 6 in the MS, fol. 3r-6r), titled in the MS "salut et solace par l'amour de Jesu."

11. On the "dynamic character" of this body of writings (which extends beyond their textual instantiation to the perceptions of genre and user-base that informs them), see further Bella Millett, "*Mouvance* and the Medieval Author: Re-Editing *Ancrene Wisse*," in *Late-Medieval Religious Texts and Their Transmission*, ed. A. J. Minnis (Cambridge: D. S. Brewer, 1994), 9–20.

12. Mary Carruthers, *The Craft of Thought: Meditation, Rhetoric, and the Making of Images, 400–1200* (Cambridge: Cambridge University Press, 1998). Invoking a distinction developed by scholars of comparative religion, between orthodox teaching and "orthopraxis" as a set of techniques for rendering its dicta productive in lived experience, Carruthers (1) aligns this "craft" with the latter; the distinction is analogous to the relation between the propositional and "proverbial" framing of "truth" in Shapin's analysis of the "heuristics" of proverbs. See Paul Gehl, "*Competens silentium*: Varieties of Monastic Silence in the Medieval West," *Viator* 18 (1987): 125–60, esp. 157–60

and refs.; his essay also provides a useful if implicit gloss on "patient poverty" as the poet develops its scope in the later reaches of Vision 3.

13. For a comprehensive account of his life and works, see Joseph Goering, *William de Montibus (c. 1140–1213): The Schools and the Literature of Pastoral Care*, Studies and Texts 108 (Toronto: Pontifical Institute of Mediaeval Studies, 1992). On the audience for his works and on the "techniques of popularization" governing his enterprise, see 59–82; on his *Proverbia*, 334–48; on his writings for nuns, 222–26.

14. The translation is that of Goering, who cites the Latin of Oxford, New College MS 98 (=MS O), fol. 135rb: "Aiunt aliqui, summa totius predicationis hec est, bene fac et bene habebis. Set hec est ac si uiatori uiam querenti dicatur: Recta semper uia gradere, et sic poteris ad metam peruenire. Numquid sufficit hic dictum? Item dicunt quidam: Scio total summam predicationis: Declina a malo et fac bonum. Hoc est ac si dicat: Noui totam fisicam uel uniuersalem medicinam: Caue egritudinem et conserua sanitatem. Sufficit hoc dicere?" Though Goering does not note the resemblance, William here paraphrases Aristotle's foundational definition of the objective of "knowledge" in ethics (*Nichomachean Ethics* 2.2, tr. W. D. Ross, http://tiny.cc/Szittya-Aristotle -Ethics) as a cultivated practice, and distinguishes it as a philosophical pursuit from metaphysics and other "theoretical" inquiries, a point also fundamental to the dialogic quest for Dowel in Langland's third vision: "Since, then, the present inquiry does not aim at theoretical knowledge like the others (for we are inquiring not in order to know what virtue is, but in order to become good, since otherwise our inquiry would have been of no use), we must examine the nature of actions, namely how we ought to do them. . . . Matters concerned with conduct and questions of what is good for us have no fixity, any more than matters of health. The general account being of this nature, the account of particular cases is yet more lacking in exactness; for they do not fall under any art or precept but the agents themselves must in each case consider what is appropriate to the occasion, *as happens also in the art of medicine or of navigation*" (emphasis added). The similarity of this distinction to William's definition of the preacher's enterprise—especially in its invocation of the same two analogous crafts—is too pervasive to be merely fortuitous. While no complete Latin text of the *Ethics* yet existed (Grosseteste launched its complete translation after his appointment to the bishopric of Lincoln in 1235, more than two decades after William's death as chancellor there), the relevant portions of the "Latin Aristotle" were available in Paris or Lincoln from the mid-twelfth century, in the *Ethica vetus* (consisting of only books 2 and 3) and *Ethica Nova* (comprising book 1 as well as some excerpts from the other books), translated by Burgundio of Pisa (ca. 1110–93) with the aid of commentaries used in the Eastern church. For these texts see the Aristoteles Latinus Database (http://tiny.cc/Szittya -Aristotle-Ethics), vol. 26.2; on Burgundio of Pisa, see article s.n. by Pieter Buellens in *Medieval Science, Technology, and Medicine: An Encyclopedia*, ed. Thomas F. Glick, Steven John Livesey, Faith Wallis (New York: Routledge, 2005), 104–5. On the presence

of these texts in the twelfth-century schools, see "Aristotelianism, medieval" (Mark D. Jordan, 1998) and "Aristoteles Latinus" (Jozef Brams, 1998) in *Routledge Encyclopedia of Philosophy*, ed. E. Craig (online ed. Routledge, 1998–2011), http://tiny.cc/Aristotle -medievalism and http://tiny.cc/Aristotle-Latin, respectively, accessed Oct. 1, 2011.

15. His Latin form of the dictum also makes grammatically explicit, in *habebis* rather than Brinton's *habe*, the relation of cause and consequence that remains syntactically submerged in the formally "proverbial" attestations of the dictum implying a spoken English antecedent, and shows his general care for semantic precision in "those things that are read and sung in the church," as potential sources of misunderstanding and superstition—an effort also evident in his *Errorum eliminatio* (Goering 2.2, esp. 139).

16. I have argued more fully elsewhere (in an unpublished lecture, "Langland's Maxims and Ours," presented in May 2007 at the Fourth International *Piers Plowman* Conference) that the "proverb" and the "maxim" are not synonymous but belong to heuristically adjacent registers: "Far from 'primitive' or 'folk' discursive forms, historically [maxims] are characteristic precipitates of the later stages in the textual or oral pedagogical articulation of a transmissible disciplinary 'expert practice' considered as applied art or craft, and tend to function as a professional shorthand for practitioners, not, as is often assumed, as mnemonics for those entering their first schooling in it"—still less for the intended beneficiaries of their ministrations. See Peter Stein, *Regulae Iuris: From Juristic Rules to Legal Maxims* (Edinburgh: Edinburgh University Press, 1966), esp. 72–81, 140–43; also Shapin, 746, 756–7.

17. His citation thus reproduces the point of the first aphorism of Hippocrates, which contributes to the quasi-proverbial repertory of late-medieval citation the dictum "Ars longa vita brevis." Though often read by later "humanist" literati as if meant to celebrate the durability of monumental artifice against time's ravages (as Spenser professes to understand it in *Epithalamion*), this short maxim continues (as Chaucer recognizes in rendering all of it as the opening gambit of *Parlement of Foules*) with less sanguine concessions to the variety of cases and individual conditions that affect the choice of treatment, and make local tactful judgment the consummate skill: *occasio praeceps, experimentum periculosum, iudicium difficile* ("Life is short, the skill long [to acquire], opportunity fleeting, experiment perilous, judgment [i.e., inference, assessment, and decision] difficult"): *Hippocratic Aphorisms*, trans. Francis Adams, Internet Classics, http://tiny.cc/hippocrates-aphorisms (accessed Oct. 26, 2009). As Shapin notes (740), "in Aristotelian terms, proverbs belong to the process known as *deliberation*—the taking of decisions about what to do, what may be brought about by our own efforts, in the realm of the more-or-less and of the contingent—where absolute certainty is neither available nor rationally to be expected."

18. See further Katharine Breen, *Imagining an English Reading Public, 1150–1400* (Cambridge: Cambridge University Press, 2010), chap. 5 (172–221), esp. 174.

19. The quoted phrases are those of *Speculum Christiani*, ed G. Holmstedt, Early English Text Society o.s. 182 (London: Oxford University Press, 1933), 2.5–13.

20. On the ideational and exegetical connective tissue that joins this "reading" of Trajan's exemplarity to the ensuing exposition of "patient poverty," see Ralph Hanna, "Some Commonplaces of Late Medieval Patience Discussion: An Introduction," in *The Triumph of Patience*, ed. Gerald Schiffhorst (Orlando: University Presses of Florida, 1978), 65–87.

21. *Breviarium ad Usum Insignis Ecclesiae Sarum*, ed. Francis Procter and Christopher Wordsworth, 3 vols. (Cambridge: Cambridge University Press, 1879).

22. As Breen (174) has observed, the C version provides a more thorough, consistent, and tonally even account of the ways in which the universal "kynde" imperative of mutual guidance both resembles and differs from the pastoral offices reserved to the ordained. On books of pastoral care in the collections of cloistered orders, see further Vincent Gillespie, "Cura Pastoralis in Deserto," in *De Cella in Saeculum*, ed. Michael G. Sargent (Cambridge: D. S. Brewer, 1989), 161–81; also germane in this volume are essays by Nicholas Watson ("Richard Rolle as Elitist and as Popularist: The Case of *Judica Me*," 123–43), and Ann Hutchinson ("Devotional Reading in the Monastery and in the Late Medieval Household," 215–27).

23. On the A version of this impasse, see Gillespie, "Thy Will Be Done: *Piers Plowman* and the *Paternoster*," in *Late-Medieval Religious Texts and Their Transmission*, ed. Minnis (n. 11 above), 95–119; on the BC revisions of the passage, see D. F. Johnson, "Persen with a Pater-Noster Paradys Oþer Hevene: *Piers Plowman* C.11.296–98a," *YLS* 5 (1991): 77–89.

24. John Burrow identifies the poet's characteristic "gesture of substitution" of the figurative for the literal as a constitutive technique in the serial development of the poem: "The Action of Langland's Second Vision," *Essays in Criticism* 15 (1965): 247–268, esp. 263–66. On "Robert the ruyflare" and "ȝeuen ȝelde-aȝeyn" (C.6.308–24) in the Confession episode of Vision 2, see Ralph Hanna, "Robert the Ruyflere and His Companions," in *Literature and Religion in the Later Middle Ages: Philological Studies in Honor of Siegfried Wenzel*, ed. Richard G. Newhauser and John A. Alford, Medieval and Renaissance Texts and Studies 118 (Binghamton: SUNY Press, 1995), 81–96, esp. 83, 91–94. On Patience and Will as paired diners at the Banquet (B.13.46–61a; C.15.40–65a), and the Paternoster as the "vitaille" Patience draws forth from his "poke" for Hawkyn, see Gillespie, "*Piers Plowman* and the *Paternoster*," 102–4; and John A. Alford, "Langland's Exegetical Drama," in *Literature and Religion*, ed. Newhauser and Alford, 97–117, esp. 103–6. On the doubling of Patience and Hawkyn Activa-Vita as providers of bread for human "byleue," as Hawkyn's occupation enacts in a different register a reprise of that of Piers, see Watson, "Pastoral Theology and Spiritual Perfectionism," esp. 94–97.

25. On Langland's method as serial anatomy of the constitutive genres and discursive registers of the poem, see Steven Justice, "The Genres of *Piers Plowman*," *Viator* 19 (1988): 291–306; also Elizabeth Kirk, "Langland's Plowman and the Recreation of Fourteenth-Century Religious Metaphor," *YLS* 2 (1988): 1–21.

26. The account of the parable in the *Glossa Ordinaria* is drawn almost entirely from Bede, I.i (*PL* 91:937ff.): "Notandum autem, quod Vulgata editio pro Parabolis, quae Hebraice Missae vocantur, Paroemias, id est, proverbia dicit. Sed nec ipsum nomen abhorret a vero. Quae enim parabolae recte nuncupantur, quia occulta sunt, possunt non incongrue etiam proverbia vocari, *quia talia sunt, quae merito saepius in ore colloquentium versari, ac memoria debeant retineri*" (emphasis added); cf. the Gloss on Proverbs 1.1 (*PL* 113:1079).

27. "Allegory without the Teeth: Reflections on Figural Language in *Piers Plowman*," *YLS* 19 (2005): 27–43, esp. 29–33.

28. Jill Mann, "The Nature of Need Revisited," *YLS* 18 (2004): 3–29, p. 13.

29. See my essay "Piers Plowman, the Monsters, and the Critics: Some Embarrassments of Literary History," in *The Morton W. Bloomfield Lectures, 1989–2005*, ed. Daniel Donoghue, James Simpson, and Nicholas Watson (Kalamazoo, Mich.: Medieval Institute Publications, 2010), 94–115, esp. 97–99. Ralph Hanna has suggested that in its summary assay of the ordinary practical resources most useful to pastors and poets, Ymaginatif's heterogeneously "scrappy" didactic repertory implicitly offers a similar embarrassment to "the recent tendency [of critics] to bring high medieval learnedness to bear" on the remit of this figure: "Langland's Ymaginatif: Images and the Limits of Poetry," in *Images, Idolatry, and Iconoclasm*, ed. Jeremy Dimmick, James Simpson, and Nicolette Zeeman (Oxford: Oxford University Press, 2002), 81–94, at 93.

30. Hans Belting has discussed the ideational and ideological reach of this figure, especially in later-medieval defenses of ecclesiastical dispositive and interpretive power; see his essay "The New Role of Narrative in Public Painting of the Trecento: *Historia* and Allegory," in *Pictorial Narrative in Antiquity and the Middle Ages*, ed Herbert L. Kessler and Marianna Shreve Thompson (Washington, D.C.: National Gallery of Art, 1985), 151–168, esp. 154–57.

31. Raimundus de Pennaforte, *Summa de paenitentia*, tomus B, ed. Xavier Ochoa and Alfonso Diez (Rome: Universa Bibliotheca Iuris, 1976), dist. 3, tit. 34, para. 23–29, cols. 817–27.

32. *Decretum* II pars, causa 33, q. 3, dist. 1–7: *Corpus Iuris Canonici*, ed. Aemilius Friedberg (1879; repr. Graz: Akademische Druck- u. Verlagsanstalt, 1959), 1.1159–1247 (hereafter *CIC*). Two concentrated runs of penitential dicta drawn from this treatise have been identified in the poem. One is Ymaginatif's sequence of Latin citations at B.12.29a–154 (as well as the introductory adage, at B.8.20–23, "Sepcies in die cadit iustus"), traced to this source by Ernest Kaulbach, in a (still unpublished) 1997 paper,

"Piers Plowman B.12: The Penitential Canons in Ymaginatif's Reply," presented at the annual meeting of the International Congress on Medieval Studies in Kalamazoo, Michigan. A second set, at B.13.45a–135a (C.15.50a–137), rehearses the "metes" served by Scripture at the Banquet; in the Gratian treatise the latter sequence is headed by *Agite penitentiam* (B.13.49; C.15.55; cf. Matt. 3:2; Acts 2:38–41), Canon 44 of dist. 1 of the treatise (*CIC* 1.1168), which reorders cap. 3 of Ps-Aug. Sermo 392, *Ad conjugatos* (*PL* 39:1711). In the *Decretum* the treatise is inserted without transition amid its section on the moral law of marriage, a placement that has long puzzled canon-law scholars, but may help to explain Wit's lengthy excursus on marriage, followed by an exposition of the Flood, in his account of Dowel; see M. Teresa Tavormina, *Kindly Similitude: Marriage and Family in Piers Plowman* (Cambridge: D. S. Brewer, 1995), 78–90.

33. See New Advent, http://tiny.cc/Jerome-two-epistles, for translation of Jerome's two epistles; for that of Tertullian (*PL* 1:1233), see *Tertullian: Treatises on Penance*, trans. William P. Le Saint (Westminster, Md.: Newman Press, 1959): "Do thou . . . lay hold on it [*poenitentia*] and grip it fast, as one who is shipwrecked holds to a plank of salvation. It will buoy you up when you are plunged into a sea of sin and bear you safely to the haven of divine mercy." The translator provides (149, n. 54) a useful account of the early history of the figure; its classical antecedents include Plato, *Phaedo* 85d; Seneca, *De beneficiis* 3.9.2, "dare tabulam naufrago"; and Cicero, *De officiis* 3.23.89, "tabulam de naufrago arripere." The translation of Seneca quoted here is that of Aubrey Stewart, 1887, from the edition of M. C. Gertz, Berlin, 1876, at Ancient History, http://tiny.cc/Seneca-translation.

On the medieval fortunes of the body of dicta on the interior life ascribed to Jerome, and often transmitted together in MSS of pastoral counsel to religious, especially women, see further Katherine Gill, "Women and the Production of Religious Literature, 1300–1500," in E. Ann Matter, ed. *Creative Women in Medieval and Early Modern Italy* (Philadelphia: University of Pennsylvania Press, 1994), 64–85, esp. 79–81. The epistle to Demetrias in a Middle English translation for those embarking on a nonregular religious vocation survives in five MSS; see further E. A. Jones, "The Heresiarch, the Virgin, the Recluse, the Vowess, the Priest: Some Medieval Audiences for Pelagius's Epistle to Demetrias," *Leeds Studies in English*, n.s. 31 (2000), 205–27. The importance of this epistolary corpus for Langland's poem is further attested by another citation from it only recently identified: C.9.213a, quoting Ep. 69.5 to Oceanus (*PL* 22:658). Though the CSEL edition is now the standard reference for the genuine epistles of Jerome—*Opera*, ed. I. Hilberg, vols. 54–56 (Vienna 1910–18)—here I continue to refer to the texts in the *Patrologia Latina* chiefly for convenience, as those still cited most often in studies of their medieval afterlives.

PENN R. SZITTYA AS SCHOLAR AND TEACHER /
JO ANN HOEPPNER MORAN CRUZ

I would like to thank John C. Hirsh, who has made a number of helpful suggestions for this chapter.

1. Penn R. Szittya, "The Angels and the Theme of *Fortitudo* in the *Chanson de Roland*," *Neuphilologische Mitteilungen* 72 (1971): 193–223.

2. Penn R. Szittya, "The Living Stone and the Patriarchs: Typological Imagery in *Andreas*, Lines 706–810," *Journal of English and Germanic Philology* 72 (1973): 167–174.

3. Penn R. Szittya, "The Friar as False Apostle: Antifraternal Exegesis and the *Summoner's Tale*," *Studies in Philology* 71 (1974): 19–46; "The Green Yeoman as Loathly Lady: The Friar's Parody of the *Wife of Bath's Tale*," *PMLA* 90 (1975): 386–94; rejoinder to Carole K. Brown and Marion F. Egge, "The *Friar's Tale* and the *Wife of Bath's Tale*," *PMLA* 91 (1976): 291–93.

4. Szittya, "The Friar as False Apostle," 27.

5. Szittya, "The Green Yeoman as Loathly Lady," 392.

6. There were other signs by which the friar-like Pharisees could be recognized and condemned. Among the charges against them is that they loved the first place at dinners, the first seats (i.e., the pulpit) in the synagogue, and salutations (recognition) in the marketplace. They feigned sanctity and austerity and enticed young boys into their order. Szittya, "The Antifraternal Tradition in Middle English Literature," *Speculum* 52, no. 2 (1977): 294–301.

7. These false apostles try to supplant the role of the traditional descendants of the apostles (the bishops and the parish clergy); they are *penetrantes domos*, cannot endure having their probity tested, beg and wander about, preach the gospel for gain, preach vain stories, seduce women, increase in numbers beyond measure, and so forth. Szittya, "Antifraternal Tradition," 303–11.

8. The multiplicity of friars in fourteenth-century England (not supported by historical investigation) signaled, in the antifraternal literature, theat they were those coming at the end of time. Szittya, "Antifraternal Tradition," 311–12.

9. Penn R. Szittya, "'Sedens super flumina': A Fourteenth-Century Poem against the Friars," *Mediaeval Studies* 41 (1979): 30–43.

10. Penn R. Szittya, "Metafiction: The Double Narration in *Under Western Eyes*," *English Literary History* 48 (1981): 817–40.

11. Michael Greaney, *Conrad, Language, and Narrative* (New York: Cambridge University Press, 2002), 183n1. Szittya's essay has been reprinted in *Critical Essays on Joseph Conrad*, ed. Ted Billy (Boston: G. K. Hall, 1986); and *Joseph Conrad, Critical Assessments of Writers in English*, ed. Keith Carabine (Bromley, England: Christopher Helm, 1992).

12. Keith Carabine, *The Life and the Art: A Study of Conrad's "Under Western Eyes"* (Amsterdam: Rodopi, 1996), notes that "Conrad's treatment of Razumov's essay and

his anticipated career has received scant critical attention," with but two exceptions, one of which is Penn's article (104).

13. "The Trinity in Langland and Abelard," in *Magister Regis: Studies in Honor of Robert Earl Kaske*, ed. Arthur Groos (New York: Fordham University Press, 1986), 211–12.

14. Penn R. Szittya, *The Antifraternal Tradition in Medieval Literature* (Princeton: Princeton University Press, 1986). Two of the chapters contain portions reprinted from the earlier articles published in *Speculum* and *Studies in Philology*.

15. As Christina von Nolcken points out, "These are usually obscure, for the most part unedited, often extant in single manuscripts, and it can take considerable detective work to identify some of the authorities they cite." Review of *The Antifraternal Tradition in Medieval Literature*, by Penn Szittya, *Modern Philology* 86 (1989): 293.

16. Penn R. Szittya, "Domesday Bokes: The Apocalypse in Medieval English Literary Culture," in *The Apocalypse in the Middle Ages*, ed. Richard K. Emmerson and Bernard McGinn (Ithaca, N.Y.: Cornell University Press, 1992), 374–97.

17. Penn R. Szittya, "Kicking the Habit: The Campaign against the Friars in a Fourteenth-Century Encyclopedia," in *Defenders and Critics of Franciscan Life: Essays in Honor of John V. Fleming*, ed. Michael F. Cusato and Guy Geltner (Leiden: Brill, 2009), 159–75.

18. See Szittya's review of *Omne Bonum: A Fourteenth-Century Encyclopedia of Universal Knowledge, British Library MSS Royal 6 EVI–6 EVII*, by Lucy Freeman Sandler, *Speculum* 74, no. 2 (1999): 491–93.

19. Szittya, "Kicking the Habit," 175.

THE DESIRE TO WRITE THINGS DOWN: A POETIC PALIMPSEST ON CERTAIN REMARKS BY PENN SZITTYA / MARK McMORRIS

The tale of the minor civil servant was composed from my recollection of the lecture on *Omne bonum* given by Penn for the Lannan Center in the fall of 2006. The theme of the larger event was The Poetic Book: Medieval, Modern, Postmodern, and it included talks by Jerome McGann, Johanna Drucker, and Caroline Bergvall. In keeping with this theme, Penn's lecture focused on the visual dimensions of the encyclopedia and other documents such as *mappae mundi*, to discuss the representation of metaphysical ideas through pictorial design and in geometric spaces. Fortunately, a video recording of the lecture exists, which I consulted in order to minimize the chance of misrepresenting his thought here. To gain a more comprehensive, and a more exact, understanding of the encyclopedia and its author, I also consulted the work of Lucy Freeman Sandler in her magisterial *Omne Bonum: A Fourteenth-Century Encyclopedia of Universal Knowledge: British Library MSS Royal 6 E VI–6 E VII*, 2 vols. (London: Harvey Miller, 1996).

The man I refer to as the minor civil servant is shown by Sandler to have been one James le Palmer. In the years when the encyclopedia was being written and illustrated, James held in the exchequer a position known as clerk of the great roll (*clericus magni rotuli*), or engrosser of the exchequer. Sandler discusses the details of this job (responsibilities, number of days worked per year, remuneration, etc.) and considers the substantial cost of the vellum that James used in making the encyclopedia, a costly private project of his own. How did he come to possess it? That the clerk may have stolen the vellum, or had its cost charged to the king's exchequer, is not an assertion made by either Sandler or Szittya. It's only a suggestion gleaned from their words, a mere possibility—one that I eagerly embraced for my own purposes and of my own accord.

CONTRIBUTORS

SEETA CHAGANTI is an Associate Professor in the Department of English at the University of California, Davis.

JO ANN HOEPPNER MORAN CRUZ is Dean of the College of Humanities and Natural Sciences and Professor of History at Loyola University New Orleans.

KARA DOYLE is an Associate Professor in the Department of English at Union College.

RICHARD K. EMMERSON is Dean of the School of Arts and a Professor in the Department of English at Manhattan College.

MOIRA FITZGIBBONS is an Associate Professor in the Department of English at Marist College.

NICK HAVELY is an Emeritus Professor in the Department of English and Related Literature at the University of York.

JOHN C. HIRSH is a Professor in the Department of English at Georgetown University.

J. PATRICK HORNBECK II is an Assistant Professor in the Department of Theology and the Medieval Studies Program at Fordham University.

MARK MCMORRIS is an Associate Professor in the Department of English at Georgetown University and founder and former director of the Lannan Center for Poetics and Social Practice.

ANNE MIDDLETON is a Professor Emerita in the Department of English at the University of California, Berkeley.

JOHN T. SEBASTIAN is an Associate Professor in the Department of English at Loyola University New Orleans.

INDEX